The Dambuster Raid

The Möhne dam in the early morning of 17 May 1943. A bouncing bomb has created an enormous breach in the reservoir of the Ruhr area. The seemingly impossible has become reality: millions of tons of water are thundering down into the valleys, bringing death and destruction.

The Dambuster Raid

A German View

Helmuth Euler

Pen & Sword
AVIATION

First published in Great Britain in 2015 by
Pen & Sword Aviation
an imprint of
Pen & Sword Books Ltd
47 Church Street
Barnsley
South Yorkshire
S70 2AS

ISBN 978 1 47382 802 5

A CIP catalogue record for this book is available from the British Library

Typeset in Ehrhardt by
Mac Style Ltd, Bridlington, East Yorkshire
Printed and bound in India by Replika Press Pvt. Ltd.

Pen & Sword Books Ltd incorporates the imprints of Pen & Sword Archaeology, Atlas, Aviation, Battleground, Discovery, Family History, History, Maritime, Military, Naval, Politics, Railways, Select, Transport, True Crime, and Fiction, Frontline Books, Leo Cooper, Praetorian Press, Seaforth Publishing and Wharncliffe.

For a complete list of Pen & Sword titles please contact
PEN & SWORD BOOKS LIMITED
47 Church Street, Barnsley, South Yorkshire, S70 2AS, England
E-mail: enquiries@pen-and-sword.co.uk
Website: www.pen-and-sword.co.uk

Contents

The Möhne Lake, the great reservoir of the Ruhr area, is overspilling; an event occurring occasionally during spring, when the inflow from the drainage area in the Hochsauerland is above average due to snowmelt and strong rains.

Water War: 17 May 1943: Bouncing Bombs Against the Dams on the Möhne, Eder and Sorpe Rivers

The battle for the Ruhr waters controlled by barrages began in September 1937, when British military officers of the London Air Ministry considered the demolition of these water reservoirs of the German arms industry. Six dams of the Möhne, Eder, Sorpe, Ennepe, Lister and Diemel rivers were on the target lists of the British Bomber Command. The heart of the German armament industry, the Ruhr area with the interlinked waterways serving the transport of war material, ought to be dried out with one strike, simultaneously taking out the hydroelectric plants. Barnes Wallis was not the first to have this thought, but he succeeded in demolishing the dam walls with the aid of an ingenious idea. So the deployment of the 617th Bomber Squadron under Wing Commander Guy Gibson came about, an elite unit for special operations and precision attacks braving considerable flight risks. During the night of the 16 May 1943 the German water front broke, when bouncing bombs tore apart the gigantic retaining walls on Möhne and Eder during spectacular low-level flight operations. During Germany's longest night, more than 1,400 people died, and eight of the nineteen Lancaster bombers of "Operation Chastise" did not return to England. The explosion of two bombs on the Möhne and Eder dams triggered two of the greatest disasters of the last century. Only the dropping of a nuclear bomb in Japan exceeded the scale of the destructive power of the individual "conventional dam buster bombs". Dozens of road and railway bridges were torn off, hundreds of buildings destroyed, hydroelectric and other power plants rendered inoperative, and almost two hundred square kilometres of land flooded and laid waste. Yet the arsenal on the Ruhr River continued its production without interruption, the strategic advantages of the allied forces did not materialise. The holders of power at that time imposed a gagging order regarding the drama in the valleys and withheld the names of the "damaged" barrages in the daily report of the Armed Forces High Command. Now the author of "Als Deutschlands Dämme brachen" [When Germany's dams broke] complements his first book on the bombardments of the barrages with the supplement volume "The Dambuster Raid: A German View". This account is based on official documents held in international archives recently released and testimonies from further witnesses of this event who either played a leading role in the preparation and execution of the airstrike or experienced the misery in the river valleys on the German side. The Möhne, Eder and Sorpe dams made world history. They attracted the attention of many interested people, including historians and members of the military, and held their attention for decades after the event. For the second time, an authentic German report is presented here with more than 300 very rare photographs, documents and arresting eye witness statements, collated in an effort to fully illuminate the background and ramifications of the "secret Möhne and Eder catastrophes" during the destructive Dambuster Raid.

The same night, one hour after the breaking of the Möhne dam, the Eder dam suffers the same fate, a double strike of the Royal Air Force against the German reservoirs. The air raids on the Sorpe and Ennepe dams fail.

Preface

After the publication of "Als Deutschlands Dämme brachen" (Motorbuch Publishing), many eye witnesses from Germany and abroad contacted the author with statements, photographs and film material of the nocturnal airstrikes against the Möhne and Eder dams. Almost sixty years after the attacks on the barrages, international archives have opened up further, and important documents previously unseen have been released to the public. These are the basis for this book. "Operation Chastise" rewrote military history. In the English speaking world it became legend through the press, radio and television, as it possessed all the classic military attributes such as originality, surprise, heroism and dramatic events. In Germany the dam disasters remain unforgotten.

On the night of the 16/17 May 1943, a bomber formation of nineteen Lancaster crafts of the newly installed 617th Squadron of the RAF attacked four barrages in West Germany in very low-level flight. Within one hour bouncing bombs broke two main targets, the gravity defying walls of the Möhne and Eder dams. The Sorpe dam was damaged, but the Ennepe dam withstood the attack. Eight Lancaster bombers did not return from this sortie. Only the dropping of a nuclear bomb over Japan exceeded the scale of destruction of the individual conventional dam buster bombs (Upkeep). During Germany's longest night more than 1,400 people in the river valleys lost their lives which, at this point, was the highest number of casualties taken during an air raid. More than 200 square kilometres were flooded. The airstrike was a feat of engineering technology, but it proved something of a failure for the RAF and Bomber Command. It was based on an experimental series of tests, with an exact prediction of results, and was aimed against the arsenal of the Nazi empire in the Ruhr area.

The expected strategic advantages for the allied forces failed to materialise and production continued without interruption. Did the costs in material, time and the loss of eight bombers with fifty-six aviators pay off in terms of strengthening the wartime morale of the British civilian population? Churchill needed victories in the aerial battle of the Ruhr, too. How did the British view the demolition of the dam walls of the Mohne and Eder, which together retained 336 million tons of water? After the consultation of the original documentation, it is established that in the light of a looming new war the British Air Ministry had recognised German reservoirs and barrages as potential targets by September 1937, and that it had named the Möhne and Sorpe resevoirs in October of the same year. At the outbreak of war, Bomber Command intensified the notion to neutralise the heart of the German armament industry in the Ruhr area by destroying the barrages, to virtually cripple the nerve centre of the defence economy on the principle of paraplegia and to decisively shorten the length of the war.

Until the beginning of 1943 many suggestions from RAF personnel were discussed, decided upon and listed. The verdict: the reservoirs in Germany could not be bombarded with conventional methods. Even torpedoes, remote-controlled hydroplanes filled with explosives, synchronised detonations of sea mines or sabotage units deployed by parachutes were to be used successfully against the Möhne dam. Initially Barnes Wallis believed in a ten ton earthquake bomb, but it could not be transported and used accurately enough to initiate a collapse of the retaining wall in May 1943. Barnes Wallis was not the first to recognise the German reservoirs as important targets, but he had an ingenious idea, the technology of the bouncing bombs, which would unleash the deluge of water behind the Möhne and Eder dams.

For three years, Barnes Wallis tinkered with his bomb theories, lastly against the resistance of the aviation technocrats. The 617th Squadron, under the leadership of Wing Commander Guy Gibson, needed only seven weeks of low-level flight training. When the decision was made on 26 February 1943 to start "Operation Chastise", no specific detailed drawings of the special weapon even existed.

Three days before the attack, the first and only test with a live bomb succeeded. The decision on the preference of "Upkeep" (dam buster bomb) over "Highball" (anti-ship weapon) was not made in the London Air Ministry, but in Washington where the British general staff of the Air Force met the "colleagues" of the US Air Force during conferences. On 14 May 1943, upon request, the Air Ministry in London received the desired signal for attack from overseas. The latest date to successfully carry out "Operation Chastise" with the required water levels in the reservoirs was 20 May 1943, the last suitable night of a full moon period. At the Möhne reservoirs the earth satellite was in the southern night sky. During the time of the strike it illuminated the retaining wall from the water side.

The Eder dam: its overspill is always a worthwhile spectacle, with cascades of water reaching a width of twenty-five metres and a height of almost forty-three metres. The construction of the Eder barrage was a joint effort by Prussia and the principality of Waldeck and Pyrmont. On the valley side, the south tower bears the royal Prussian coat of arms, an eagle with the letters FR (= Friedericus Rex) on its breast. On the north tower the coat of arms of the Waldeck-Pyrmont principality with the Waldeck star and the Pyrmont cross is displayed.

The History of the Reservoirs

The construction of reservoirs counts amongst the most important technological achievements of mankind. Engineers have always tried to store water in great volumes in order to supply towns with drinking water, to irrigate the fields during draughts or to protect inhabited areas from flooding. The building of artificial water reservoirs is not an invention of the nineteenth and twentieth centuries. Already, in antiquity, important barrages had been erected. Contemporary authors report on the hydrological wonder of Lake Moeris south of modern Cairo in Egypt, which stored the Nile inundation for the dry period in a natural depression with the aid of dams and canals. Two and half millennia before Christ, one of the most fertile provinces of ancient Egypt was thus created by extensive hydrological measures with a dam at its core. Other historic barrages, with dams and walls resting between two mountainsides, had been constructed as early as the fourth and third millennium BC in Armenia and Jordan. The construction of barrages has been closely associated with the development of cities and states for thousands of years. The setup of early larger settlements in the history of mankind was always linked to the concern about a sufficient supply of drinking water.

The history of reservoir construction is also an important part of cultural history. In Germany, important dam constructions developed in the sixteenth and seventeenth centuries in the Harz Mountains, where hydraulic power was utilised in ore mining for smelting and metal processing. Similar to the territory surrounding the Harz Mountains, the Sauerland and the Bergisch Land regions were areas where metal working represented an important economic factor. For hundreds of years, hammer mills, smithies and mills in the valleys had harnessed the power of the numerous streams and rivulets in the area. This changed with the onset of modern industrialisation, when villages became towns. The rapidly growing enterprises and the swift population increase demanded ever larger quantities of water, which could no longer be provided by the traditional pump stations.

Before the turn of the twentieth century, new technical developments took place within the construction of water barrages, which caused some cities to plan the construction of their own reservoirs for drinking water. The great pioneer of German barrage construction was the engineer Dr Otto Intze, professor at the Technical University Aachen. Without planning permission, the town of Remscheid in the Bergisch Land completed Germany's drinking water reservoir in the Eschbach valley in 1891. This was the first barrage retaining water behind a wall. The town fathers of Remscheid created a fait accompli. Professor Intze had designed the plans for the construction of the retaining wall according to the latest hydrological insights. The royal government in Düsseldorf was continually updated on the progress of the works. It controlled the building project, but did not want to assume responsibility for the construction, in terms of it actually being able to withstand the pressure of the water, by granting planning permission. The success which the town of Remscheid had with its new drinking water reservoir encouraged the neighbouring town of Lennep to also build a reservoir. Professor Intze and the government building officer Albert Schmidt from Lennep paved the way for this project. The construction of the Panzerbach reservoir was just completed, when the building permission of the government agencies arrived. Soon further reservoirs came into being in the Bergisch Land, which can be called the birthplace of modern barrage construction. The area along the Wupper became a land of artificial lakes. This reputation was soon contested by the Sauerland. In the second half of the nineteenth century a rampant growth of industries and population took place in the region between Emscher and Ruhr. From a predominantly rural region, the Ruhr area emerged in the course of only a few decades as a centre of German heavy industry, the district of coal and steel. In order to supply the rapidly growing cities and their industrial complexes with sufficient water, the river giving this region its name was exploited to the point of exhaustion. Pump stations sprang up like mushrooms in the Ruhr valley. Little consideration could be given to hygienic requirements in the extraction of water. Thus in 1901 a typhoid epidemic took place in Gelsenkirchen due to the insufficient quality of the central drinking water provisions. During some summers, a catastrophic lack of water prevailed along the lower Ruhr sections, when the rainfall dipped below average.

Until the turn of the twentieth century the Ruhr River had been able to bear this burden without artificial supporting measures. Only when the extracted volume increased dramatically within a few years from ninety million cubic metres (1893) to 135 million cubic metres (1897) and even over 500 million cubic metres, the natural water resources no longer sufficed. The demands became so vast that they could no longer be secured without artificial intervention by barrages. In 1896, with the aid of the towns of Altena and Gevelsberg, the first two reservoirs for drinking water came about in the drainage basin of the Ruhr River, the Fuelbeck reservoir with a holding capacity of 700,000 cubic meters and the Heilenbecker reservoir (450,000 cubic metres).

Yet the thirst of the Ruhr area grew and grew. So on 10 December 1899 the Ruhr Reservoir Society was founded with the aim "to improve the water level of the Ruhr both in volume and quality by promoting the construction of reservoirs in the drainage basin of the river." The society supported smaller reservoir cooperatives with significant grants. In 1904 the Hasper reservoir, the Fürwigge reservoir, the Glörtal reservoir and the Ennepe reservoir could be inaugurated, with a total volume of 16.1 million cubic metres.

The union within the Ruhr Reservoir Society of those withdrawing water and the owners of the drinking water along the Ruhr was originally voluntary, but underwent legal regulation in 1913 by the Ruhr Reservoir Law. The "forced cooperative by public law" could now call on all parties involved in the water economy for financial contributions. Due to the growing demand on drinking water, the Ruhr Reservoir Society agreed in 1906 on the construction of the large-scale project Möhne reservoir, with a volume of initially around 130 million cubic metres. With this it burst the conceivable dimensions in European reservoir construction so far. The retaining wall, centre piece of the Möhne reservoir, traced an arc of 650 metres across the valley floor. It rose 37.7 metres above the ground. The foundation of the wall did not only reach the bedrock, but penetrated it a further three metres to prevent a shift of the wall by water pressure. So a total height of 40.3 metres was reached with a width of 34.2 metres at the base. The width of the crown was 6.25 metres.

The Sorpe reservoir is situated fifteen kilometres away from the Möhne reservoir, at that time the second largest catchment lake of the Sauerland. In contrast to the Möhne and Eder retaining walls, the Sorpe dam is a flattened earthwork made of rock fill containing a concrete core. For a long time, the sixty-nine metre high Sorpe dam was Germany's highest earthwork. The length of its crown is 700 metres with a width of ten metres. The Sorpe reservoir, with a strong capacity of seventy million cubic metres, forms a water reserve to supplement and support the network of the remaining reservoirs in the tributary area of the Ruhr, in the event of so-called "double dry years", i.e in the event that, over two consecutive years, the amount of rainfall falls below the annual average, and the other reservoirs prove insufficient for the provision of the Ruhr area. Put into service in 1935, the Sorpe dam consists of 3.25 million cubic metres of rock fill and 130,000 cubic metres of concrete. The Sorpe reservoir shows another special feature: it is a so-called carryover storage facility, i.e. the reservoir capacity is larger than the water volume flowing in from the drainage area in its annual average. The water caught in this reservoir needs to be managed with particular care, since replenishment takes a correspondingly longer amount of time. Since the 1950s, the volume of inflow has been further improved by diversions from neighbouring river basins. The generation of electric energy is insignificant at the Möhne and Sorpe reservoirs.

Roughly seventy kilometres south-east of the Möhne Lake on Hessian territory, the Eder Lake is located. It owes its existence to a Prussian law from 1905 concerning the planning and construction of the Mittelland Canal, a law, as it was stated, "to improve the national culture, to minimise flood damage and to develop the waterways network". In order to secure a sufficient water supply for the newly created Mittelland Canal – a great west-east waterway and an important link for the inland navigation to the Ruhr area – guaranteed amounts had to be withdrawn all year round from the Weser without endangering navigation on that river. This regulation required the construction of reservoirs in the drainage basin of the Weser. So the Diemel reservoir and the Eder lake came into being, the latter of gargantuan dimensions at the time, having a volume of 202 million cubic metres. Although the retaining wall is 200 metres shorter than the wall of the Möhne reservoir, still the volume of stored water is higher by seventy million cubic metres. The Eder retaining wall is eight metres higher, a slimmer construction without loam skirting in front. A further reason for the construction of the twenty-seven kilometres long Eder Lake was flood protection, since the Eder showed itself to be Hesse's wildest river. Floods in the years 1840, 1881 and 1890 had wreaked terrible havoc. In the free capacity of the Eder reservoir these floods are contained and stored until demand during dry periods. The water surface slope is used for the generation of electric energy by power stations at the retaining wall and at the end of the equalising reservoir. Furthermore the equalising reservoir in the Eder valley serves as lower reservoir for the pumped-storage power plant Waldeck I.

The technical data and the importance of the reservoirs for the German centre of armament in the Ruhr area were well-known to the enemies at that time, the British air force officers. On the fateful night of the 16/17 May 1943 six dams in West Germany should be destroyed. Four dams were attacked according to plan, a fifth accidentally by a nuisance raider. The Möhne and Eder retaining walls broke and caused devastating floods in the valleys. Direct hits by bombs damaged the Sorpe dam.

British Bouncing Bombs Shock Berlin

On 17 May 1943 at 2pm, before the news, the Greater German Radio aired the official Wehrmacht report with the unvarying announcement: "From the headquarter of the leader; the High Command of the Armed Forces announces: …". After a verbose list of insignificant German successes at the eastern front, the Greater German Radio reported the air strikes on the retaining walls in embarrassed words, in the following, low-key manner, which at once both down-played and obscured the true face of things: "Weak British air forces intruded last night onto the territory of the German Reich and dropped a scant amount of explosive bombs in some places. Two reservoirs were damaged and many casualties among the civilian population were caused by the ensuing deluge. Eight of the attacking planes were shot down, a further nine enemy crafts destroyed above the occupied western territories, among them one by army troops…" Nothing more was revealed to the Greater German public. Not even those in the effected territories. The authorities refused access to the disaster zones to foreign correspondents on grounds that the reservoirs would now count as non-visitable restricted areas, as the English had turned them into targets. A cloak of silence, spread by the Nazi leadership, covered the events at the barrages. Blank spaces in people's understanding of events churned the seething rumour mills into action.

Despite all secrecy, a shock wave travelled through the German population which perhaps caused more damage than the floods in the valleys. Fear went about, for the military experts in the Reich Air Ministry had thought the heavy walls to be indestructible. How had the impossible become a reality? Where were the weapons of retaliation so often promised? In the "confidential reports", with which the "district press offices" directed the newspapers on a daily basis at that time, it was written: "No line is allowed to be reported on the bombardments

The Möhne reservoir is a Westphalian sea in the Sauerland, enjoyed by the population of the Ruhr area. Elegant in its architecture, the dam blends into the landscape. In 1912 it became the first great barrage of Europe, and the destination of millions of tourists.

The Eder Lake is situated amidst an enchanting landscape in Hessen, with the Waldeck castle in the foreground, the historical landmark of the region. The Eder dam, completed in 1914, was one of the last great technical monuments of the Second Reich, the last "giant" of the imperial age. Responsible for the technical scheme was the government building officer Dr Sympher, for the artistic design the government building adviser Dr Mayer who matched the dam to the neighbouring Waldeck castle; a vast stone wall with the character of an impregnable fortress. Eder dam and Möhne dam are of the same construction type, developed by the reservoir specialist Dr Otto Intze of the Rhine-Westphalian Technical University, Aachen.

More swiftly than the masons, the designers of the postcard production companies presented a new tourist attraction. The Möhne reservoir, in this postcard idyll, shows two symbols of progress in the twentieth century, the dam and, above it, an airship by Count Zeppelin. During World War I, Emperor Wilhelm II's airships had dropped bombs on Belgium, France and England. Twenty-five years later, during World War II, British night bombers destroyed German dams and made the impossible possible.

On 17 August 1912 Emperor Wilhelm II and his wife Auguste Victoria visited the construction site of the Eder dam. The imperial couple had arrived by car in the modern fashion; on the right the main power station at the equalising pond of the Möhne Lake.

of the reservoirs." On 19 May the German Press Agency had to come clean after all. After the terse mentioning in the armed forces report, now the regional newspapers were reporting, within whose areas of distribution the catastrophes could not be concealed at any rate, and in which the obituaries of entire families revealed the misery: "Concerning the attack on the reservoirs the German Press Agency learns that the losses among the civilian population turned out to be less than originally assumed. The number of casualties amounts to 370 citizens of the German Reich according to recent official assessments, in addition, 341 prisoners of war of various nationalities perished." This was only half the truth but, after a mere two days, no exact numbers could be given anyway. An exact number of victims cannot be determined even today, but it is probably more than 1,400. Corpses of many missing persons were never found. The news about the destruction of the reservoirs must have hit the Berlin governmental circles like a bomb. This is revealed by private notes in the diary of the Minister of Propaganda Joseph Goebbels from 18 May 1943. Yet even these lacked information and contained many errors, due to the short span of time that had elapsed since the events.

Dr Goebbels noted: "The English flew in with thirty to forty crafts dispersed over a large area, at heights between fifty and three hundred metres; the return flight took place at 3,000–5,000 metres. Among others, the Eder reservoir, the Möhne reservoir and the Sorpe dam were attacked and severely hit. The Eder reservoir was illuminated with headlights by the enemy crafts circling above it for some time, and then two torpedoes were dropped into the basin, which was filled until it hit the brim, at which point, the retaining wall was ripped apart to a width of forty metres across. The water masses disgorged with rapid flow into the surrounding area. Thirty villages were flooded. In part, they are no longer visible at all. Some people were able to save themselves by climbing onto the roofs. A rescue mission has not been possible so far, because even the pioneers could not reach them due to the rapid current. Great loss of lives has to be expected. Great losses in cattle and crop shortfalls have to be taken into account, too. The power station was damaged, but the shortfall in electric power is currently still calculated. Also at the Möhne reservoir the dam was demolished from the inside out by aerial torpedoes, and the power station was torn away. Considerable damage was done to the supply of drinking and extinguishing water in the Ruhr area, equally a substantial power failure had to be noted. At the Sorpe reservoir the dam was likewise damaged, the vicinity badly flooded. As the telephone lines are destroyed, no exact information is at hand so far."

After a note on the war in Serbia the Minister of Propaganda further writes: "The past night has brought us heavy damage in the aerial war. The attack of the British bombers on our reservoirs has experienced great success. The Leader is extraordinarily impatient and angry about the lack of preparation on the side of our air forces. At first very dramatic reports were transmitted from the districts concerned, yet the impact of the attack reveals itself to be not quite as devastating in the course of the day. For a while, several thousand victims were mentioned. The damage to production brought about can be considered as exceeding the usual. Naturally the leaders in the districts, in which reservoirs not attacked so far are located, are very much concerned, since the air defence at the reservoirs is entirely inadequate. The reports coming in from the districts affected by the flood disaster speak a very clear language. Unfortunately some people of the ministry's staff adopt certain imaginations induced by panic, especially Berndt (journalist), who is bombarding me the whole day with telephone calls, but from which nothing factual can be gleaned. Of course they brag mightily about the achieved success in London. Some English reconnaissance planes have already determined that the attack on the reservoirs has succeeded. Incidentally we admit this openly in the report of the Armed Forces High Command. It is only a small consolation that London experienced air-raid alarms three times last night, too. We were above the British capital only with nuisance raiders and could not cause any exceptional damage. The English now make it big with the reporting on the aerial war. They exaggerate in a manner which gets on one's nerves. Admittedly they can call upon remarkable successes. They predict further very severe air raids and propagandise an intensification of the aerial war which will certainly bother us considerably during the next weeks and months."

On 19 May 1943 Goebbel's private chronicle reads: "There is hardly another topic with the English and the Americans than that of the aerial war. Their successful attack on the German reservoirs is the great sensation both in London and in Washington. They are of course very much in the know in terms of what they have achieved with this attack. The former Berlin Reuters correspondent Bettany explains that the plan for this attack originated from a Jewish immigrant from Berlin. I am having this explanation summarised for a short report to be issued in the Reich territory, especially in the areas affected by the disaster. Therefore we see here, how dangerous the Jews are and how right we are to take them into secure custody. (The English Reuters report was a false story.) The Americans naturally turn the flooding of a large part of the vicinity into the most stunning sensation imaginable. Admittedly the ensuing consequences are quite devastating for our armament. The casualties are – thank God – not as high as we had feared in the beginning. The English and the Americans already speak of 10,000 dead. In reality the number lies between 1,000 and 2,000. It seems clear to me that concerning the attack, treason was at work even within the Reich territory, as the English were so unerringly orientated and have such a detailed knowledge of what damage they have

An image from the peaceful Twenties at the Möhne Lake: a hydroplane with floats and a motor power of 450hp, type Junkers F 13 (W), has landed at the public bathing beach of Delecke to take onlookers on board and to advertise aviation. In the background the tree-studded dam leading to the bridge at Delecke is visible.

Bathers observe the hydroplane take-off from the springboard of the beach. Today an air show on the lake would no longer be possible. In those years many excursionists from the Ruhr area visited the newly discovered recreational area of the Möhne Lake for camping and bathing.

Between the First and Second World War, leading aeroplane manufacturers competed to build increasingly powerful hydroplanes with more powerful engines. Flying competitions thus promoted the technological development. Hydroplanes and airboats offered the potential to launch from any body of open water without the need to build expensive airports with runways.

The construction of the Möhne dam was based on an idea by the German reservoir pioneer Prof Dr Otto Intze of the Technical University, Aachen, who developed the principle of the curved gravity dam at the end of the nineteenth century. It counters the pressure of the dammed-up water by its own weight. 267,000cbm masonry mass virtually rides out the water pressure. Today the Möhne Lake is a reservoir with 134.5 million cubic metres of drinking water for the conurbation of the Ruhr area. The government architect, Dr Ernst Link, a student of the reservoir pioneer Otto Intze, calculated the statistics and the technical details of the construction, the first barrage of the Ruhr Reservoir Society. The competition for the external design of the dam was won by the Cologne architect Franz Brantzky, among seventy-two applicants. His prize-winning towers with copper roofs had served as platforms for anti-aircraft batteries since the beginning of the war.

From a holding pattern above the Arnsberg forest, the Lancaster bombers flew straight towards the dam, over the wooded peninsula formed by the Möhne and Heve basins. From the opposite shore to the retaining wall their flight lasted just fifteen seconds. Only during this short span of time could the two centimetres anti-aircraft guns fire effectively at the attacking aircraft.

caused even after the attack, that we can hardly assume that they could have determined this solely by aerial reconnaissance."

After a few diary entries on the history of war, Goebbels further writes about the reservoir disasters: "The devastations caused at the reservoirs show themselves to be not quite as severe as we had initially expected. Yet all the same they suffice to create considerable difficulties for our industries at Rhine and Ruhr. At first roughly five thousand to seven thousand casualties were listed, now it has come to light that there are only roughly 700 in total, of which half are Russian prisoners of war. The reports by Berndt which caused me such headache during the first day reveal themselves to be wholly exaggerated and hyped. Apparently Berndt took his information from Radio London. We see herein once more, how impractical and irrational it is to pass on such alarmist reports to the higher leadership posts. Firstly they burden the latter tremendously, and secondly they are not correct in most cases. I am issuing a short notice on the casualties of the attack on the reservoirs, primarily because the English and Americans are turning this matter into a huge sensation and are speaking of thousands of dead and hardly repairable devastations. Most likely the communiqué issued by us will turn out to be a slap in the face of these illusions."

On 20 May 1943 Goebbels notes in his diary: "In the evening Speer calls me and gives me a report on the reservoirs catastrophe. He flew there immediately and has inspected the damage inflicted. Thank God it is not as severe as Speer had initially assumed. He has taken a series of far reaching measures, especially by withdrawing a large contingent of workers from the Atlantic Wall and assigning them to clear the inflicted damage, in total there are 6,000 to 7,000 men who are already on their way and will soon be called into action. Speer expresses the hope that we will succeed in getting production into motion again to some degree by the beginning of next week. By the end of next week it ought to be in full swing once more. Speer is a veritable genius for organisation. He does not allow himself to be stumped and ruffled, even by great calamities, he immediately takes the adequate measures and doesn't ever shy away from dictatorial arrangements, if they serve the cause. The Leader has given him absolute authority, and he has made full use of this, too."

This covers the comments on the reservoirs attacks in Goebbels' diary.

"Reports from the Reich"

The secret situation reports of the Security Service of the SS also dealt with the reservoirs attacks in the "reports from the Reich". One of the tasks of the Security Service of the SS was the operation of a domestic police intelligence service within the Reich Security Head Office for the purpose of investigating the public opinion on many aspects of life and on the impact of measures by the government. From numerous individual reports from the judiciary, administration, economy, culture and informants, the "polling body of the dictatorship" formed its opinion analyses and situation reports, which Heinz Boberach published in 1984 in 17 volumes from the holdings of the Federal Archive in Coblenz. The "Reports from the Reich" (NT 385) from 24 May 1943 report under the heading "Miscellaneous":

"Among the military events the current development of the aerial war is, according to the existing reports, most frequently discussed by all parts of the population with great concern. The impact of the attack on the Möhne and Eder reservoirs, in its extent often very much exaggerated, has gotten around the entire Reich territory very quickly, and partly alarmed the population to a high degree, especially since the armed forces report mentioned the loss of lives as high. Particularly during the first days, the most nonsensical rumours were spread among large parts of the population, e.g. 10,000 to 30,000 casualties were named. After the official numbers of dead were announced, a certain calming took place, although the reported numbers are met with a very deep distrust. Yet they are considered as the benchmark for the fact that the numbers spread by rumour must be too high. Large sections of the population believe themselves to be informed by the circulating tales on the devastations caused by the floods and the economic damages, too, and see therein proof for a 'cold-blooded planning of the aerial war in the enemies' camp'. The attack on the reservoirs has demonstrated that we can be hit most severely from the air by comparably minimal means. Frequently the inflicted destructions achieved by an attack on the reservoirs have been called more serious than the impacts of the terror attacks on the Ruhr area. Many fellow Germans look for an explanation as to how such an attack could be possible at all; they fear that the securing of the reservoirs by anti-aircraft batteries and barrage balloons was not sufficient." The Security Service of the SS knew the vox populi concerning the reservoirs catastrophe.

A District President Makes a Report

Not only did the population ask itself why the retaining walls fell victim to the bombs, but also those responsible unofficially looked for an excuse or an explanation for the reservoirs disaster. District president Eickhoff in Arnsberg writes to the Reich Minister of the Interior, Dr. Frick, in Berlin on 24 June 1943: "The attack of the enemy Air Force on the Möhne reservoir, its military success and its catastrophic consequences gave rise to the following questions: How could it happen that this attack was carried out in this manner? How could it lead to such a success on the retaining wall? Why couldn't the loss of human life have been avoided, after the inevitable material damage had occurred, with the possible exception of the loss of cattle? In accordance with these questions, the issue follows if and where responsibility lies, whose negligence has led to culpability in the event as a whole or in its catastrophic extent. As far as this problem points to military matters, these have to be left aside entirely, as they cannot be the subject of this report. Such matters can only be considered here as given facts which cannot be verified from the outside.

The idea of an air strike on reservoirs is not novel and not unknown. This is demonstrated by a publication of Camille Rougeron (eminent French technical writer for military aviation of the pre-war period) with the title: 'Aviation Bombing', in which such an attack is discussed in detail. As such, all authorities concerned with reservoirs, both military and civilian, must have been aware of the possibility. They were therefore obliged to do everything in their power to prevent such an attack or to mitigate its consequences. Incidentally, the administration had even alerted the military authorities to this publication. The Ruhr Reservoir Society, in agreement with the district president of Arnsberg, addressed the petition, attached here as a copy, to the commander of the Air Force, district VI Münster, on 28 August 1939, and sent a copy of this letter to the General Command A.K. on 5 September 1939. Herein the publication of Camille Rougeron is referred to explicitly. The purpose of this petition by the Ruhr Reservoir Society, which actually clearly predicted the disaster that came to pass, was to obtain military protection for the reservoirs. At that time the district Air Force Command initially rejected a securing of the reservoirs by flak entirely. (Letter of the Military District Command from 15 September 1939, dept. Ic no. 339/39.)

Therefore, if the possibility of an air strike on a reservoir was known to the military authorities, and they were pointed to this prospect by the administration immediately at the outbreak of war, so these authorities were alerted to this event more particularly by the fact that the English executed an air raid on the largest reservoir of Sardinia. About this the district air force command VI Münster has also been informed by a letter of the Ruhr Reservoir Society from 1 February 1941.

The decision as to whether this possibility could become an actual enemy operation in our land, and which military counter-measures had to be taken for the protection of the reservoirs, now lay solely with the military authorities. Most of all it was their duty to inform the administration about the military options and means for an attack as well as their impact on the retaining walls, so that the latter was enabled to take the necessary counter-measures in its area. This information was not provided to the possible and necessary extent.

With the aid of twenty-two letters, meetings and negotiations with representatives of the Reich Air Ministry and the armed forces authorities in Münster, the senior mayor of Essen, Justus Dillgardt, also chairman of the Ruhr Reservoir Society, achieved in a tenacious struggle some defence at the Möhne dam. Justus Dillgardt's efforts are dated from the 28 August 1939 before the outbreak of war until 12 May 1942. Tirelessly he alerted the military authorities of the endangerment of the reservoirs by air, and sent graphic illustrations of the connections between storage contents and storage levels of his reservoirs in order to point out the increased danger of catastrophe during full capacity. On 12 June 1941 the district Air Force Command VI Münster answered the Ruhr Reservoir Society: 'Regular reports on storage level and volume in the two reservoirs are no longer necessary to be sent here!' The Ruhr Reservoir Society also emphasised in its warnings that the size of the bombs dropped by the enemy increased steadily and so the possibility of a destruction of the dam crest rose. Also the district president in Arnsberg, Eickhoff, had alerted the Reich Air Ministry in Berlin emphatically to the endangerment of the reservoirs by air. Yet this predicted disaster was considered impossible by the military authorities. At the behest of the Ruhr Reservoir Society the following protection against air strikes was set up at the Möhne reservoir:

1. At the outbreak of war, flak protection was installed. Even platforms for the installation of artillery pieces were erected. Until the start of the offensive in the west in 1940, medium-sized anti-aircraft guns and spotlights were stationed at the Möhne reservoir.

2. After the beginning of the western offensive in 1940, the flak protection was withdrawn in its entirety.
3. In autumn 1940, two centimetre flak arrived which was withdrawn in spring 1941.
4. In autumn 1942, two centimetre flak was installed once more which remained until the attack.
5. From spring until autumn 1942, a balloon barrage was positioned all around the Möhne Lake. It was withdrawn without replacement.
6. At the beginning of 1943, torpedo nets were cast in front of the retaining wall. No smoke screen installation existed until 17 May 1943 at any reservoir nor were any of the reservoirs connected to the air raid warning network until then."

The district president in Arnsberg further writes to the Reich Minister of the Interior in Berlin: "As the administration was convinced that an air raid on the reservoirs was achievable and also would take place, as the attack on Sardinia demonstrated, it was its task to ascertain the extent of the impact of such an attack in order to take appropriate protective measures. The documents for this had to be provided by the military, as only these authorities knew the type of the enemy weapons and the extent of their effects." On 10 October 1939 the Ruhr Reservoir Society received an express letter from the Reich Air Ministry with information on the anticipated scale of the opening due to destruction at the Möhne retaining wall after an air strike. The assumptions expressed by the Air Force on the extent of the destructive potential were in part based on detonation tests at the decommissioned Bever dam undertaken at the instigation of the Reich Air Ministry. On 17 October the Ruhr Reservoir Society via the district president of Arnsberg sent to the Reich Air Ministry a detailed report on the expected damage of the flood waves, which would arise from the destruction of the Möhne reservoir.

On 14 November 1939 all retaining walls in the administrative district Arnsberg had been examined for the possibility of destruction through site visits. From the mural crown the Möhne dam broadens from 6.25 metres to 34.20 metres at the base. According to information from the Reich Air Ministry a destruction of the wall to the width of seven metres could occur with the effect that a gap of 6.70 metres breadth would come about. The volume of water then draining away would have been roughly 625 cubic metres per second according to the calculation of the Ruhr Reservoir Society. That would have corresponded to approximately double the amount of the highest flood to be expected. This was the basis provided by the expert authorities in charge of the measures taken by the administration.

In order to be entirely sure, a water volume of 1,000 cubic metres per second was taken as the basis. This amount would have resulted in a flood of threatening extent, but nowhere near the disaster that actually took place. 120 million cubic metres drained from the Möhne reservoir, initially with an amount per second of over 8,800 cubic metres. So a destruction of the retaining wall of entirely unexpected extent occurred as a consequence of the hitherto unknown explosive effect of the enemy aircraft ammunition. According to the escaping water volume calculated as 1,000 cubic meters per second and the speed of its travel, a warning service was installed at the reservoirs. Already some years before the war, special attention had been given by the government of Arnsberg to the problem of protecting the reservoirs not only with a view to the water management, but in particular also in the light of safeguarding the population against the dangers to be feared from damage to the reservoir dams. So regulations were put into place for the warning service by civil servants of the administration and the knowledgeable and experienced Ruhr Reservoir Society. These were announced per circular by the district president of Arnsberg NI. 336/40g on 5 June 1940.

For each reservoir a schedule exists which lists the communication from the reservoir guard to all places threatened by the water. The communication is drawn largely on the collaboration of the Reich Postal Service. In the case of imminent danger the guard of the Möhne reservoir informs the trunk exchange in Soest, number zero. The trunk exchange then calls the endangered towns and administrative bodies along the course of Möhne and Ruhr in the sequence of their endangerment. In this case, in order: town of Neheim, department of Werl, department of Fröndenberg, department of Menden, town of Schwerte, town of Westhofen, flood control centre of Hengsteysee. From this control centre the commissioners of the participating districts, the district president, the water supply works and the towns and departments situated further downriver are informed. The purpose of this facility is that the initially endangered places are informed as soon as possible without regard to the administrative connections and responsibilities. The participating authorities were obliged to pay special attention to securing the correct procedure of the warning and information service. The Reich Postal Administration Dortmund confirmed by letter on 6 June 1940, to which trunk exchanges the reservoir guards had to send their information and which numbers had to be dialled. This information was passed on to the guards. The Reich Postal Administration Dortmund further informs in its letter that it would check the telephone connections of the reservoir guards daily at the start of work for their operability, as per arrangement. With this the system of the warning service was installed. The experience made during the break of the Möhne dam has shown that this warning system was sufficient for an erupting water volume of 1,000 cubic metres per second, as calculated. The imagined amount would not have travelled at such a speed so as to impede a timely warning, directed at the endangered inhabitants of the valley.

The explosive effect of the hitherto unknown weapons used in the attack on 17 May 1943 (probably mines with underwater detonators) was of such force that a much larger hole was torn into the wall. Instead of the calculated breach of 6.70 metres breadth to a depth of the wall of seven metres, an almost rectangular gap of seventy-seven metres breadth and twenty-two metres depth was rent. The water volume streaming into the valley was thus considerably larger and sped along at twenty to thirty kilometres per hour, depending on the width of the valley. With this speed in play, the intended warning service had no hope of keeping pace, let alone keeping ahead.

Nevertheless, thanks to the generally good organisation of the warning service and the timely intervention of the government of Arnsberg (district director Niewisch), a warning of the permanent special service reached the police administration in Neheim before the arrival of the flood wave. The scheduled report from the reservoir guard to the trunk exchange Soest and from the latter to listed police administrations in the valley occurred correctly, too. Yet it was delayed by the fact that due to the enormous vibrations of the retaining wall the telephone installation of the reservoir guard was destroyed, as was the telephone line in his living quarters, and he had to speak from a different location. Due to this loss of time, and the fact that, due to the speed of the flood wave, the telephone installations in the valleys were put out of order, the message from the trunk exchange at Soest did not get through. The single official warning which reached Neheim via the government in Arnsberg was transferred by another means. The reservoir guard and senior forestry official Wilkening, who had a main telephone connection via the centre below the retaining wall, could not make a connection to the trunk exchange Soest, either, as the centre had been destroyed by the impact of the bombs. After the loss of valuable minutes, he could reach the trunk exchange Soest via the exchange Körbecke and cable the message "catastrophic flood" between 1.10 and 1.15am.

According to the postal clerk, this call came through around 1.30 or 1.35am. Due to an electric blackout the postal clerks were impeded and had to work by candle light. The connection to Neheim ran via Menden and was disrupted. Perhaps the trunk exchange Neheim was already under water and made getting through impossible. The motorist intended as a substitute was not able to get the message through either, due to the speed with which the flood rushed down into the valleys and washed over the streets.

The government of Arnsberg immediately requested military support units for the endangered communities. Three Arnsberg government officials arrived at 1.20am at the Möhne reservoir which was still under attack. From the hotel "Möhne Lake Terraces" they tried to pass on messages to police departments situated down in the valleys, but this did not succeed. By time-consuming detours the officials reached Neheim at 3am. In the police department, which was situated in the higher-lying part of town, they met the commander of the regular police force and the Reich defence commissioner, vice district leader Hoffmann, as well as the vice district president in order to initiate further supportive measures. "During the night of the attack I (the district president) was on an official trip in Berlin and after my return I adopted without delay, together with the Reich defence commissioner, the measures necessary as a result of the on-going events. If in hindsight considerations are given whether alternative or better possibilities of warning existed, the following has to be said in response: The material damage, as unfortunate as it is, could have been prevented only to a very insignificant degree – e.g. the timely rescue of grazing cattle – with any other conceivable warning system, too, as the residences, industrial complexes, sheds, barns etc. in the endangered area must remain in the danger zone. The deeply regrettable loss of human life couldn't have been prevented in a danger zone of five kilometres below the retaining wall with any other warning system, since nothing could have been saved from the enormous force of the assaulting wave in front of the retaining wall.

Concerning the areas situated further down the valley, a large part of the people killed in the disaster could probably have been saved, theoretically speaking, if they had been warned in time. Yet this was unfortunately not possible in the given situation, as the potential extent of the explosive effect of enemy bombs was given incorrectly by the authorities in charge. Based on this, the warning system was set up on the assumption of a much lower travelling speed of the water. If the authorities in charge had only made a report in time, that a much higher explosive effect had to be considered and hence a much higher water eruption, so it

Hidden between the mountains of the Waldecker Land lies the Eder reservoir. The lake of twenty-seven kilometres width, not spanned by any bridge, is dammed by the almost forty-seven metre tall retaining wall. Twenty-four million gold marks including the acquisition of the grounds were spent on the reservoir of 202.4 million cubic metres, serving as water supply for the Weser. The Waldeck or Hemfurth reservoir, as it was initially called, was constructed between 1908 and 1914. At that time Germany's largest reservoir, it is today number three after the Bleiloch reservoir (215 million cbm) in Thuringia and the Schwammenauel reservoir (205 million cbm) in the Eifel.

The inauguration on 25 August 1914 with its invitation to His Majesty Emperor Wilhelm II fell victim to the outbreak of World War I on 1 August 1914. The air raid during the fateful night of 17 May 1943 was flown through the ravine past the Waldeck castle, across the headland of the Hammerberg towards the dam (white line). Neither torpedo nets nor anti-aircraft installations protected the barrage.

The Sorpe dam rises sixty-nine metres above the valley ground, rock fill with a concrete core, damming seventy million cubic metres of water. For many years the highest dam in Germany, it was opened to the public on 20 April 1936 by the inauguration of the 700m long dam road.

The white lines mark the approaches of the Lancaster bombers. McCarthy approached the target without headlights in parallel flight, coming from Langscheid. Kenneth Brown attacked the dam with blazing headlights from the lake side on a route not stipulated. Their bouncing bombs were released conventionally without rotation. They both exploded almost at the same spot, below the crest at the centre of the road, at a depth of four to six metres at the sloping Sorpe dam. Here the hydrostatic fuse set to 9.1 metres did not react. The Sorpe dam withstood all air raids of the Second World War.

would have been determined with the particular thoroughness and diligence, with which such matters are always dealt with here, that a warning system based on telephone reports by the reservoir guards could not keep pace with the speed of the flood wave. Thus a speedier and more secure warning system would need to have been installed, as far as one was possible in terms of available technological capabilities. Or the endangered areas had to be evacuated for the duration of the war. Immediately after the advent of the disaster I have examined with the telephone office in charge the possibility of a warning system uninfluenced by the failure of the regular telephone network. The idea of the telephone technician was to the effect that a cable is embedded into the retaining wall, which changes simultaneously with any alteration within the substance of the wall and thus triggers an alarm to all endangered districts independently and without the necessity of human involvement. The examination is not concluded yet. Difficulties arise in the obtaining of materials and the layout of the line. Meanwhile a warning system has been installed at all reservoirs, so that the people in the endangered areas can leave the danger zone in time."

Here ends the report of the district president Eickhoff to the Reich Minister of the Interior Dr. Frick who visited the Möhne reservoir shortly after the attack with a delegation. One could not speak of a warning system before the attack on the Möhne reservoir. It was merely a warning installation with a messaging schedule according to the "snowball system". A water alarm plan with rules of conduct for the valleys' inhabitants during a flooding was missing, also special recognisable acoustic signals to prompt the population to leave the bomb shelters, furthermore, signs for escape routes to higher ground. Informing the administrations and police departments was futile, as they had no hope of getting the population out of the bomb shelters during an on-going air raid alert. The German Air Force considered a successful air strike on the Möhne reservoir impossible, but pointed to danger by sabotage from the ground. Therefore the district president of Arnsberg installed object protection, together with the commander of the regular police force Münster. Already on 1 September 1939 the district commissioners in Arnsberg, Soest, Olpe, Altena, Schwelm and Meschede were instructed by decree to place the reservoirs in their districts under object protection. The command responsible for ground protection at the Möhne reservoir consisted of twelve men and was controlled during the war years by a staff officer of the uniformed police or a police officer for air defence matters.

The "Bomber Committee" Facing Many Problems

Against the background of the looming Second World War, the British military also paid attention to the German dams. At the eighteenth meeting of the "bomber committee" on 26 July 1938 in London, at the Air Ministry, the topic of discussion was: air raids on reservoirs and barrages. The prevailing opinion of the past was that targets of the aforementioned kind could only be attacked from the air with extreme difficulty and little economic success. Therefore the significance and far reaching consequences of a successful attack on certain barrages in potential enemy countries had not been fully appreciated until then. These targets found no mention in the current edition of the handbook of air tactics. The chairman of the "bomber committee" said that more recent studies had shown that certain barrages in Germany and Italy formed something of an "Achilles heel" in those countries, because the industrial power potential is based on energy which was generated almost exclusively from those sources. Therefore the aim of this meeting would be to study the possible extent to which the dams and other similar targets could be attacked from the air.

The information available at that time was briefly summarised and circulated as B.C. Paper no. 16. It describes the construction types of mural crowns, the effects of different assault weapons and evaluates the accuracy of a bombardment from great height. The meeting's protocol records: the whole of Germany uses only three times the amount of water as the Ruhr region by itself, and a large part of this water is solely provided by one large reservoir called the Möhne barrage, dammed up by a simple gravity retaining wall.

By the destruction of the Möhne reservoir, electric power would be cut off, primarily through flooding of the hydroelectric power stations in the Ruhr valley. Another five reservoirs were mentioned, which in part supply the waterways in Germany. A disruption of these water reservoirs would cause the waterways to dry up. As water transport has great importance for the German transport system, additional traffic would have to be diverted onto roads and railways. This would lead very soon to chaotic situations. Squadron Leader Burge then presented photographs of various German barrages to the members of the bomber committee for evaluation. The committee decided to deal with the gravity dams first, since this type was easier to attack from the air. An important question was whether the attack should be carried out against the valley or the water side. A discussion of the methods of attack and types of weapons followed. It was suggested to drop heavy bombs from a great height, a propeller-driven bomb of the SAP type of at least 250kg, or torpedoes. Then, however, doubts arose as to whether a weapon of that calibre could cause sufficient damage to the wall. Group Captain Bottomley asked about the greater explosive effect of a 500kg bomb. Dr Ferguson of the research department Woolwich explained that a heavy bomb would have to be detonated on the water side with a time lag in order to promise some success. Bombs of 1,000kg with high explosive power were not yet available, Wing Commander Rowley answered. It was discussed whether any plane could even carry a 1,000kg bomb. The Wellington bomber was a year away from being ready.

A representative of the admiralty pointed out that the bundling of several small torpedoes would have the same effect. Torpedo nets made of dense wire mesh laid out in front of the retaining walls by the Germans could cause problems. Item 51 of the protocol explores the possibility of similar barrages existing in England, which could potentially be attacked by the enemy in a similar manner. Further, what defensive measures had been taken at the reservoirs in Wales which serve the supply of Birmingham and Liverpool. Nothing was known of any defensive measures. Item 65 of the eighteenth meeting of the bomber committee records the decisions in summary: Due to identifiable reasons, a full practical series of trials of assault methods and weapon types against a viable target, which was discussed during the meeting, is impractical in conditions of peace. Yet the technical data and theoretical implications have to be viewed logically with the possibility of modifying in response to future developments.

The bomber committee was of the opinion that the destruction of barrages by attacks from the air could be a feasible operation with certain qualifications.

1. Attacks from low altitude above water or shallow diving depth are viewed as the most successful and desirable from the operation's viewpoint.
2. A gravity retaining wall is the type exacting an attack. The recommended weapons on the basis of the currently existing information are, in the order of importance:
   a) a number of torpedoes,
   b) 250kg general purpose bombs,
   c) 250kg anti-submarine bombs,
   d) large 500kg or 1,000kg bombs, as far as these are developed.

The chances of success with the aforementioned torpedoes are viewed as less favourable. Yet in the case of pressing necessity in the immediate future, the 250kg general purpose bombs and the 250kg anti-submarine bombs would be the only weapons available; so far the protocol of the eighteenth meeting of the bomber committee on 26 July 1938.

Already from September 1937 the British Air Force had detailed intelligence material on the largest German reservoirs of the potential war opponent gathered. The design of the High Command of the Royal Air Force was the arsenal of the Reich at the Ruhr, the heart of the German arms industry with the connecting waterways of the Weser and the Mittelland Canal on which war material was transported. The Ruhr area should be dried up in a single strike and the hydroelectric power stations along the Ruhr should be neutralised in order to shorten the length of the war. The Bomber Command paper no. 16 "Air Attacks on Reservoirs and Dams" contains some map exercises and studies which were frequently discussed, but impossible to realise, given the conventional means of the pre-war years. All suggestions turned out to be impractical. Remote-controlled planes laden with explosives were supposed to float against the retaining wall, before detonating. Hydroplanes were to be sunk in front of the dam, with their explosive load detonating under water.

An attack with conventional aircraft bombs promised little chance of success, since bomb drops from high altitude showed scatterings of 100 to 200 metres. Hits by torpedoes would merely scratch the retaining wall. Thousands of kilograms of explosives would be necessary to destroy such a gigantic wall. This amount would have to be detonated in one go. The only possible method to destroy the stone masonry by an air strike would be the deployment of 100 heavy "M" sea mines at the top edge of the retaining wall with the simultaneous detonation of a high explosive bomb. The practical difficulties of this method were considerable and in the end not feasible.

After the outbreak of the war the High Command of the Royal Air Force intensified the war games around the destruction of German reservoirs. At the beginning of May 1940 the dropping of super-heavy bombs with 9,080kg weight were considered, which were supposed to explode in front of the retaining wall at depth of thirteen metres, and then the wall might "go". Even if the load were made to detonate in ten units of 908kg, each in short succession, this could lead to the same result. It was speculated whether a container could be developed, loaded with explosives, which operated on the surface of the water like a hydroplane or even

In March 1930, a letter to the editor against the construction of the Bleiloch reservoir was published in the newspaper "The National Socialist" in Weimar. In a forecast, it presented similar considerations as those given later in Great Britain, concerning the possibility of dam destruction and its consequences.

underwater like a torpedo. A low flying plane was supposed to deploy the container 1,000 metres before the retaining wall at a speed of 130km/h. With this weapon, even targets protected by torpedo nets in German marine harbours at the Atlantic Coast would be open to attack.

The deployment of forty torpedoes detonated simultaneously – each with 200kg of explosives, so 8,000kg in total – must lead to success at the Möhne dam. On 2 June 1941 the deployment of a glider loaded with dynamite was debated, that would contract its wing after landing on the Mohne Lake, before jumping the impeding torpedo nets. The carrier plane would have to descend from 7,000 metres altitude to 2,000 metres at night, fly to the wall in a right angle and trigger the explosive glider eight kilometres before the target. The latter was supposed to land 800 metres before the retaining wall, and a motor was supposed to propel it further over the torpedo nets against the wall. After the impact on the wall, it must sink and explode at the pre-installed depth of thirteen metres. Fifteen crafts must attack consecutively in this manner. According to this plan, several such glider weapons were supposed to wait for each other underwater and made to detonate at the same time by an initial explosion. So the attacking crafts would remain outside the reach of the anti-aircraft guns.

One suggestion referred to the new two-motor Wellington bomber which could carry a 1,360kg bomb to the target under each wing. Ten planes whose bombs would be made to explode close to the wall at a depth of thirteen metres, even with time delay, could bring the desired result. Even the deployment of a sabotage command dropped off by parachutes was taken into consideration. Until the end of 1942 no planes were available in England which could transport super-heavy bombs and drop them accurately, moreover against the Möhne reservoir protected by flak and balloon barrages. The suggestions of the first general plan for the destruction of the German reservoirs revealed themselves to be impractical. Furthermore, British water management experts believed in the indestructibility of such huge stone walls, too. Wallis added later that English politicians unfortunately had insufficient scientific education to realise the great importance of the reservoirs for the German arms industry.

The Civilian Barnes Wallis Goes to War

When the war broke out, Wallis was chief of the aeronautical research and developing department of the British Aircraft Corporation in Weybridge. Here, entirely independent to the Air Ministry, he had devoted himself to the question of how the Axis Powers' energy sources in Germany and Italy could be destroyed. The archived expert literature provided Wallis with the necessary documentation, especially on the German reservoirs. He firmly believed in the possibility of stopping the steel production of the German armament industry through the loss of the water reservoirs of the Ruhr area. The importance of the reservoirs was obvious, since 100 tons of water were necessary for the production of one ton of steel. German publications in the "Journal for Civil Engineering", "Journal for the Entire Water Management", "Journal of Civil Engineering" within "Swiss Water Management" and "The Field of Gas and Water" showed Wallis the most intricate technical details of Germany's water reservoirs. With his study "Note on the Method of Attacking the Axis Powers" dealing in detail with the destruction of German reservoirs, Wallis gained the attention of military leaders and politicians, who were at first suspicious of his motives. Wallis believed that at the end of 1940 or the beginning of 1941, a heavy bomb, weighing ten ton, and dropped from an altitude of 13,000 metres, would penetrate deeply into the ground near the retaining wall, explode, and cause edifices to collapse due to the shock waves striking their foundations. (Wallis would realise this idea in 1945, when his ten ton "Grand Slam" bombs destroyed submarine bunkers on the Channel Coast and railway viaducts in Bielefeld and Arnsberg). Yet at this time neither an "earthquake bomb" nor a plane able to drop it accurately were available. At the beginning of the war the British military had a low opinion of the large bomb theory. Some could not be convinced, others were of the opinion that the project was technically unachievable. Nevertheless, from August 1940 onwards, Wallis succeeded in testing streamlined model bombs in a wind tunnel in Teddington. Also in the Road Research Laboratory Harmondsworth, led by Dr. W.H. Glanville, a series of trial detonations were run from October 1940, which were connected to the destruction of the Möhne dam.

The aim was to find out how close to the retaining wall a ten ton bomb, dropped from operational altitude by a huge "Victory" bomber, had to explode to cause it to collapse. The Road Research Laboratory was deeply involved in military projects since the outbreak of war and had considerable experience in model building for predicting specific explosions and their impact. The director of the institute, Dr. Glanville, discussed with Wallis the latter's problems and agreed spontaneously to arrange a trial series on different barrage models. The idea of the dam model test was very simple. The starting point was to use the same material, in proportion to the size of the Möhne dam. The original in Germany would react in the same manner during the explosions. Dr. Glanville gathered a team under the direction of Dr. Collins for the study of the dam model tests. Responsible for the measurements and the explosion physics was the scientific advisor (Officer) D.G. Charlesworth. Dr. Collins remembers: "The dams at Möhne and Eder consist of massive stone masonry, and this is very stable by nature, even if it is breached. Of the two retaining walls, that on the Eder shows a greater height, but the Möhne retaining wall – built more conservatively – possesses on the water side a loam skirt reaching up to almost half the height. We therefore decided to recreate the Möhne retaining wall for both barrages in the scale of 1:50 as model, even with two dummy towers. The first Möhne retaining wall model was created as accurately as possible, as an uncertainty arose during the experiment concerning the actual gravity of the dam. Under the direction of Dr. N. Davey, lots of small stone blocks were produced by his team members in Garston in the "Building Research Station" and built up by hand into a Möhne wall model. A concrete model built later has been preserved and can still be visited today.

Wallis had suggested an explosive charge of seven tons for his ten ton bomb; true to scale, this would mean fifty-six grams of explosives for the model. He assumed that, with the deployment of a six-motor stratospheric bomber still only existing on the drawing board, a bomb would drop at a distance of forty-five metres before the retaining wall. These parameters were chosen as a starting base for the tests, also for the following concrete models. The first test ran with a detonation of fifty-six grams of gelatine dynamite at a distance of 0.90 metres before the model wall, corresponding to a forty-five meter distance on the water side of the original dam to the wall. The result was a vertical rent in the middle of the dam and a horizontal rupture below the dam crest.

A shock wave recording device installed at the model wall and working like a seismograph registered the movements of the model wall on the horizontal level which had vibrated almost up to the calculated frequency of ten Hz. For a retaining wall with foundations, even a to-and-fro motion of the retaining wall's centre piece of twenty Hz could be expected. The main vertical rupture in the model was ascribed to longitudinal stress resulting from a backlash effect from the dam curvature. The team felt that an explosive charge triggered at a specific distance would enable the induction of the collapse by making use of the wall curvature and of the strong water seal, and that the middle part would drop out of the retaining wall. The opinion was held that equivalent explosive charges at the Möhne and Eder dams would cause the same damage and would bring about repair works and a reduction of the storage capacity. Yet the result was not good enough to risk an air raid, moreover since the bomber targeting devices at that time only allowed hits at a distance up to forty-five metres. A closer distance would have been sheer luck. The test series with different explosion distances of 60.96cm and 30.48cm continued to run. The tests demonstrated, however, that a very difficult and extremely precise attack would have to be flown, and this was very unlikely to be put into practice. At no time was it considered to abort the trials. More and more models were needed. Due to time constraints the Road Research Laboratory manufactured concrete models with the aid of templates. So the production time was reduced to barely two weeks per model.

The scientist Barnes Wallis, the inventor of the bouncing bomb, in his office at Burhill, Walton-on-Thames, in which his bomb theory took shape; in a film interview with the author in 1969, he said: "The first thing an engineer thinks of as an effective means to stop the war is to look for an opportunity to obstruct the enemy's steel production. For almost 100 tons of water are necessary to produce one ton of steel ..." On the office wall hangs a large photograph of the Möhne dam with the washed-out torpedo nets. On 30 October 1979 Sir Barnes Wallis died at the age of ninety-two in England. In 1968 the Crown rewarded him with a knighthood for his service to Great Britain.

Author Helmuth Euler shows Barnes Wallis new images from the destroyed dams. In exchange, Barnes Wallis provided Helmuth Euler with many 35mm test films, photographs and documents free of charge. For twenty years they were top secret. In part they are stamped "most secret" or "under lock and key". In 1969 Dr Wallis explained in a film about the "Dams raid" made by the author: "The most regrettable matter of the whole project was the fact that a large number of women and children drowned in the valleys, as they were sitting locked inside the air raid shelters without warning. About this we are very sad, for that was not our intent; we firmly believed we would be able to stop German steel production by the destruction of the dams."

Parallel to the tests with the spherical projectiles in the water tanks of Teddington, the trial series with detonations at dam models were running at the Road Research Laboratory in Harmondsworth and in the Building Research Station in Garston. Dr A. R. Collins directed the tests for Barnes Wallis and discovered by chance the possibility of destroying the dam wall with a relatively small explosive charge by wall contact; in the aerial photograph Harmondsworth features in the aerial photograph above (top right of the trial field). This was were the detonations of scaled-down dam models took place.

Barnes Wallis fired different models from his "sample case" against a simulated dam wall across the water surface of an almost 200m long test tank at the National Physical Laboratory in Teddington, Middlesex. Wallis tried to discover the optimal weight, size, design, surface and speed for an ideal bouncing technique. All experiments were filmed on the surface and underwater.

A dam model at the scale 1:10 near the Nant-y-Gro dam in Wales is prepared for a trial detonation by the Road Research Laboratory in Harmondsworth.

A model of the Möhne dam at the scale of 1:50; special apparatuses, similar to seismographs, are attached to the model's wall. They are supposed to record the vibrations of the wall during underwater explosions at different distances.

A model of the Möhne dam still stands today on the testing ground of the Building Research Station in Garston near London, but with a hand-made breach; a commemoration of the trial series in spring 1943. The author filmed the old model in 1993.

During low water levels, a concrete model of the Eder dam rises from the lake near Nieder-Werbe. It was a display object by the hydraulic engineers for model tests before reservoir construction. Basic release and high water overspill at the dam were examined and documented with photographs. The trial object possesses a strong similarity to Barnes Wallis' dam models.

A super slow motion film with 222 images per second shows the explosion at a concrete model with enhanced curvature of the wall. Frames from this test film demonstrate the development of the breach in the dam. The aim of the research was to realise the connections between explosive charge, depth of the explosion at the wall and height of water level. The large-scale trials at the decommissioned Nant-y-Gro dam in Wales were filmed, too. A first detonation within the lake in front of the wall brought no result. The second large-scale trial with a 224kg water bomb having wall contact tore a hole into the fifty-five metre long and nine metre tall retaining wall and thus proved the correctness of the model theory. One instant too late, Dr A.R. Collins activated his slow motion camera and missed the phase of the successful detonation.

We had new doubts as to whether the concrete models with their thin foundations on loam reacted like the real retaining walls founded on rock on Möhne and Eder. Also we needed to find out if the simplified concrete models were like the masonry ones in terms of statics. The simplified models showed themselves to be slightly weaker than the accurately built ones. They were then adjusted in such a way as to show the same strength in relation to the retaining walls in Germany."

Members of the "Dam Buster Committee" followed the trials. At the end of 1941 Dr. Stradling suggested to the committee after an agreement with the proprietor, the Birmingham Corporation, to use the small decommissioned Nant-y-Gro dam for trials true to scale. The retaining wall was approximately nine metres high and fifty-five metres long, built straight without curvature from heavy concrete. It was situated in a quiet area and could be demolished without the water causing damage. Models were built and tested also from this dam at the scale of 1:10. Trials showed a different reaction between straight model walls and the curved ones of the Möhne models. Here, there was no recoil resulting … but the proof of a vertically bending movement in which the blocks within the wall structure were spun up by the explosion, to then fall back again into their original positions. Twenty-eight grams of explosives, triggered at a distance of 300mm and a depth of 300mm before the model wall of the Nant-y-Gro dam, showed the same damage as later twenty-eight kilograms detonated at three metres distance and at a three metre depth before the original dam. Ruptures had formed in the wall construction, and parts of the mural crown had become loose. The first large-scale trial ran satisfactorily, but an explosive charge of 13,600kg at a distance to the wall of fifteen metres would in all cases be necessary to cause damage at the Möhne and Eder dams.

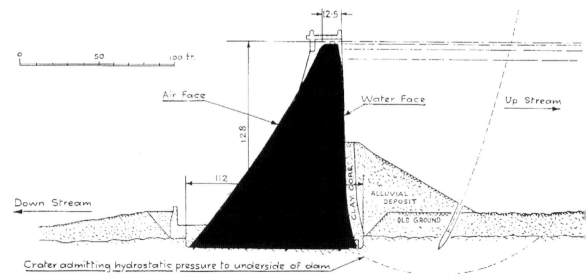

This drawing from Wallis' study "Note on the Method of Attacking the Axis Powers" shows the trajectory of a ten ton bomb towards the ground in front of the Möhne dam. Earthquake-like tremors triggered by the explosion were supposed to cause the construction to collapse.

Barnes Wallis had always had the idea to operate at the retaining wall with a contact charge, but the 'Dam Buster Committee', consisting of scientists and military officers, didn't consider this suggestion to be feasible in practice. But then 'Master Chance' came to the rescue. Shortly after the first large-scale test before the Nant-y-Gro dam, the research team had to remove a used dam model and decided for reasons of convenience to work with a contact charge. The impact proved itself to be unexpectedly high. Model parts had flown more than six metres down the valley, a 'giant rent' had opened the dam wall. At first, further tests ensued with contact charges of different sizes and in varying depths of water. On Friday, 24 July 1942, the second large-scale test at the Nant-y-Gro dam began, now with a contact charge of 127kg of explosives delivered by a water bomb of 224kg. Triggered in a depth of 3.48m, the explosion tore a spectacular breach of 18.29 width and 7.32m depth into the retaining wall. The model predictions were exceeded considerably in width and depth. Now they began to study the correlations of explosive charge, explosive depth at the wall and the height of the water level in the reservoirs. Soon all information was at hand, and the test series could be concluded. The basic research established: gravity dams can be destroyed by a single contact hit in a specific water depth of 9.1 metres with an explosive load of three to four tons. This weight could be transported to the German reservoirs by the Lancaster bomber newly taken into service, but a precision bombardment to the point seemed impossible.

English leaflets falling from the sky in Germany at that time
1939   "We will not surrender the Ruhr area to a single aerial bomb!" (Göring in Essen, 10/08/1939)
1940   "And if the British air force drops 2- or 3- or 4,000 kilograms of bombs, then we will drop in a single night 150,000, 180,000, 230,000, 300,000, 400,000 and more kilos! And if they declare they will attack our cities on a large scale, we will eradicate their cities!" (Hitler in Berlin, 04/09/1940)
1942   "From now on I will retaliate once more strike by strike!" Hitler in Berlin, 26/04/1942)
1943   "One day I will remember exactly what they have brought about in our country and I will possess sufficient pitilessness to pay back the strike." (Göring in Berlin, 30/01/1943)
1943   *On 18th February the Minister of Propaganda Dr. Joseph Goebbels in the Berlin Sports Palace demanded total war. He received the thunderous applause of the crowd, when he posed ten questions. "Total war – the briefest war" was the name of the game, and the people rose.*

The Reservoirs in the Sights of Bomber Command

On 28 March 1943 the general staff of the RAF once more summarised the targets in Germany and explained the economic and moral effects of the destruction of the Möhne reservoir and the increased impact of the simultaneous eradication of the Sorpe and Eder dams. The primary reservoirs situated in the drainage basin of the Ruhr are listed in the table.

Name	Year of Construction	Capacity/ million m³	Type	Height of wall/dam
Möhne reservoir	1908–1913	134	Stone wall	40.3 metres
Sorpe reservoir	1926–1935	70	Earthwork with concrete core	69 metres
Lister reservoir	1909–1912	22	Stone wall	40 metres
Ennepe reservoir	1902–1904	12.6	Stone wall	50.9 metres
Henne reservoir	1901–1905	11	Stone wall	37.9 metres
Total capacity		**249.6**		

Another seven smaller reservoirs with a total volume of twelve million cubic meters of water are found in the same drainage basin and bring the total capacity up to over 260 million cubic metres. It has to be stated that the Möhne reservoir alone holds fifty per cent of the Ruhr drainage basin, together with the Sorpe reservoir, seventy-five per cent. This fact proves: the Möhne and Sorpe reservoirs are the main water suppliers for the provisioning of the Ruhr area with non-potable water for industry and drinking water for the population. For the ever growing industry a strong increase in pump stations came about at the end of the nineteenth century, for the seasonal water shortage endangered the sufficient supply of drinking water to the region's population and threatened many industrial enterprises as well as the hydroelectric power stations along the Ruhr.

In this context it has to be noted that the water from other rivers in the Ruhr area, like Wupper and Emscher, is not suitable for the production of drinking water. As a consequence of this, a great reservoirs program was developed to gain natural water supplies. However, the program permanently lagged behind the demands. It is known that before World War II additional storage of 180 million cubic metres was planned. The effects of the destruction of the Möhne reservoir can be viewed under the following aspects:

1. direct destructions by flood waves,
2. loss of non-potable water for the industry and outage of electric energy (hydroelectric power stations),
3. wipe-out of railway lines and waterways in the Ruhr valley,
4. termination of supplies of drinking water and water for fire-fighting,
5. impact on the morale of the civilian population.

Direct destructions

Immediately after the breaking of the Möhne dam, considerable damage will take place in the Möhne-Ruhr valley. The extent can only be predicted with difficulty, but will be sufficient. Before the barrages were built, the average amount of water in the Ruhr amounted to 82.5 cubic metres near Mülheim, the highest flow rate was 153.5 cubic metres per second. Before the regulation of the river by barrages, lower lying areas were exposed to extensive floods, among them also districts of Schwerte, Herdecke, Wetter, Kettwig, Mülheim and Duisburg.

In case of the assumption that the breakage of the Möhne dam will lead to a complete drainage within ten hours, the average flow rate will amount to 3,720 cubic metres per second, peak rates will exceed this by far. The capacity of the Möhne reservoir alone suffices to trigger a catastrophe of the greatest extent in the Möhne and Ruhr valleys.

Impacts on the Ruhr industry

An extensive loss of electric capacity will occur through the destruction of thirteen known hydroelectric power stations situated between the Möhne dam and Mühlheim. The total output of these power plants amounts to 250,000 kilowatt. The pumping station near Herdecke alone produces 194,000 kilowatt. Even if the power stations are not destroyed in their entirety, their working capacity will be severely hampered by siltation and uncontrolled flow. In addition the coal power stations which need large amounts of non-potable water for cooling purposes, especially during the summer months, will decline in performance. The water shortage must also have an impact on the heavy industry, as furnaces, coking plants, mines and chemical plants need enormous amounts of water for their production. Insufficient amounts of water have a double effect on the industrial production:

1. the direct effect through the "water gap" for the running production,
2. shortage of electrical energy due to water shortage for the generators.

Impact on the transport system

The tail water of the Ruhr upriver until Herdecke seems to be navigable. The loss of water control would doubtlessly disrupt the shipping traffic for the heavy industry. The railway network crosses the Ruhr in many places and runs parallel almost the entire length from the Möhne Lake until the Rhine. In the narrow valleys the flood water from the broken Möhne dam would bring considerable damage to railway tracks and bridges the entire length of the river. Drinking water would fail in large parts of the Ruhr area, well into Hamm and Ahlen at the north-east end of the region.

Effect on the morale of the civilian population

After a series of bombing attacks in the last months, the general morale of civilian population must already have been heavily affected, especially by the two devastating air raids on Essen. Without a doubt, the destruction of the Möhne dam with all its consequences would further lower the morale of the population. The increased danger to the people of the Ruhr area through the lack of fire-fighting water could be extended to the political conduct of war and offer an excellent opportunity to spread panic among the civilian population. The destruction of the Eder dam would result in spectacular effects on the popular mood, especially if its breakage should take place together with the Möhne and Sorpe barrages. The economic effects would not be as great at the Eder reservoir.

The Sorpe dam

The Sorpe dam stores half as much water as the Möhne reservoir. Yet the dam construction is such that greater difficulties in breaking it have to be overcome! That is not impossible, as the tactical problems are no different from those of the Möhne and Eder dams. The destruction of

Möhne and Sorpe dams together would take away seventy-five per cent of the water supply to the Ruhr area, and would have a paralysing effect on the Ruhr industry and lower the morale there even more.

The Eder dam

The Eder dam, built over a four year period from 1910 to 1914, possesses a storage capacity of 202.4 million cubic metres of water. Its stone masonry retaining wall reaches a height of forty-seven metres. The water store collects the winter rainfalls from the drainage basin above the lake and thus regulates the high waters of the river Eder. Before the construction of the Eder dam, Eder, Fulda and Weser were very restless rivers which overflowed regularly during the winter months and caused floods. The main task of the Eder Lake, however, lies in the supply of reserve water which is released in the summer, partly in boosts, into the Weser for the regulation of shipping traffic. Therefore the lake is also responsible for the filling of the Mittelland Canal. Electric energy is produced by the Eder Lake by means of two power stations at the retaining wall as well as a pumped-storage station and a power plant at the equalising pond in Affoldern. The same tasks that are carried out at the Eder Lake are taken on by the neighbouring Diemel dam, holding twenty million cubic metres of water. This is held in place by a stone brick wall of 34.5m height, built 1912–1923. Although the destruction of the Eder dam would be sensational, a great economic effect might be debatable: no significant industrial area would be cut off from its water supply, the loss of electric energy would be secondary, and the impact on navigability of Fulda, Weser and Mittelland Canal would probably not be of long duration. From an economic viewpoint, the Eder dam was not a first class target.

The Möhne reservoir

On the other hand, the Mohne reservoir was of prime importance in terms of the water supply to the Ruhr area. Its destruction would have several effects on the armaments industry and lower the morale of the civilian population most significantly. The simultaneous destruction of the Möhne and Sorpe dams could evoke a serious, critical situation for the Ruhr industry. The destruction of the Eder dam would bring spectacular results, and the moral effects would become more intense in context with the simultaneous eradication of the Ruhr dams. The economic impact through the break of the Eder dam would be less significant.

The Ingenious Idea of Mr. Barnes Wallis

The suggestion to attack the German reservoirs with conventional means seemed to be dead already when Barnes Wallis appeared at the Road Research Laboratory in Harmondsworth and brought the idea back to life. The tinkerer in Barnes Wallis could not be discouraged, and he was convinced that a contact explosive charge at the retaining walls would bring success. Parallel to the trial series with the dam models in a water tank of 195 metres length at the "William Froude Experimental Tank Laboratory" in Teddington, he catapulted spherical projectiles the size of tennis balls made from wood, aluminium, steel and lead with different surface textures, at a bouncing pace across the water surface, against a simulated dam wall. Hereby the best weight, size, design, speed and bouncing distance of the spheres on the water surface should be tested in order to find out the ideal values for the hopping technique. Wallis's inspiration came from watching children skipping stones across the surface of a river. The idea of his ingenious bouncing bomb was born and needed refinement to deploy a relatively small explosive charge accurately. Extensive experiments showed that the number of bounces, and thus also the reach of an ideal spherical bomb, could be increased if it was dropped from low altitudes at high speed and with high-speed reversal rotation. The high rotational speed allows the projectile to jump, impeding torpedo nets or tearing them with ease. After the massive impact on the mural crown it forces the "bouncing bomb" to take a course towards the retaining wall once more, to crawl down along it in close contact, until the critical depth, at which the explosion triggers an earthquake-like tremor within the wall structure.

During the test series in the 'Experimental Tank Laboratory' at Teddington, Wallis had filmed above and under water at normal speeds and in slow motion. The experiments with the cunning little spheres caught the attention of Admiral E. de F. Renouf, the director of the special weapons research department within the admiralty. Right away he ordered 250 weapons operating according to this principle, which were built and tested under the code name "Highball". The British military navy wanted to deploy this smaller rotational bomb with fast Mosquito planes against shipping targets. Ricocheting canon balls have been utilised since the sixteenth century. They were used in naval artillery in the seventeenth and early eighteenth century to improve the range of powder guns. In 1903 the German physicist Carl Wilhelm Ramsauer studied the behaviour of very fast moving bodies during impact on a water surface. He fired brass spheres with a diameter of eleven millimetres and a muzzle velocity of 610 metres per second onto a water surface. Already these experiments demonstrated that the sphere did not resurface, if the angle of contact (angle of entry) exceeded seven degrees. At an angle of less than seven degrees the sphere bounced across the water surface.

The mathematicians Cranz and Becker have rendered these results into formulas. Carl Julius Cranz is the creator of modern ballistics. His student Karl Becker made essential contributions to internal and external ballistics. Naval artillery and Ramsauer's experiments were, however, carried out without rotating the projectiles. Although the implication of a speedy rotation is used in many ball games (e.g. tennis) to achieve certain effects, the potential outcome on the flight of a spherical projectile during ricocheting was not recognised, until this topic was examined, for the first time, by Barnes Wallis.

Experimentally, Wallis proved, for the first time, the possibility of increasing the running distance of ricocheting weapons on a surface of water, if these weapons are given a lifting force at impact by the reverse rotation. The "Magnus effect" acts like an "aerodynamic lift" and thus multiplies the number of bounces. Projectiles with forward rotation immediately sink on the surface of the water.

Green Light for the Prototypes "Highball" and "Upkeep"

It wasn't until 25 August 1942, at Vickers House in London, that Barnes Wallis was able to convince representatives of the Air Ministry, members of the Ministry for Aeroplane Production,

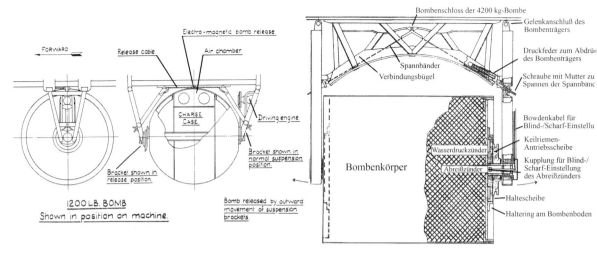

This drawing shows the mounting and the propulsion of a spherical rotational bomb at an aircraft for a 500kg "Highball". On the right, the assembly drawing for a cylindrical 4.2t dam buster bomb "Upkeep".

and the company Vickers Armstrong Ltd, that his ideas were viable. They decided to undertake trials with a spherical bomb at the coast near Chesil Beach. On 4 December 1942 Wallis flew as bombardier in a Wellington with the test pilot Mutt Summers from Weybridge to the "First Trial" across the sea before Chesil Beach. The coastal flak opened fire, since the modified Wellington with the protruding bomb could not be recognised as a friendly craft. Wallis eluded defeat. Yet his "spheres", as Wallis called the bombs, burst on impact when they hit the water. On 9 December the next trial series began. A flash from the cockpit of the Wellington signalled to the observers and the RAF camera operator J. Woolls the launch of the bomb, on which a white stripe made the rotation visible. On 15 December 1942 further test drops followed from an altitude of fifteen and seventy metres at a speed of almost 400 kilometres per hour and rotations between 250 and 750 turns per minute. All the bomb bodies were heavily damaged. New trials with wood-clad bomb bodies ensued, but all turned out negative.

The reservoir bomb had received the code name "Upkeep". The admiralty were urged to further develop the smaller model of the dam bomb "Highball" first, as it could seemingly be made ready for series production more quickly and should be urgently deployed against the German super-battleship "Tirpitz". On 23 January 1943 during the "Fourth Trial" a "wooden sphere", dropped from an altitude of fourteen metres, ran backwards with 485 rotations in thirteen satisfactory bounces across the sea before Chesil Beach. Besides the rotational bombs "Upkeep" and "Highball", Wallis was supposed to develop a third version under the code name "Baseball" in order to launch it from a naval torpedo boat against military ships. All bouncing bomb types ran under the overall name "Golf Mine". At the end of 1942 Barnes had finished his memorandum "Air Attack on Dams" and had presented it to some high military officers and politicians. On 28 January 1943 Wallis also showed his test films of the trials before Chesil Beach in Vickers House (London) to the highest ranking members of the Air Ministry and the admiralty and to the representatives of the Ministry of Aeroplane Production. Admiralty and the Ministry for Aeroplane Production gave highest priority to the initiation of "Highball". Yet Wallis wanted to deploy his "Upkeeps" against the German dams first, which he considered to be more important than the German battleships. A premature usage of "Highball" could reveal the secret of the rotational bombs to the Germans who then would upgrade their barrages to unassailable fortresses. Wallis suggested the simultaneous development of both weapons.

Wallis' Private War against Aeronautical Technocrats; Bomber Harris "Explodes"

The first serious bureaucratic setback to hit Wallis occurred on 10 February, 1943. Air Vice Marshal F.J. Linnell, chief of the research and development department in the Ministry for Aeroplane Production, brought him the news that all work on the reservoirs project had to be stopped immediately. A small comfort: the work on the "Highball" program was allowed to continue, especially with regard to the usage of a Mosquito, which was supposed to become the carrier of two small rotational bombs. On 13 February the chief of the British bomber command, Sir Arthur Harris, was filled in completely on the reservoirs project by Group Captain S.C. Elsworthy. On this day, members of the dam buster committee harboured doubts as to whether an operational rotational bomb could be produced by April. On 14 February Air Vice Marshal Saundby summarised the operation against the reservoirs once more, based on the Wallis study "Air Attacks on Dams", and presented the written document to Bomber Chief Harris for a final decision by 15 February. This paper demanded the establishment of a new squadron that would require a training period of three to four weeks. The assault tactics would not be difficult, and the operation should be flown during a clear night with a full moon, utilising the new radio altimeters.

   Sir Arthur Harris, Bomber Chief, answered Air Vice Marshal Saundby with a crushing handwritten letter on 14 February 1943. Harris, who loved carpet bombing and no precision assaults, "exploded" in withering criticism: "This is a totally crazy idea. There are so many ifs and buts, and there is not the slightest chance that it will actually work. Assuming the bomb was perfectly balanced around its axis, the vibration at 500 turns per minute would cause the plane to crash or, at least, the bomb to sheer off. I do not believe a single word of the presumed ballistic properties of the bomb on the water surface. It would be much easier to drop a ship than bomb onto the water, to detonate its prow at contact, to let it sink and then explode. On account of the costs, stop the holding in readiness of Lancaster bombers which only weakens our bomber fleet's offensive strength by going on this wild goose chase. Let them prove the practical deployment of the bomb first! The war will be over before this is possible and it would never be possible!"

   On 18 February 1943 "Bomber Harris" threatened the Air Chief Marshal Sir Charles Portal: "I am prepared to bet my last shirt that:

1. the weapon will not be available even as a prototype for a test in six months time,
2. it will not show the predicted ballistic behaviour on the water,

The mission of the bouncing bombs began with this catapult. With it Barnes Wallis fired marbles onto a filled rain barrel and had his children measure the jumping distances of the projectiles. Barnes Wallis' inspiration was a pebble skipping across the surface of the water, a children's game.

A sample case of Barnes Wallis' "test tennis balls". The trial spheres, of around five centimetres in diameter, are made of lead, aluminium, ash, beech or pine wood and show different surface structures and weights. Some resemble oversized golf balls.

First tests with bouncing bombs were flown by Captain Mutt Summers, test pilot with Vickers Armstrong Ltd, in a Wellington bomber at Chesil Beach near Portland. Most of the tests with the bouncing bombs were unsuccessful. At the beach of Reculver a Mosquito dropped a "Highball", the smaller model of the "dam buster bomb", onto the sea. The "sphere", as Wallis called the bomb, initially bounced according to plan, but then spun out of control and raced closely past the intrepid cameraman J. Woolls. The bouncing bomb was marked in black and white in order to make its rotation more visible on film.

The "Highball" (code name) weighed c.500kg and had a diameter of eighty-eight centimetres. This weapon was supposed to be deployed against ship targets, with an operational reach of up to five kilometres. It never reached the stage of series production.

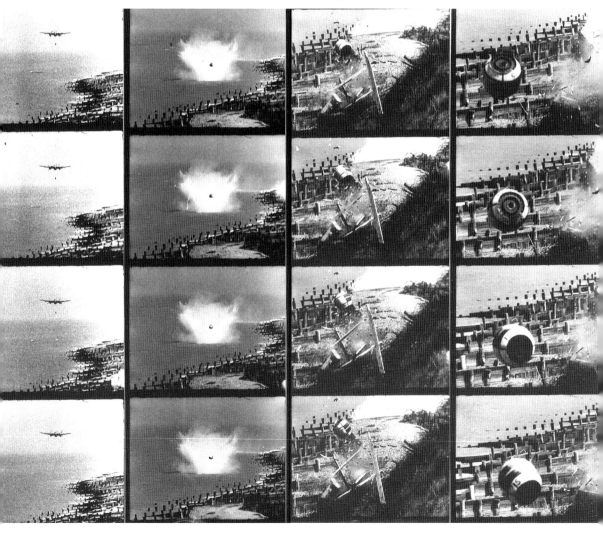

"Bomber Harris", chief of the British Bomber Fleet, knighted for his war service, nearly became the involuntary saviour of the German dams. Behind the scenes he fought a running battle with Barnes Wallis to stop the latter's reservoirs project. On 14 February 1943 he wrote, in a personal letter to Air Vice Marshal Robert Saundby, that the latter ought to terminate the trials immediately.

Handwritten letter of "Bomber Harris" to Air Vice Marshal Robert Saundby against the "Dams Raid Project".

Air Vice Marshal Sir Ralph Cochrane: the Air Officer Commanding No. 5 Group worked out the assault plans against the dams. It was his idea to install the new radio devices in the Lancasters as a secure aid for executing the operation above the dams. Cochrane also suggested having four crews, who had not achieved the highest standard in accuracy during the trial drops, attack target Z, the Sorpe dam. The attack methods utilised here allowed the crews an opportunity to prove themselves.

Overnight Guy Gibson, a young man of twenty-four, here with a tobacco pipe in a studio portrait, became a national hero after destroying two giant dams in one historic night. Of his squadron, fifty-six men did not return from this sortie. With the comrades who did return, he celebrated by throwing a big party. He could not sleep; the engine noise pursued him for hours. He had flown many missions against Germany and Italy, and had participated in the first 1000-bombers night raid on Cologne. He shot excellent film material of the burning Mainz for the British newsreels. Tragically, he did not see the end of the war. Sixteen months after his triumph at the Möhne and Eder dams he was shot down during an attack on Mönchengladbach-Rheyd. His Mosquito, which he had flown as target marker, shattered in Dutch Steenbergen.

The title image of the successful book "Als Deutschlands Dämme brachen" [When Germany's dams broke] by author Helmuth Euler shows the attack of a Lancaster bomber on a dam. Two spotlights enable the maintenance of the exact altitude during the release of the bomb. If the beams touched each other on the water surface and formed a recumbent eight, the required height of 18.3 metres was attained. The roll axis of the aircraft had to be absolutely horizontal at the moment of release. If the position of the craft did not fulfil that requirement, the bomb fell onto the water in a tilted manner, was thus hindered in bouncing accurately, and veered off from the calculated trajectory. It then detonated near the shore or jumped over the dam. Almost 400 metres before the target the bouncing bomb had to be released onto the water, to jump across the water in sixty metre leaps which became gradually shorter, over the torpedo nets, until it impacted on the mural crown. The backward rotation let the bomb slide downward in continual contact with the wall, until it detonated at the calculated depth of 9.1 metres, creating a 500m tall column of water.

Author Helmuth Euler stands next to an "Upkeep" concrete bouncing bomb in the Imperial War Museum London. Almost fifty years after its release, it was recovered from the sea near Reculver.

3. such a weapon cannot be kept balanced in rotation by an aircraft,
4. it will not work, when we have it. After all, we have undertaken tests to fly successful low-level attacks with heavy bombs. They were all, without exception, costly failures."

A final decision from Bomber Harris was not forthcoming at first. Yet Wallis did not give up. He received support from the First Sea Lord Sir Admiral Pound who considered the smaller rotational bomb "Highball" a promising secret weapon against the "Tirpitz". On 19 February 1943 the chief of the general staff of the Air Force, Portal, informed the leader of Bomber Command, Harris, that he would provide three valuable Lancaster bombers for test purposes, until the rotational bomb was ready for series production. The trial series would have to be continued, too. Yet Wallis did not know this news yet. In those days he busied himself in the "film business". He showed his test films in strict secrecy on different occasions to very high military officers of the Air Ministry and of the admiralty – and convinced them.

On 22 February 1943 Wallis travelled to the lion's den, to the headquarters of the British Bomber Command in High Wycombe. Here he met an almost hostile Harris who bellowed at him while crossing the threshold: "What in the devil's name do you inventors demand? The life of my boys is too valuable to be thrown away by you!" – but "Bomber Harris" could be persuaded at last to see the test films.

In order to answer any aeronautical questions, Wallis had brought along his test pilots Mutt Summers and A.O.C. Cochrane, who later organised the attack against the reservoirs. Air Vice Marshal Saundby operated the 35mm film projector. The films showed the top secret tests of the rotating spheres, how they ran in multiple bounces across the water and sank. Despite the unpleasant atmosphere, Wallis explained the different types of bombs and the targets. Underwater shots of a five centimetres trial sphere scaling down a model wall in an experimental tank at Teddington aroused little curiosity in Harris. When Wallis broached the subject of rallying a new squadron, with modified Lancasters, the Bomber Chief remained sceptical about "chasing an almost five ton steel lump across a lake". After the unpleasant visit to Bomber Headquarters, Wallis was finally rewarded with a sense of achievement; the Ministry for Aeroplane Production had authorised the modification of two Mosquito fighter planes for "Highball" trials. On 23 February the "hammer" hit Wallis. The director of the research department in the Air Ministry, Mister Linnell, demanded that he "stop all work on the nonsensical reservoir bomb immediately!" Sir C. Craven explained that Wallis was considered a great nuisance by the Air Ministry. The inclusion of the armament company Vickers Armstrong Ltd supposedly weakened, directly or indirectly, the interests of the firm. Mr. Linnell did not yet know, however, that the chief of general staff Portal had already made the decision to have three Lancasters modified for trial purposes.

At a conference on 26 February in the presence of representatives of the Air Ministry, the Ministry for Aeroplane Production and the company Vickers Armstrong, the sudden turnabout came for Wallis' reservoir bomb "Upkeep". Mr. Linnell suddenly sought the greatest secrecy, explaining that the Chief of the General Staff of the Air Force, Portal, wished to undertake every effort to develop the planes and bombs in question in order to deploy them in the spring of 1943. Something unexpected had happened. Wartime Prime

Minister Winston Churchill had read the Wallis study "Air Attacks on Dams" and given the order to execute the "reservoir project". Wallis was very pleased to be able to continue his work, after having spent such a long time researching and collating his ideas, not to mention the months of trials. The rotational bombs had to be refined through tests, and only eight weeks remained for this. The project received the highest priority at Vickers Armstrong Ltd and the AVRO aircraft factories. Besides the three Lancaster bombers already being modified, another twenty-seven should follow and 150 "Upkeep" rotational bombs would be commissioned. The AVRO aircraft factories had to alter the missile bay in the Lancasters, to strengthen the fuselage design in this place, to construct the release fixture equipment and to install the hydraulic motor for the bomb propulsion. Vickers Armstrong should construct the retaining jig for the bomb and the bouncing bomb. Three weeks were calculated for the filling of the bombs with explosives. On 28 February Wallis had completed the entire construction drawing of the bomb on the drafting table. Water pressure and self destructive fuses could be obtained from the navy. The 20 May was the last date for attack in 1943, based on the full moon phase and the water level in the reservoirs.

Bouncing Bombs Do Not Want to Jump

Wallis and the suppliers worked at full speed. As high-quality steel for an ideal spherical form of the bombs was not available, Wallis had to draw on a steel cylinder which he encased spherically with wood. After trials with wood of different degrees of hardness and structure, all of which burst on impact, Wallis noticed how the cylinder continued to hop as required. All trial bombs were filled with concrete and balanced around their axis of rotation, their

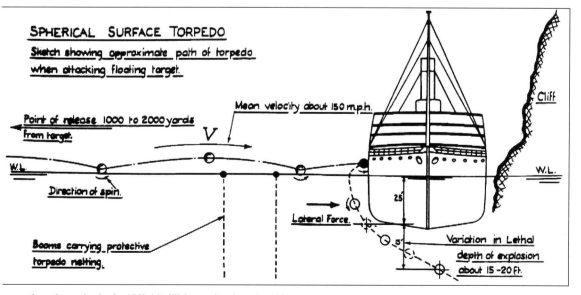

Attack method of a "Highball" bouncing bomb (450kg) against a war ship protected by torpedo nets; the explosion was supposed to occur beneath the vulnerable, unarmoured hull of the ship.

colour, battleship-grey. The live "Upkeeps" later had a black-green coating. On 18 April 1943 two "spheres" sank after impact on the water, a third bounced for 700 metres after shedding its wooden mantle. Wallis decided to remove the wooden casing. On 21 April the first naked cylinder fell, again a failure. Wallis ordered a lower altitude during the flight. On 28 April, a "Highball" test took place at Reculver. On the 29/30 April the first functional bounces with a cylinder bomb came through. Under the strictest secrecy, US experts attended the trials on 12 April, too.

On 11 May test pilot "Shorty" Longbottom performed two perfect drops at the coast near Reculver. After many failed attempts, only five days before the attack on the dams, the optimal coordination of speed of the Lancaster (380km/h), flight altitude (18.3m) and speed of rotation of the "concrete cylinder", was achieved. Some of these test bombs were recovered from the sea thirty-two years later and exhibited, e.g. in a hangar at Duxford airfield, England. On 13 May, for the first time a live "Upkeep" bouncing bomb was dropped at the North Foreland coast by test pilot Longbottom. The now operational "Upkeep weapon" possessed in the final version a total weight of 4,196kg (mantle length 1.52 metres, diameter 1.27 metres). At 500 turns against the direction of flight, it crossed a distance of 800 metres in seven bounces, sank to the depth of 9.1 metres and exploded after four seconds. The explosive force set free 2,994kg of research department explosives (RDX) and created a column of water that towered, over 300 metres high, for ten seconds. The "Highball" trials did not run quite as successfully, as the release equipment did not work perfectly and there were problems with the target device. US military officers had already shown enthusiasm about the "Highballs" on 27 March, which they wished to deploy in the Pacific Ocean against the Japanese Fleet.

Secret Squadron X Trains Low-Level Flight

On 15 March 1943 Bomber Chief Harris ordered Vice Marshal Cochrane to organise the attack against the dams. The latter knew that only select bomber crews were capable of performing and endeavoured to set up a new squadron, under the name X. He suggested the experienced fighter and bomber pilot Guy Gibson as Wing Commander. Base camp of the squadron, which was given the number 671 on 24 March, was Scampton in the vicinity of the city of Lincoln. On this day volunteers from different squadrons gathered on the Scampton airfield, between twenty and thirty-two years of age. They came from various countries of the Commonwealth: Great Britain, Australia, New Zealand, Canada, and even the USA. On 24 March, seven teams were formed, another seven teams on 25 March, and a further seven between the 26 and 31 March 1943. On 27 March the squadron already had an operational force of 100 men. The training began immediately with Lancasters borrowed from other squadrons. On the agenda were low-level flights at day and night, "as low as possible", across lakes and landscapes in England and Scotland. At the end of April, Gibson reported that all pilots in low-level flights by night could fly from landmark to landmark, navigating by map. From 5 May the low-level flight was shortened to an altitude of eighteen metres. The maintenance of the altitude with the spotlights worked excellently. The speed of flight had been determined at 380km/h by Wallis. On 26 April a storm blew over the tower dummies erected at the bombing test area Wainfleet, two panels of seven by ten metres, separated by 230 metres. On 3 May these targets were reinstalled at the Uppingham Reservoir.

Light exercise bombs fell onto the training targets by the hundreds, but the crews did not know the real targets, which were labelled by the military; X for the Mohne, Y for the Eder, and Z for the Sorpe. Between 23 and 27 April alone, 289 training bombs with only thirty-nine missed hits were dropped. The crews speculated about the targets and suspected submarine bunkers at the French Channel Coast or the large German battleship, the Tirpitz.

Ben Lockspeiser, director of the scientific research department of the Ministry for Aeroplane Production, had solved the problem of the exact altitude above water. He had an Aldis lamp installed into the camera hole at the front of the Lancaster and another into the fuselage behind the bouncing bomb, shifted slightly towards starboard. If the beams touched each other on the water surface forming a lying eight, the required altitude of 18.3m had been reached. While combating submarines in Coastal Command, he had undertaken similar, but unsuccessful attempts.

The version of events shown in the English feature film "The Dam Busters" of 1955, where two spotlights sweep a chorus girl and give Gibson the idea of an altimeter, seems to be pure fiction. Actually some pilots reached the same conclusion after a visit to a burlesque show in the London Windmill Theatre. At that time only five nights allowed authentic night flight training on the British Isles. Therefore during the day a synthetic night flight had to be simulated. With the aid of amber-coloured glasses and blue transparent window dressings in the cockpits a virtual moonshine landscape was created. On 29 March 1943, after a training flight across the Derwent Reservoir in the Midlands, the towers of which had always been used as targets, Guy Gibson guessed the true targets. At the beginning of April the organiser of the

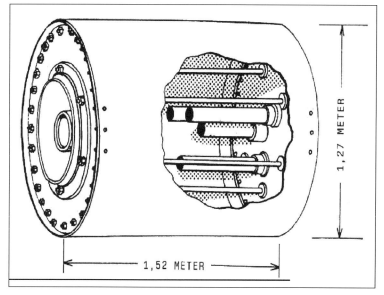

1,27 METER

1,52 METER

The dam buster bomb "Upkeep" in a cross-section drawing with three hydrostatic and one self-destruction fuse. Total weight = 4,196kg, explosive charge = 2,994kg.

Tests with concrete-filled bouncing bombs in original size took place off the Kentish coast near Reculver. The region had been declared a restricted area in order to keep out unwanted spectators. Furthermore the Manston airfield for the operation of heavy Lancaster bombers was not far away. The former church on the beach of Reculver with its twin towers served as a landmark for the pilots' orientation. Not far from the church ruin, two posts with large white sheets had been erected on the beach to represent the dam towers. Among the observers of the tests, Barnes Wallis is on the very left, next to him Guy Gibson. A heavy bouncing bomb jumps onto the beach very close to them.

Almost all tests with the bouncing bombs, from the "Highballs' to the "Upkeeps" were filmed. The film material with the title "Dam Busting Weapon" shows the trials in spring 1943. On 13 May of that year, for the first time, a dam buster bomb filled with explosives was dropped from a height of eighteen metres onto the sea off the coast of North Foreland near Broadstairs from a Lancaster flown by the test pilot Longbottom. The cylindrical bouncing bomb turned with 500 rotations against the flight direction, jumped almost 800m in seven leaps and sank to the predetermined depth of 9.1 metres. After four seconds the explosive device detonated, and a water column, almost 300 metres tall, rose from the sea. It demonstrated the force of the 2,994kg RDX explosives of the 4.2t bouncing bomb, now ready for action. Only three days after the successful "dress rehearsal" these devilish water columns rose in front of the walls of German reservoirs. Some fifty years after the war "Highball" and "Upkeep" training bombs filled with concrete were recovered from the sea near Reculver for museum purposes.

On 26 May 1943 Siegfried Werner made a detailed drawing of the defused British rotational bomb found near Haldern-Herken. The cylindrical bomb has no tail unit to stabilise the trajectory. The diameter measures 1270mm, the length 1530mm. The two front discs are attached with thirty screws and angles each. The thickness of the cylinder's wall is 12.5mm. It is loaded with high performance explosives of around 2,600kg. Three hydrostatic fuses and one

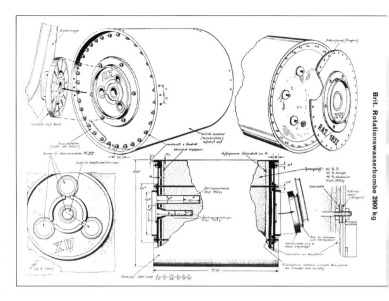

tear-off detonator triggered the explosion. The latter was to be used against unexploded ordnance on land.

The air force nearly lifted the secret of the weapon with the aid of the bomb find and the statements of the captured aviators. The knowledge of the explosion depth at wall contact remained undiscovered.

A simple isosceles plywood triangle with two pins at the ends served as aiming device for the bombardier. During sighting, the two pins had to align with the wall towers. Thus the exact release point was reached at that moment; geometry of death. As this method was very shaky during flight, Len Sumpter and Edward Johnson developed the chinagraph method as another aiming device in the "triangulation business".

Two forty-four centimetre long cords are attached to the Plexiglas forward gunner compartment of the Lancaster and brought to the nose of the bombardier. As in a Chinese shadow play, two black line markings on the windscreen at a distance of twenty-two centimetres drew near to the two wall towers during the approach. With the alignment of the towers and markings, the exact point of bomb release was attained. At the Eder dam this aiming device led to success, at the Möhne dam the wooden triangle sight.

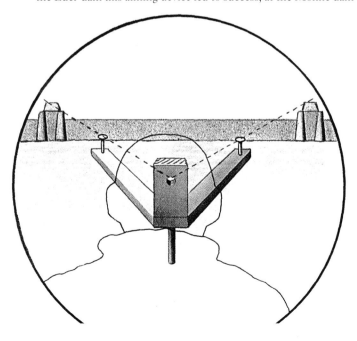

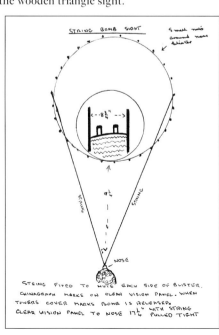

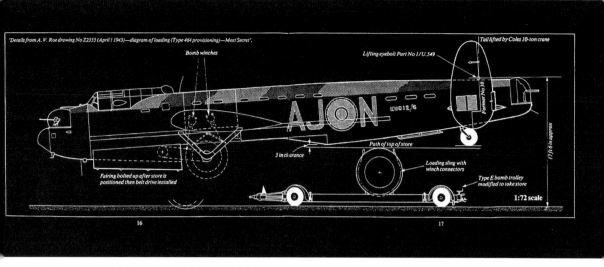

'Details from A. V. Roe drawing No Z2353 (April 1 1943)—diagram of loading (Type 464 provisioning)—Most Secret'.

Bomb winches

Lifting eyebolt Part No 1/U.549

Tail lifted by Coles 10-ton crane

Former No.38

Path of top of store

3 in clearance

Loading sling with winch connectors

Fairing bolted up after store is positioned then belt drive installed

Type E bomb trolley modified to take store

17 ft 6 in approx

1:72 scale

16   17

Design no. Z2353 (April 1943) of the AVRO Lancaster Type 464 Provisioning; at the scale of 1:72 the drawing shows the loading of the aircraft with the bouncing bomb. In order to achieve the height required for the bomb's transport beneath the Lancaster, the tail had to be lifted with a ten ton crane to c.5.33 metres. Then a modified bomb trolley drove the weapon to the position below the clutches. Two winches pulled the explosive device onto the clutch apparatus with wire cables attached to angles fixed to the bouncing bombs. After the mounting of the bomb, the front fuselage fairing was bolted up and a belt drive placed onto the drive wheel and disc of the bouncing bomb.

Before the mounting, the "Upkeep" steel cylinders had to be very accurately balanced and equilibrated with small weights. If the bombs did not rotate faultlessly with 500 turns per minute against the flight direction ten minutes before release, strong vibrations in the aircraft occurred which prevented an accurate release.

The bouncing bomb looked like an oversized "tomato tin". Two V-shaped clutches mounted to the sides of the sliced fuselage carried the heavy weapon, as shown here on Gibson's Lancaster AJ-G.

The hydraulic drive of the bouncing bomb was induced by the right internal motor of the Lancaster. Ten minutes before the command to attack, the radio operator opened a valve and started the hydraulic motor. A drive wheel at the front right side of the fuselage below the cockpit put the bouncing bomb into rotation per fan belt. When the bombardier pushed the trigger, the clutches folded away and let loose the rotating projectile.

dam operation, Air Officer Commanding, Air Vice Marshal Ralph Cochrane, showed him, as the first man in the 617th bomber squadron, the models of the barrages in the headquarters of the 5th British Bomber Fleet in Grantham. Wallis explained to the surprised Gibson, who at first had also thought of the Tirpitz, the principles of operating his bombs.

On the basis of triangulation Wing Commander C.L. Dann had developed his bombing target device for the retaining walls, a plywood triangle with two nails and a peep hole. As the distance between the towers on the wall was known, likewise the point of release for the rotational bomb, the angle of the plywood triangle could be easily calculated. Two bombardiers, Len Sumpter and Edward Johnson, developed a different aiming device, the "Chinagraph Method", also on the basis of triangulation, only more "vibration-free". At the beginning of May, all Lancasters were equipped with frequency-modulation radio transceivers, on 7 May a total ban on taking leave was instated.

From 11 May 1943, the training flights for "advanced" crews began, and for the first time concrete-filled, balanced practice bouncing bombs in the original "Upkeep" format were launched against targets on the beach of Reculver. Guy Gibson noted in his diary: "'Upkeep' rotational bombs dropped from a height of eighteen metres, good run across 600 metres." Pilot Munro damaged the stern of his Lancaster ED 921/G, because he released his "Upkeep" below eighteen metres and the bomb body jumped at the Lancaster. This machine could be repaired in time, Maudslay's severely damaged Lancaster could not.

On 13 May 1943 the following bombs were available: fifty-six "Upkeeps" filled with explosives in Scampton and two in Manston. Concrete-filled practice bombs: thirty-seven in Scampton, nineteen in Manston, two in Weybridge and four empty bomb shells.

At the same time there were ninety-nine "Highballs" filled with explosives and 104 "Highballs" filled with concrete. Forty-eight hours before the attack against the dams, nineteen available Lancaster bombers, of the type 464 Provisioning modified, flew for the last time, during a joint squadron exercise.

Launch took place at 9.50pm. For four hours the training flight was led once more across the training targets – the reservoirs Uppingham Lake, Colchester and Derwent Lake. As yet, none of the pilots suspected what would face them, except Gibson who knew the targets were in Germany.

Encoded Radio Report with "Tulip" and "Mermaid"

The radio operators of the 617th squadron were told that for a mining mission a good air-to-air communication in altitudes of fifteen to 300 metres would be necessary. Cochrane recommended the new frequency-modulation radio as a suitable means of communication. On 28 March 1943 the test started during daylight at altitudes of 700 metres in which ranges of sixty-five kilometres were achieved. On 7 April further trials followed with the radio set T.R. 1196 between two crafts in altitude between 150 to 1,000 metres up to a range of fifty kilometres. When night flying training began, however, disruptions of the radio communication occurred through interferences. On three wavelengths the reception was better, but there were problems with loud background noise. The installation of the new frequency-modulation sender and receiver of the T.T. 1143 type, as it was used in fighter planes, brought success. All Lancasters received this radio equipment.

On Sunday evening, 9 May, a radio test with two Lancasters took place. One craft was flown by Squadron Leader Maudslay on a course of 180 degrees at an altitude of 150 metres, the other by Squadron Leader Young circled above the Scampton airfield at the same height. Hereby good communication without "black-outs" was achieved up to a distance of ninety kilometres. Gibson found the intercommunication system of the modified Lancaster satisfactory. The success of the whole operation also depended on good radio communication, both plane-to-plane and, with the means of Morse code telegraphy, with the leadership at the group headquarters at Grantham. All crafts were set to the radio wave 4090 for the link to base. As it was of vital importance that the enemy did not pick up this wave, too – all radio communications across England were of course intercepted – only a series of V signals at regular intervals were sent during the tests. On 16 May 1943, at 10am, the leading officer of the radio unit learned that operation "Chastise" would start on the following night. Immediately he began to copy the lists with the code names in order to be able to hand out a sufficient number to all radio operators involved.

For the Morse code	channel the following code names have to be used
PRANGER	Attack on target X (Möhne dam)
NIGGER	Target X Möhne dam broken, continuing flight to Y (Eder dam)
DINGHY	Target Y Eder dam broken, continuing flight to Z (Sorpe dam)
DANGER	Attack on target D (Liste dam)
EDWARD	Attack on target E (Ennepe dam)
FRASER	Attack on target F (Diemel dam)
MASON	All planes back to base
APPLE	The first wave of attack listens at button A
CODFISH	Interference of button A, switch to button C
MERMAID	Interference on all ultra-short wave frequencies, switch to Morse code on short wave
TULIP	Craft 2 takes over lead at target X (Möhne)
CRACKING	Craft 4 takes over lead at target Y (Eder)
GILBERT	Attack alternative targets as arranged
GONER 1	Special weapon released, unexploded ordnance
GONER 2	Special weapon released, jumped retaining wall
GONER 3	Special weapon released, explosion more than 100 metres before the retaining wall
GONER 4	Special weapon released, explosion 100 metres before the retaining wall
GONER 5	Special weapon released, explosion 50 metres before the retaining wall
GONER 6	Special weapon released, explosion five metres before the retaining wall
GONER 7	Special weapon released, explosion with wall contact
GONER 8	No visible break
GONER 9	Small break in the retaining wall
GONER 10	Large break in the retaining wall

With the distributed code names, the radio operators had a "dry" run on the ground of communications with their operational base and amongst each other via a loop. The radio regulations for "Operation B 976" were: frequency-modulation communication is the primary method above the reservoirs. For the frequency, button A is used. The frequency of button C is used by the second attack wave and serves as reserve frequency. The code name CODFISH sent via Morse code frequency indicates the switch to this short wave frequency. From the launch until the position "Zero Hour" above the North Sea all aircrafts have to listen attentively to the T.R. 1196 radio receiver on button D. Ten minutes before reaching the target area it is switched to frequency-modulation communication and used until one hour after the attack, then the operators switch back to button D of the T.R. 1196 device.

Via frequency-modulation all reports are sent unencrypted in clear text. Thus, that shall be practised what has been trained on the ground. If a frequency-modulation device on a plane is disrupted, this craft has to inform the attack leader twice via the Morse code frequency with the code word DEAFNESS. In the case of a failure of the frequency-modulation system of the attack leader, he will transfer the control of the attack via Morse code communication to the craft two or four. All crafts should listen to the frequency 4090 during the flight until the signal "operation completed". In the case of a failure of the entire frequency-modulation systems (buttons A and C) the leader of the first wave of attack will send the code word MERMAID via Morse code channel, which means interferences on all ultra-short wave frequencies. So only a lead via Morse code communication is possible for the first wave of attack.

Shortly before the launch, at Gibson's request, the letters for the targets XYZ were changed to ABC, as they were also used during training above the English reservoirs. Here the example of an encoded radio report: GONER 78 A means special weapon released, explosion with wall contact, no visible break at the Möhne retaining wall.

The attack leader had to send the corresponding code names to the group headquarters via Morse code communication according to the "I Method". From here the entire radio report is repeated twice at full transmitting power. Should Morse code be used, each plane of this attack wave has to report immediately after arrival at the target to the attack leader via short wave. All crafts have to switch to the normal operational frequency of the group of 3680Hz, as soon as their bomb has been released. They shall then immediately send the associated code group with a numeral combination plus letter suffix of the target to the operational leadership. After the confirmation of the radio report by the headquarters at Grantham, all operators should switch to the set group frequency of 4090Hz. If in the target region the entire radio communication fails, optical communication becomes effective. The attack leader or deputy then fires green flares. They mean that each pilot shall wait until he flies towards the retaining wall in the optimal position of attack, and after its break, the crafts not deployed yet fly to the next target.

"Fir Trees" Trouble the British Assault Strategists

The reconnaissance flights D/561 6–366 on 4/5 April 1943 showed, on aerial photographs, inexplicable construction activities at the crest of the Mohne dam that gave cause to some speculation. Those who evaluated the aerial photographs described the objects and their shadows as shaped posts. They seemed to have at the top a diameter of no more than thirty-three centimetres, widening towards the base. Some groups of the erect objects, whose size could not be exactly determined, stood partly at street level next to the parapet or were found in front of the parapet above the water level along the retaining wall. These constructs at the barrage could be explained as follows:

A) as an answer to rumours of an imminent air raid,
B) necessary repair works,
C) an elevation of the wall to increase water capacity.

The activities regarding the tightening of the torpedo nets in front of the Möhne dam are still no proof of any news leak in the Air Ministry that the secret plans had become known. Just in case, the location of the torpedo nets was re-examined once more on photographs from 19 February 1943. They revealed themselves to be slightly neglected, and on 4/5 April they lay tightened and orderly. Some spacers between the chains had been replaced, usually seasonally, when the water during the winter months had risen up to the spillway. The water stood at sixty centimetres below the spillway of the Möhne dam, and the time had come to readjust the torpedo nets.

In addition, a study from 1942 troubled the British aviation military. In it, the demolition trials of the Road Research Laboratory in Harmondsworth and at the Nant-y-Gro dam are described in detail. Seventy copies of this illustrated paper, in which even the Mohne reservoir was mentioned by name, werecirculated amongst the military. Four of them went to the USA to rouse interest in super bombs and carrier planes. Most of the copies lay securely in safes, but one got into civilian hands in September 1942. It was presented to Dr von Karman, California Institute of Technology, who also worked on a super bomb theory. So, it is possible that this paper was no secret in the USA. Perhaps it reached Germany and, due to the known details, precautionary measures were taken against a wall demolition by shock waves.

It was incomprehensible that the British government should have allowed the circulation of this study. Due to the immense size of the structural shell of a retaining wall, defensive measures against shock waves are not easily possible. They can only be produced in the form of a protective shield to break the waves and to spread the energy through reflection and disruptions before they hit the main structure of the dam. This could possibly be achieved by closely spaced concrete columns, standing on a loam bunk in front of the wall with its foundations.

Similar protection could also be offered by huge concrete-filled steel pipes if they are driven into the Möhne dam from the street side. With a diameter of 1.5m they withstood shock waves with great resistance. The last aerial images show that this type of work did not take place. Yet it might be that the objects in the pictures could be part of repairs, since the retaining wall is thirty years old after all. Due to overspill, considerable erosion damage might have occurred.

Usually autumn is set aside for repairs, when the water level of the lake is low and warm weather favours the construction work. Against this might stand the increased demand for water in the Ruhr area as a result of the continued war, with the desire for overfull reservoirs. Yet these actions do not seem to be the visible works at the dam. Further considerations led to the question – were the mysterious bodies anti-aircraft missiles? Heavy defensive installations should rather stand on the road across the Möhne dam which is closed to traffic, furthermore alternative routes needed to be at hand. The difficulty of finding a secure stand during the firing of the rocket, with its recoil, would make it more likely to place such a battery in the middle of the road. The unknown objects, however, stood at the sides of the parapets. Whatever the reason for the works on the Möhne dam may be, the analysis of these measures does not find any protection at the retaining wall against a bouncing bomb and no prevention of a flyover above the Möhne dam.

At the time the English could not solve the mystery of these objects, even with further aerial photographs. Actually they were artificial "fir trees" with which the German air force wanted to camouflage the Möhne dam as a forested headland at the transition to the Arnsberg Forest. On 9 May 1943 there was another photo call for the reservoirs in the Sauerland and the Waldecker Land to check on the water levels and potential defensive measures. At the Möhne dam, a broken black line still snaked along the mural crown. It might have been a drainage channel or a wire belt, and did not allow for an exact interpretation. The towers on the Möhne retaining wall had tent-shaped roofs, as visible on pre-war photographs. Already some time previously, they had been dismantled to a platform of five by seven metres each. At the northern dam access another platform can be seen on aerial photographs. On each of these platforms a light anti-aircraft gun stood. Three further anti-aircraft guns lay in waiting in boxes of six by six metres on a meadow in the north-west below the Möhne dam. They are surrounded by walls of sandbags or similar material. The reconnaissance flight D/68 showed no changes, not even in the vicinity of the reservoirs. The exact measurements between the dam towers have been transferred, true to scale, from the aerial photographs onto the barrage models.

Technique and Tactics with "Upkeeps"

On 5 May 1943 another meeting of highest-ranking military officers and scientists took place in the Air Ministry with the topic of discussion "Upkeep weapon". Wallis explained that he – like Dr. Glanville who had performed detailed studies of this issue – considered a detonation point at the wall at a depth of 9.1 metres, with contact to the wall structure, to be optimal. The chances of destruction decrease significantly during an explosion at greater depth, as the walls strengthen towards the base. The water level in the lakes was discussed, too.

Dr. Glanville confirmed, by experiments recently carried out, that the explosive effect would decrease rapidly with diminishing water levels in the reservoirs. With a water level of 1.5 metres below full capacity an effective loss of explosive force of five per cent would occur, and with a water level of 3.5m below full capacity the loss of efficiency would be twenty per cent. The scientists Wallis and Glanville agreed that a water level of 1.5 metres short of full capacity must be adequate to destroy the Möhne dam. Air Marshal Bottomley talked about the accuracy of the hydrostatic detonator at a depth of 9.1 metres. Wallis confirmed that detonator tests had showed a depth detonation with deviations of thirty to sixty centimetres.

The water level in the reservoirs should not be higher than a metre below maximum, since sufficient wall surface was needed for the impact of the bomb.

The cumulative effect of several explosions was also the subject of enquiry. The scientists considered this possible, but not predictable in its extent. It was attested in the dam model trials, but one contact detonation alone would trigger the destruction. Air Marshal Bottomley spoke of the necessity to schedule the attack for the full moon period between 14 and 26 May. Wallis and Glanville explained that the water-level reports by the aerial reconnaissance had to be awaited, as exact stereo-images would permit an accurate estimate. On 19 February 1943 the water level was twelve metres below the capacity target, on 4/5 April, sixty centimetres below full capacity.

Air Marshal Bottomley once more stressed the need for secrecy. It was agreed to issue new regulations for the security of further photo flights and to instruct the pilots to render all exposed negatives unusable to the Germans by light exposure, if they had to exit over enemy territory or to crash land. It was decided to choose a date for the attack in May, as the risks were substantially increased from June on, due to the water level dropping each month by three metres. The next aerial photographs should bring the decision. Also, for reasons of secrecy, an earlier date would be desirable. Wallis then spoke about the Sorpe dam. No model tests were made with this type of dam, but there was a very good chance of damaging it and thus initiating its final destruction. A leak in the upper watertight part with a break of the inner concrete core of the dam would suffice. The hole in the dam would be enlarged rapidly by the draining mass of water and could not be closed. However, this would not be easily recognisable for the bomber crews.

The Decision is Made in the USA

The Chiefs of the General Staff of the British Air Forces were in Washington at the end of April, and remained so into early May 1943. By telegraphy they were constantly informed under strict secrecy on the progress of the trials with the "bouncing weapons" by the Air Ministry.

US Air Force General Arnold wanted to have plans and weapons in the USA at the earliest possible date, especially with view to the "Highballs" and their deployment in the South-West Pacific. With the British delegation, Winston Churchill had come, too. The Vice Chiefs of the general staff of Bomber Command (RAF) now urged the deployment of "Upkeep" without waiting for "Highball" to be ready for serial production. On 13 May 1943 they asked the chiefs of the general staff in Washington in a cypher telegram, reference number 204, to make a decision on the preference of "Upkeep" over "Highball".

The vice chiefs of the general staff in England recommended an immediate launch of the reservoirs operation from 14 May 1943 onwards. The reasons for the immediate decision of the Vice Chief of the General Staff of the RAF were the following: a deployment of "Upkeep" ahead of schedule would no longer endanger the security of "Highball"; for "Upkeep" now a "container bomb" is deployed and released at short distance.

The method of attack could lead to the belief that it was a special water bomb dropped between the torpedo net and the wall. For purposes of deception an aircraft could furthermore

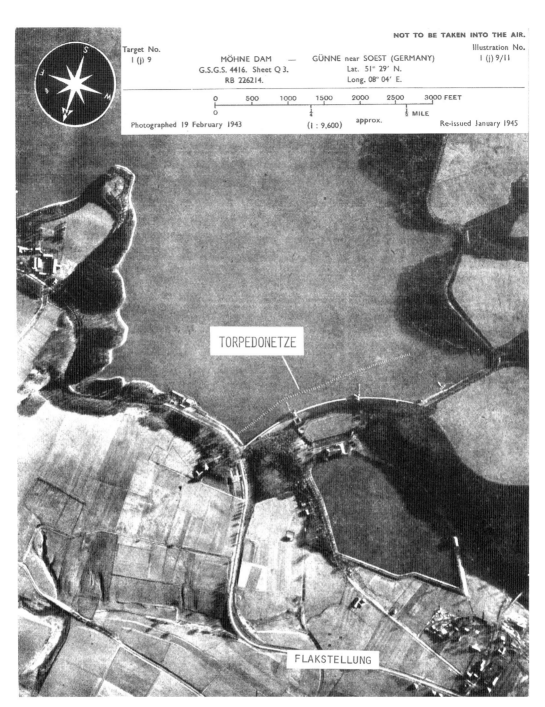

Target No.
I (j) 9

MÖHNE DAM   —   GÜNNE near SOEST (GERMANY)
G.S.G.S. 4416. Sheet Q 3.   Lat. 51° 29′ N.
RB 226214.   Long. 08° 04′ E.

Illustration No.
I (j) 9/11

0   500   1000   1500   2000   2500   3000 FEET
0   ¼   ½ MILE

Photographed 19 February 1943   (1 : 9,600)   approx.   Re-issued January 1945

British long-distance reconnaissance planes flew over the German reservoirs without attracting attention, in changing directions of approach. In preparation of the attack a specialist at the aerial photography interpretation office of Medmenham had studied the images of the dams amidst the greatest secrecy. Often the expert puzzled for hours over unidentifiable details, enlarged the photos to the film's grain size, and viewed them under bright lights with magnifying glasses of microscopic strength in order to identify potential camouflaged spotlights or air defence positions. This shot from 19 February 1943 shows the double chain of torpedo nets in front of the dam with the batteries on the towers, below on the sloping meadow three light anti-aircraft guns and buildings of the village of Günne. The light patches along the shore around the peninsula with Delecke House (top left) reveal that the reservoir had not yet reached the full capacity required for a bombardment with the "Wallis method".

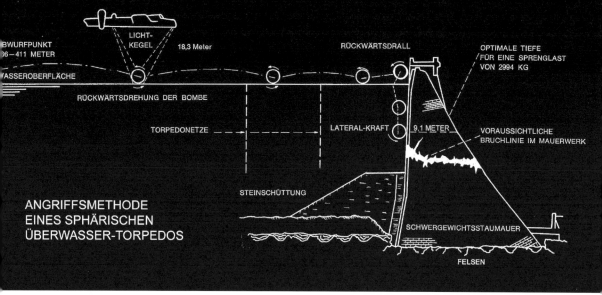

ANGRIFFSMETHODE
EINES SPHÄRISCHEN
ÜBERWASSER-TORPEDOS

ABWURFPUNKT
366–411 METER

LICHT-KEGEL

18,3 Meter

RÜCKWÄRTSDRALL

OPTIMALE TIEFE
FÜR EINE SPRENGLAST
VON 2994 KG

WASSEROBERFLÄCHE

RÜCKWÄRTSDREHUNG DER BOMBE

TORPEDONETZE

LATERAL-KRAFT

9,1 METER

VORAUSSICHTLICHE
BRUCHLINIE IM MAUERWERK

STEINSCHÜTTUNG

SCHWERGEWICHTSSTAUMAUER

FELSEN

Drawing from a study by Wallis in which he supplies scientific evidence for the possibility of destroying a dam with a single bomb. Just under 400 metres before the target, the backward rotating bomb cylinder is released at an altitude of 18.3m and is driven over the torpedo nets against the top of the dam in sixty metre leaps which become successively shorter. After the rebound from the freeboard of the wall, the bomb makes contact again due to its backward rotation and scales down the wall in four seconds, until the hydrostatic fuses set to 9.1m trigger the explosion whose shock waves initiate the destruction of the construction in the manner of an earthquake.

Reconnaissance photos from 4/5 April 1943 worried the British military. Within a number of weeks unidentifiable objects had appeared along the mural crown. Could the German air defence have learned of the imminent attack and moved defensive forces into position? The unidentified objects were artificial pine trees with which the German air defence tried to camouflage the wall as a wooded headland.

R.* Y. Form 683. **SECRET.** (L) 10346. Wt. 23086-1335. 120M. 8/12. T.S. 700

CYPHER MESSAGE. *1 A.*

To—		Date	15.5.43.
HQ Bomber Command		Receipt	Despatch
		Time of	1130
FROM— Air Ministry Whitehall AX457 15th May		System	

MOST SECRET Serial No. Y3976

Operation CHASTISE immediate attack of targets X Y Z approved.   Execute at first suitable opportunity.

T.O.O. 150900Z
MOST **IMMEDIATE** T.O.R. 151125B

R.A.F. Form 683. **SECRET.** (L) 10346. Wt. 23086-1335. 120M. 8/42. T.S. 700

CYPHER MESSAGE. *6 H*

To—		Date 16.5.43.
Officer Commanding Scampton (R) Bomber Command.		Receipt	Despatch
		Time of 1610	1645
FROM— 5 Group A 7 16th May.		System	

Serial No. Y3990.

Executive operation Chastise 16/5/43 zero hours

22/48B.

T.O.O.161510B
T.O.R.1607/16

G/C OPS [signature] 1 6 MAY 1943

Mission telegrams for "Operation Chastise" against the German reservoirs. At the beginning of May 1943 the Chiefs of the General Staff of the British Air Force were in Washington. By telegraph they were continually kept informed on the progress of the trials with the "jumping weapons" by the Air Ministry amidst the greatest secrecy. On 14 May 1943 the Chief of the General Staff of the RAF, Sir Charles Portal, gave green light for "Operation Chastise" from the USA with the cipher telegram T.O.O. 1440 Z/14.

On 15 May the Chief of Bomber Command, Arthur Harris, received by telegram the Air Ministry's decision to execute "Operation Chastise" at the next possible date and to attack the targets XYZ (Möhne, Eder, Sorpe).

The telegram with the mission order to launch the attack that night came on 16 May from 5 Group A7 to the Officer Commanding Scampton (R) Bomber Command Withworth.

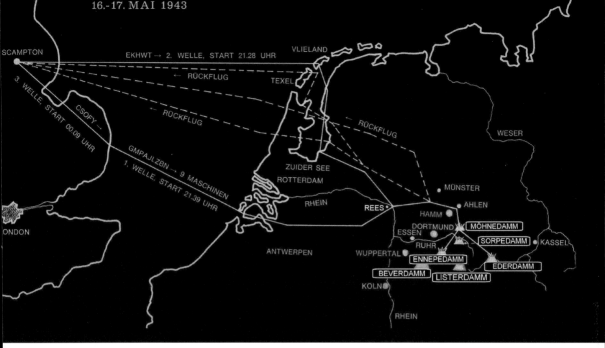

Flight schedule for Operation Chastise. It shows the outbound and return flight of the nineteen Lancaster bombers deployed against the dams in West Germany. Eight aircraft with fifty-six aviators did not return from this raid. Fifty-three crew members died in crashes, three were taken prisoner. The proximity of the reservoirs to each other facilitated the nocturnal attacks.

With this Lancaster as reserve craft (serial number 825/G), seen here without squadron identification, the American McCarthy flew to the Sorpe dam without delay. Due to lack of time, no spotlights had been installed in the aircraft yet. So McCarthy bombed the Sorpe dam without altimeter.

The call of RAF photographer, Flying Officer Bellamy, caused Guy Gibson to pause briefly on the ladder of his Lancaster bomber during the sunset launch against the German dams. Surprised, Gibson turned around and the shutter clicked. The photographer took the camera into his left hand and saluted. Gibson vanished quickly inside the bomber. However, a short while later he reappeared at the hatch. "Hey there", he called to the photographer, "remember to send a print to my wife!" The crew laughed loudly, the ladder was drawn up, and the door slammed shut. Outside one could hear the men taking their positions, laughing and making jokes about the Wing Commander's remark, as if he would not return. None of the crew members survived the war. Left to right: Trevor-Roper, Pulford, Deering, Spafford, Hutchison, Gibson, Taerum.

Taken one day before the attack: the deceptive calm at the "anti-aircraft sanatorium Möhne Lake", as the soldiers called their position. Battery chief Lieutenant Jörg Widmann had admonished them time and again: "Children, children, you don't know what responsibility you bear, what depends on the reservoir, the water supply of the armament industry in the Ruhr area". The Möhne Lake is full to its brim; a double chain of torpedo nets is lying protectively in front of the wall camouflaged by artificial trees.

On a tower of the dam, air defence soldiers are servicing their two centimetre gun. The Möhne flak fired with red and green tracer ammunition.

fly parallel along the wall. Leaps across a short distance strongly resemble the normal bouncing effect, if a bomb hits the water at a flat angle. It is unlikely that the enemy would link "Upkeep" with a spherical bomb, to "Highball", which requires a much greater distance of release for the deployment against ship targets. The rotation principle could possibly be revealed in case of the downing of a plane over enemy territory.

Aerial photographs, taken today, show optimal water levels in the reservoirs, a fact which allows an attack in this ideal full moon phase.

Twenty-three Lancaster bombers are "frozen" for the special operation against the targets XYZ. A postponing of the attack to June means the loss of bomber deployments for a month. The last bomb test has shown that the weapon is operational. The crews have reached their peak form, they are "hot" for a "suicide mission". The "Highball" tests still show marked weaknesses. Waiting for "Highball" would mean a year-long delay for the dam attacks. The decision on the date for the attack against the German reservoirs was made in Washington, 5,500 kilometres from London.

On 14 May 1943 the Chief of the General Staff of the RAF, Sir Charles Portal, gave the green light for operation "Chastise" against the German reservoirs in the cypher telegram T.O.O. 1440Z/14.

Briefing, Operation Order No. B 976

The mission order "No. 5 Group Operation Order B 976" took centre-stage at the briefing on 16 May 1943. Firstly, the crews were therein informed of the significance of the reservoirs for the Germans and the expected effects by the flood on the armament industry and the population. A list of the targets with their locations and the itemisation of the anti-aircraft measures at the Möhne dam followed as well as the tactics of operation "Chastise".

The task:
The destruction of the retaining walls in the order of their importance:

1st target	"X"	(GO 939)	Möhne dam	"A"
2nd target	"Y"	(GO 934)	Eder dam	"B"
3rd target	"Z"	(GO 960)	Sorpe dam	"C"

Last resort targets:

1st target	"D"	(GO 938)	Lister dam
2nd target	"E"	(GO 935)	Ennepe dam
3rd target	"F"	(GO 933)	Diemel dam

The first wave consisting of nine planes will launch in flights of three aircraft at intervals of ten minutes and fly on the southern route to the Möhne reservoir. The second wave with five planes takes the northern route to attack the Sorpe dam. It transverses the enemy coast in Holland at the same time as the first wave. The third wave forms a flying reserve under direct radio guidance by the headquarters of the 5th Group at Grantham. It will fly to the targets along the southern route. Its launch time is coordinated in a manner that it can be still called back before reaching the enemy coast in Holland, if all targets have been destroyed by the first two waves. The orders for the third wave are sent on a special group frequency. Before the reserve planes pass over the enemy coast, the targets to be attacked by them shall be communicated. If this radio communication is not received, the aircraft attack the dams according to importance on the target list, namely those which are not destroyed yet.

Above England they fly at an altitude of 500 metres, above the North Sea of 18.30 metres with the use of the new altimeter. An exact approach of the Dutch coast is very important, but no aircraft should fly back again, if the point of approach was not accurate. The chosen routes are as free of anti-aircraft installations as possible. Good map reading and cooperation in the cockpit will keep the aircraft on course. It has to be flown as low as possible, only for orientation the altitude can be occasionally slightly higher. At a distance of fifteen kilometres from the Möhne reservoir the leader of each group shall climb to an altitude of 300 metres. Then all Lancasters will turn on their frequency-modulation radios and report to the assault leader.

Ten minutes before the attack the bouncing bomb has to be put into rotation. The assault leader attacks first and then controls the other attacks against the Möhne and Eder dams. Leader no. 2 of the first wave serves as deputy for the assault leader. Planes which have released their bombs at the Möhne dam return to base except for the deputy assault leader. The direction of attack against the Möhne dam is at a right angle to the length of the target, a general line going from south-east to north-west. No aircraft will fly to the Eder dam before the Möhne dam has

The main target: the Möhne reservoir, rendered as a lifelike model according to reconnaissance photos, scale 1:6000. There was also a display piece of the Sorpe reservoir for the briefing of the pilots and crews, only the model of the Eder reservoir arrived too late for the instructions of the crews.

broken. If this has happened and sufficient bombs are still available, two further breaches shall be made into the wall, but three planes need to be ready for the Eder dam.

The destruction of the Möhne dam shall be observed very carefully, so that no confusion with overspilling water will arise. A continuation of flight will only follow if the Möhne dam is broken without a doubt. Time shall be taken. After the destruction of the Möhne dam all remaining craft of the first wave fly to the Eder reservoir, which is treated with the same tactics concerning the frequency-modulation radio, the target device, the altitude (18.3m) and speed (385km/h). The second wave flies in low-level flight on the northern route to the Sorpe reservoir. Its aircraft cross the enemy coast in quick succession, but not in formation, at the same time as the leading group of the first wave on the southern route. These planes communicate with each other on another ultra-short frequency. The bouncing bombs against the Sorpe dam will not be put into rotation. The aircraft have to attack the Sorpe dam from north-west to south-east, parallel to the length of the dam, and shall hit its centre five to seven metres before the border of the shore. Here the release of the bombs had to take place from as low an altitude as possible at a speed of 290km/h.

After the release of the bombs the aircraft shall fly back to base immediately. Three return routes are intended. All Lancaster bombers attack according to the method practised. The pilot is responsible for the line of approach, the navigator for the altitude, the bombardier for the accurate distance during release, the board engineer for the exact speed. The intervals between the individual drops should be at least three minutes. At all three reservoirs a holding pattern in left turn is flown, as low as possible, while waiting for deployment.

The timing of the attacks on each target is unimportant. It may vary with the approaching waves. Of the utmost importance, however, is the time of the simultaneous crossing of the enemy coast by the two waves. "Zero Hour" given in the launch order is therefore the time when the flight of three craft of the first wave is found at a position sixty kilometres west of the Scheldt island Goeree above the North Sea with course towards the enemy coast. Thirty minutes after dusk would be the optimum time. At this point in time the vanguard of the second wave, which had a longer route, must be approximately at a position sixty-five kilometres west of the isle of Vlieland. "Zero Hour" is the point in time at which the attack is final. No recall of the planes will occur after this point.

Diversionary Attacks

The whole success of this operation depends on the element of surprise. In order not to unnecessarily attract increased attention from the German air defence, the diversionary attacks have to be timed very carefully. The Headquarters Bomber Command has coordinated the maximum number of diversionary attacks. They start twenty minutes after the leading group of the first wave has crossed the enemy coast and it has been detected by German short-range radar and other tracking devices. The British main night bombing fleet remains on the ground. An hour before the launch of the third wave, no diversionary attacks shall be flown. Fifteen minutes after the third wave has passed over the enemy coast, diversionary attacks on the Reich territory and the occupied countries shall occur with great force and last until such a time as the third wave has left enemy territory again. Diversionary attacks below 650 metres shall not be flown in the following restricted areas: along a line west of Rotterdam, Terschelling, in the wider area south of Bruges, Wildenrath, south-east of Kassel, north-east of Detmold until west of Groningen.

Headquarters Bomber Command provided serviceable weather data, with a particular emphasis placed on the visibility conditions in the target region. This was done to such accuracy and with such efficiency that sufficient time remained to recall the Lancaster bombers before they embarked towards the enemy coast. Twenty minutes before "Zero Hour" the senders of the eastern chain are switched on to support the approach to the enemy coast at the exact time. The routes are planned accurately on the basis of conspicuous features in the landscape, such as water courses, bays, canals and railway junctions. For better orientation and facilitation of map reading it may be climbed briefly to an altitude of 150m. Before the launch of the reservoirs operation, all watches have to be synchronised with BBC time. Secrecy is of vital importance! Until the announcement of the mission order, knowledge of the operation is only accessible to the Commander of the airfield, the C.O. of the 617th Squadron and his two flight commanders.

After the instruction of the crews they shall be bound to the utmost secrecy. The possibility of a potential postponement of the operation exists, if the weather reconnaissance reports bad conditions in the target region and lets the operation appear to be inexecutable. Windows, tin foil strips for the disruption of German radar devices, are not dropped. From "Zero Hour" and for thirty minutes afterwards, the first and second waves have to keep absolute radio silence, the third wave from "Zero Hour" and for three hours afterwards. On the return flight the Lancasters shall pass over the English coast at an altitude of 500 metres, returning in the same direction that they came, and approach a base or airfield in the vicinity. A chosen code word will trigger the launch signal. It is called "Chastise".

Weather forecast of RAF meteorologists
Night of the 16/17 May 1943: high above the British Isles, spreading east

Home bases	Good conditions, moderate visibility
Denmark and German North Sea coast	Scattered medium-high cloud cover and scattered stratocumulus clouds
Extreme south and east of Germany	Occasional thunderstorms
Remaining Germany	Good conditions, good visibility
Berlin and Ruhr area	Cloudless, but in the evening occasional stratocumulus fields at 2,000 to 4,000 feet are possible in the area of the Ruhr region. In Berlin and Münster good visibility, ground mist in the area of the Ruhr region.
Frisian islands	Few stratocumulus clouds in 2,000 to 3,000 feet
France	Good conditions with moderate to good visibility
Winds	West three degrees eastern longitude north-western winds, speed less than 6mph
Target area	Winds 045 degrees/ 30-35mph
Temperature	4 to 7 degrees Celsius

Weather observed

Home bases	Good conditions during the whole night
Routes	Slightly clouded, mainly in high altitudes, moderate to good visibility
Target regions	Slightly clouded, moderate to good visibility. In the valleys after 00.30 ground mist

The almost full moon rises at 5pm; set at 4.41am

Launch of the 617th Squadron for "Operation Chastise"

Lancaster	Pilot	Launch time
1st wave – 1st flight of three aircraft		
AJ-G	Gibson	21.39 hours
AJ-M	Hopgood	21.39 hours
AJ-P	Martin	21.39 hours
AJ-A	Young	21.39 hours
AJ-J	Maltby	21.39 hours
AJ-L	Shannon	21.39 hours
AJ-Z	Maudslay	21.39 hours
AJ-B	Astell	21.39 hours
AJ-N	Knight	21.39 hours
2nd wave		
AJ-E	Barlow	21.28 hours
AJ-K	Byers	21.30 hours
AJ-H	Rice	21.31 hours
AJ-W	Munro	21.39 hours
AJ-T	McCarthy	22.01 hours
The craft of the 2nd wave launched consecutively		
3rd wave		
AJ-C	Ottley	00.09 hours
AJ-S	Burpee	00.11 hours
AJ-F	Brown	00.12 hours
AJ-O	Townsend	00.14 hours
AJ-Y	Anderson	00.15 hours
The craft of the 3rd wave launched consecutively		

The second wave was launched earlier than the first wave, as it had a longer flight route in order to cross the enemy coast at the same time as the first wave. The third wave served as a flying reserve and launched two and half hours after the first wave.

Approach of the 1st and 3rd wave on the southern route
1. Scampton base
2. Southwold at the English coast
3. "Zero Hour", a point sixty kilometres west of the Scheldt island Goeree in the Channel
4. From point "Zero Hour" to the middle of the mouth of the Scheldt between the islands of Schouwen and Walcheren

5. Roosendaal
6. South of Gilze-Rijen, past a German airfield, Tilburg, along the Wilhelmina Canal
7. Beek north of Helmond, here the Wilhelmina Canal meets the Zuid Willems vaart Canal at a right angle
8. The Rhine bend at Rees
9. A point south-west of Dülmen, west of the Borken mountains
10. Ahsen at the Weser-Datteln Canal
11. Between Heessen and Ahlen towards Uentrop
12. First target is the Möhne dam

Approach of the 2nd wave on the northern route
1. Scampton base
2. Sutton-on-Sea at the English coast
3. "Zero Hour", a point above the North Sea sixty-five kilometres west of Vlieland
4. A turning point towards the south-east ten kilometres north-west of Vlieland
5. Staveren at the Zuiderzee coast
6. Harderwijk
7. Doesburg east of Rheden in Holland
8. Rees at the Rhine, crossing point with the route of the first and third waves.
9. South-west of Dülmen, west of the Borken mountains
10. Ahsen at the Weser-Datteln Canal
11. Between Heessen and Ahlen towards Uentrop
12. First target is the Möhne dam.

The return routes
Return route number 1
1. Möhne dam
2. Uentrop
3. Between Ahlen and Heessen
4. Ahsen
5. Haltern
6. Nordhorn
7. Zuiderzee
8. Bergen
9. Southwold
10. Scampton

Return route number 2
1. Möhne dam
2. Until Haltern like route 1
3. Zutphen
4. Zuiderzee
5. South of Den Helder

  6. Southwold
  7. Scampton

Return route number 3
   1. Möhne dam
   2. Uentrop
   3. Between Ahlen and Heessen
   4. Ahsen
   5. Rees
   6. Doesburg
   7. Harderwijk
   8. Den Helder
   9. Southwold
  10. Scampton

All approaches and return flights led over the target Möhne dam.

The Attack: First Wave against the Möhne and Eder Dams

During the morning of 16 May 1943 on the Scampton airfield, the heavy "special stores" were mounted in the Lancaster bombers, tracer ammunition for the board canon and the compasses of the planes calibrated with and without bombs. The massive steel body of the rotational bomb influenced the magnetic field of the aircraft. During the briefing for the pilots and navigators in the morning and the crews in the afternoon, mainly aerial photographs were shown and analysed besides the dam models and various types of maps. Vertical shots, partly taken from an altitude of 9,000 metres, are exact mathematical documents of the highest significance. Aerial photographs from 13 May 1943 show the Eder reservoir over-spilling slightly. On 14 May air reconnaissance flew once more over the Möhne dam. During this flight Dortmund and Duisburg were photographed, too, in order to distract from the reservoirs. The images showed no alterations in the defence at the Möhne dam. The 617th Squadron had the order to attack six out of seven dams, four at the Ruhr, and two in the drainage area of the Weser, which Wallis had specified five months earlier in his study "Air Attacks on Dams".

   The Möhne dam, the target X with the reference number GO 939, is situated eleven kilometres south of Soest and fifty kilometres east of Dortmund. The Sorpe dam, target Z, reference number GO 960, lies at a linear distance of fifteen kilometres south-west from Möhne dam. A mountain ridge with the church tower of Langscheid will not directly impede a parallel approach to the Sorpe dam. Target D, reference number GO 938, is the Lister dam. The attack on the retaining wall shall lead via the location of Eichen. The Ennepe dam, target E, reference number GO 935, lies thirty kilometres south of Dortmund. At high water level a small island rises from the reservoir 300 metres in front of the retaining wall. The Henne dam as the fourth target in the Ruhr basin with the reference number GO 936 is located near the town of Meschede. However, as there might be a stronger air defence in the vicinity of the town, this dam was crossed off the target list. The other two dams are found in the drainage basin of the Weser.

The Eder dam, target Y, reference number GO 934, is located seventy kilometres south-east of the Möhne dam. The retaining wall was undefended, but the mountainous environment made a night-time low-level attack extremely difficult. Target number six was F, the Diemel dam with the reference number GO 933. It counted amongst the last resort targets, as the Lister and Ennepe dams, too.

After Wing Commander Guy Gibson had announced the targets and the assault plan to the crews, he introduced the white-haired civilian Barnes Wallis. The latter showed sectional drawings of the retaining walls, described the weapon and the arguments for a demolition of the dams. In front of a huge map of Western Europe with red ribbons pinned across to the targets, the organiser of the attack, Air Vice Marshal R. Cochrane, predicted that this night operation would make history and represented a terrible strike against the German machinery of war. After that Barnes Wallis expressed the hope that all aviators would return, and he pointed once more to the successful trial detonations. Now the dams in Germany had to fall, too.

At 9.10pm the radio operator Hutchinson fired a red flare from the cockpit of Gibson's Lancaster, the signal for launch and for the second wave to fire up their motors and to taxi to the start position on the runway.

At 9.28pm Barlow started the first plane of the second wave, which had a longer flight on the northern route than the aircraft of the first wave, over the grass runway of the RAF base at Scampton into the reddened evening sky. Operation Chastise was set in motion. After a long take-off, due to the heavy bombs on board, five planes raced booming one after another towards the east in the direction of Sutton-on-Sea at the English North Sea coast with the Sorpe dam as their aim. Due to a failed launch McCarthy had to transfer to the reserve craft AJ-T and thus to make up a twenty minute delay.

At 9.39pm the green light of an Aldis lamp approved the launch of Gibson's Lancaster, with Hopgood on his right and Martin on his left. Within twenty minutes also the second wave was in the air and forty minutes later passed over the English coast near Southwold in the direction of the Möhne and Eder dams. Below them the North Sea lay calm and still. Isolated reports were sent by lamp employing Morse code from plane to plane. Gibson approached the enemy coast in the wrong place above the heavily defended island of Walcheren in the direction of Roosendaal. Constantly the bombardier checked the course on a ground map, which led along the Wilhelmina Canal closely by the German night fighter bases Gilze-Rijen and Eindhoven. Near the town of Helmond the Wilhelmina Canal meets the Zuid Willems Vaart Canal at a right angle. From here the flight led to the Rhine bend at Rees, south of Borken and past the small lakes near Dülmen towards Ahlen. In the Borken area there was strong air defence and very many spotlights. Gibson broke radio silence and sent a flak warning to the base. This repeated the warning including the position. Also north of Hamm strong air defence prevailed in the forefield to Europe's largest shunting station. Shortly before Ahlen was the last turning point, from which the flight led in a southern direction between Werl and Soest to the Möhne dam.

The second flight of three aircraft, led by Young, with Maltby on the right and Shannon on the left, followed Gibson on the same route at an interval of eight minutes. They incurred flak fire near Dülmen, too, and arrived above the Möhne dam twenty minutes past midnight.

The last flight of three aircraft of the first wave, led by Maudslay with Astell on the right and Knight on the left, had taken off at 9.59pm. Caused by rising winds, their flight across the North Sea took a little longer. Over Reich territory Astell followed closely behind Maudslay and Knight. Near Marbeck he flew against the top of a high-voltage pole at the ordered low level without flak fire or spotlight interference.

Roswitha Reining (today a nun) saw the crash: "During the war I worked as a maid for the Thesing family in Marbeck. During some nights firelight reddened the sky above the Ruhr area, when the bombs were raining down.

On 16 May close to midnight I stood outside the farm with old Mr. Thesing and watched the low-flying aircraft of which we assumed that they were German planes. First a four-motor craft flew at a lateral pass over the neighbouring houses of Thesing. One or two minutes later a second craft came from the same western direction, but closer to us, which was followed by a third at a two-minute interval. Without burning it flew against the top of a high-voltage pole standing 150-200 metres in front of the Thesing farmhouse. Immediately a great fire erupted at the craft, the plane still lifted up slightly, passed over our house and crashed 200 metres away into a field.

After circa two minutes a bomb exploded and tore such a deep hole that a house could have been put inside. Seven men fell victim to the crash. Due to the high air pressure all windows in the house were shattered, and all doors and the roof were heavily damaged.

At the time of the crash, an air raid alarm was in force, but the anti-aircraft guns for the protection of Marl only started to fire when the bomber had already crashed. Also the spotlights near Marbeck blazed up into the sky afterwards. Yet the enemy aircraft flew at such a low level, that the spotlights could not have illuminated them.

A notable event: only fifty metres away from the bomb crater stood a figure of St. Joseph with the child Jesus on his arm at the wayside. It had remained completely undamaged, not even a finger was broken off, in stark contrast to the damaged houses further away."

Main Target X: The Möhne Dam

At 00.15 hours squadron leader Guy Gibson together with the vanguards of the first assault wave reached the Möhne Lake. One by one the Lancaster bombers gathered in a left-turn holding pattern ten kilometres south of Völlinghausen above the Arnsberg forest. Fruitlessly Gibson called plane AJ-B, with the pilot William Astell, whose wreck burnt out near Marbeck. Gibson swept the Möhne retaining wall and the anti-aircraft installations. Everything showed itself to be as predicted in the briefing, three anti-aircraft guns on the retaining wall and three in the valley. On the spot, Gibson decided how the attack should be flown: from the airspace around the "Forester's Lodge Green Hope", across the middle of the arm of the river Heve and the largely tree-covered flat peninsula between Heve basin and Delleck bridge 1600 meters across water towards the middle of the retaining wall. By radio

Spotlight position near Raesfeld in the Münsterland, in front of the Fasselt-Welchering farm, only a few kilometres south-west of the Marbeck farm, the crash site of Flight Lieutenant Astell. The Lancaster AJ-B was supposed to attack the Möhne dam. This spotlight, switched on too late, searched for the approaching planes in higher altitudes. The dam busters had long since flown by at a low level.

Near Marbeck the pilot Flight Lieutenant Astell raced against the top of a high-voltage pole and crashed. He burnt to death with his crew amidst the debris of his Lancaster. In front of a torn wing lies the corpse of a crew member. A handwritten note of the local policeman shows three names of the crew and some sparse finds: emergency rations, money, a ring, a cigarette case, a pocket watch, a bundle of keys, a Canadian lighter and an engraved wrist watch.

In total the RAF lost six Lancaster bombers on route to the reservoirs with the pilots Byers (Texel), Astell (Marbeck), Barlow (Haldern-Herken), Burpee (Gilze Rijen), Hopgood (Ostgönnen), and Ottley (Heessen); on the return flight, two aircraft flown by Maudslay (Klein-Netterden) and Young (Castricum-aan-Zee).

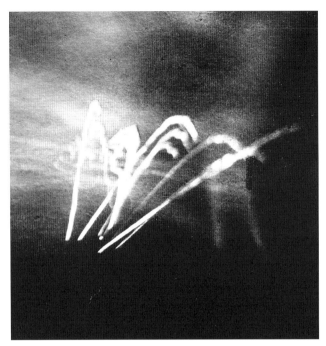

This is the only photo of the nocturnal battle of the Möhne dam. Fourteen-year-old Heinz Vogt, living below the dam at the time, fearlessly placed his 6x9 Agfa box camera on the windowsill and released the shutter. A five-minute time shot registered the trajectories of the tracer projectiles reaching for the bombers.

Corporal Karl Schütte, leaning on the two centimetre gun, together with six further air defence soldiers, was awarded the Iron Cross Second Class for the downing of a Lancaster during the attack on the Möhne dam.

Debris of the tail unit of the Lancaster shot down above the Möhne in Ostgönnen; the joker Warrant Officer Abram Garshowitz had written in chalk on the fuselage next to the hatch of Hopgood's Lancaster: "Officers entrance only". In reference to a quote by Churchill during the Battle of England, Garshowitz put the following text on one of the bouncing bombs: "Never has so much been expected of so few".

communication Gibson assigned five of the remaining eight Lancasters to the attack. He made Hopgood his deputy in case anything happened to himself.

As the first pilot, squadron leader Guy Gibson launched into attack, reached the proscribed altitude, the speed was correct, the bomb ran with 500 rotations, the bombardier saw the target in registry with the aiming device and released. Despite the heaviest resistance by the air defence, Gibson's bouncing bomb exploded at 00.28 hours. Gibson's tail gunner saw the bomb bounce three times from his "grandstand" at the back of the Lancaster. Then after some seconds a tall column of water rose, and it was believed that the wall had been broken. Yet the bomb dropped fifty metres south of the middle of the dam. Gibson's radio operator sent the message "Goner 68A" for the failed drop to the base. Five minutes later, when the surface of the water had calmed, Hopgood attacked with his Lancaster AJ-M. The Lancaster crews saw how his craft received hits by the flak; the right internal motor and the right wing were burning. The bouncing bomb was released too late; it jumped over the retaining wall and exploded inside the power station with a bright jet of flame. Hopgood's machine passed over Günne in an orange ball of flame and crashed near Ostönnen. In vain Hopgood had attempted to gain height once more in order to enable the crew members to exit with parachutes. His last sentence was: "In the name of God, disembark!" Indeed two aviators, Burcher and Fraser, could save themselves by parachute from the lowest altitude. For a third (Minchin) the chute did not open wide enough. The aviator was severely injured by flak before hitting the ground in a fatal fall.

The third attack against the Möhne dam was flown by Martin. Gibson flew at his side to deceive the air defence. Martin reported a water column fifty metres high at the northern side of the dam to Grantham (failed drop "Goner 58 A"). After landing in Scampton, it turned out that the air defence had hit an empty gasoline tank at Martin's craft. Then Young led the fourth attack against the target. For fighting the anti-aircraft guns Martin flew at a parallel course, Gibson at the same time over the retaining wall with full illumination. Again a tall water column washed over the dam (failed drop "Goner 78 A").

In the fifth craft Gibson let Maltby attack with the Lancaster AJ-J. Gibson and Martin accompanied the assault on the sides to keep the air defence occupied from the water side. A third Lancaster fired onto the anti-aircraft position on the dam from the range of hills called the Haarstrang. Maltby was right on course, everything was pitch-perfect, and the bouncing bomb jumped and hit the dam correctly. Again a water column more than 300 metres high rose from the lake, and collapsed in the light of the moon which shone from the south-east. The shock waves in the water were clearly visible. At 00.50 hours Maltby's radio operator sent another disappointing report home (failed drop). Gibson had already given the order to Shannon to fly the sixth attack. At that moment he saw how the dam broke apart. Except for one gun, the air defence had ceased to fire.

At 00.50 hours Gibson's operator sent the code word "Nigger" for a successful destruction of the Möhne dam to the central command of the 5th British Bomber Fleet. The latter repeated the radio message and asked for confirmation once more for good measure in order to avoid misunderstandings. Exactly as Wallis had predicted it, one solitary rotational bomb broke the Möhne dam, exactly at 00.49 hours. This time was recorded by a seismograph of the seismological station of the Geophysical Institute in Göttingen, more than 130 kilometres away from the Möhne reservoir. The crews of the remaining seven craft looked at their work on the ground. For them it was an indescribable sight to see how the water shot through the breach in the wall, an image which nobody would ever experience from the air again.

According to the operational plan, Martin and Maltby headed for home. The three craft which still carried "Upkeeps" – Shannon, Maudslay and Knight – flew with Gibson and Young (deputy) towards the south-east to the Eder Lake ten to twelve minutes away by flight.

At operational command in Grantham things were very tense. Harris, Cochrane and Wallis had driven to the headquarters in Grantham after the launch of the first two waves from the Scampton airfield. In a bombproof shelter they followed the details of Operation Chastise on a large wall chart. The lost and returning craft were shown with white chalk. Wallis paced up and down in excitement. Each radio message was received loud and clear. Signal Officer Dunn deciphered it and announced the message by loudspeaker. With each failed drop Wallis buried his head in his hands. It was the first time that a bomber group had radio contact with operational command above the target during an attack.

When the successful message "Nigger" came in, Wallis leapt up and threw his arms in the air. Officers shook his hands. Bomber Harris approached him, congratulated him and said 'when you came to me with your crazy ideas, I never believed them. Now, you could sell me a pink elephant'. Moments like this lived on and were never forgotten by those who experienced them. The Mohne dam was cracked.

Also **Karl Schütte**, corporal of the air defence at that time, has never forgotten the dramatic battle for the Möhne dam: "On 16 April 1943 I came to the Möhne anti-aircraft battery 3/480. On the night of the attack we received an air raid alarm report by telephone from the anti-aircraft control station at Schwansbell Castle near Lünen. After a few seconds the two centimetre guns on the wall towers and in the valley were ready to fire. Soon a dark black body materialised on the opposite horizon and hurtled in lowest-level flight across the water towards the middle of the wall. Immediately the monstrosity firing at us was taken under fire. During the exchange of fire, due to the many flying colourful spots of light of the tracer ammunition, we only saw the headlights of the craft when the plane had already approached the wall. The gunner to whom I was calling out corrections, had not aimed at the headlights, but at the entire four-motor bomber, based on the tracer. The first bomb exploded fifty metres before the retaining wall with a huge water mushroom. During the attack I saw clearly how our tracer impacted on the craft and flames formed immediately, and a motor was burning. During the flyover of the retaining wall the flame flickered and became larger. There was a shout of joy as with a success. Then a massive explosion occurred down in the valley. The bomb of the burning craft had laid waste to the power station. Such a cloud of dust rose that we could not see at first what had happened. After the direct hit on the power station, all telephone connections had been disrupted and the gun on the south tower had been broken down. The operating crew ran to the retaining wall and reported to Lieutenant Widmann.

No flak soldier was injured during the attacks, nobody could help us on the north tower, either, because after the hit on the power station the staircases were damaged and the ceilings had come down. The aircraft, in holding pattern above the forest on the opposite shore of the lake, were clearly visible, especially when they approached with the navigation lights switched on to draw the fire of the air defence. Flash bombs were supposed to blind the gunners. The impetus of the attack became stronger and stronger, as approaches ensued from all sides. Two further gigantic water columns crashed over the retaining wall. During the fourth attack our gun failed due to a non-starter. With all our might we tried with hammer and spike to remove the jam, but without success. During the fifth attack we did what we had trained to do so often: air defence by carbine. Only one gun at the access to the wall still fired on the attacking craft which now had an easy job of it. When the spray had slightly settled down after a muffled explosion, I glanced downwards over the parapet of the tower to the wall and said to my comrades: 'The wall is broken.' At first they did not want to believe it. The breach became rapidly larger. I only thought: with the next attack you will lie down there in the tempestuous floods. I did not see the bouncing bombs jump across the Möhne Lake; our attention was exclusively fixed on the attacking planes and the pursuit of the tracer ammunition.

At dawn between three and four am, once again an aircraft was passing over. It was fired upon by the last gun ready to fire at the dam's access – without success. This Lancaster with its on-board weapons shot aflame a barn in Günne. Our guns below the retaining wall could only fight the aircraft when they were leaving, as they would otherwise have endangered us on the towers. The reach of the two centimetre flak was 2,000 metres.

During the evening of 17 May the Minister of Armament Speer arrived at 8pm with a large delegation to inspect the damage. In the morning, General Schmidt from air district VI Münster showed up. We had to report. There were congratulations and awards with Iron Crosses 2nd Class, about which we were very astonished and asked ourselves for which deed we received them. The object to be defended had actually been destroyed. Apparently the superiors saw this with different eyes. Also Lieutenant General Weise, Supreme Chief of Air Defence, and the Reich Minister of the Interior, Dr. Frick, visited the demolished Möhne dam which afterwards was rebuilt into a fortress. Lieutenant Widmann had always said: 'Boys, boys, you do not even know how much responsibility you bear and all that depends on the Möhne reservoir, all the works in the Ruhr area are fed by it.' Lieutenant Widmann commanded only six light two centimetre anti-aircraft guns."

Ferdinand Nölle, assistant police constable from Günne, reports: "Just two days after Hitler had occupied the Rhineland, we stood guard on the Möhne dam in plain clothes. In evening classes we were trained. A lieutenant colonel advised us to wear a uniform. We therefore put on our fire brigade uniform. The guardroom was situated inside the power station in front of the retaining wall. Already some time before the attack citizens from Neheim had complained by telephone that the reservoir should be slightly drained to lessen the danger in case of an attack. Yet nothing happened.

One day the dam was blocked by crossbar for all civilian traffic. Soon after, a commission sent from Air District VI Munster arrived, with General Schmidt, to inspect it. The gentlemen stood between the two wall towers and pointed to the Heve basin. I came up closer and heard

Christian Tilenius received the order to examine the secrets of the crashed bombers from the Reich Air Ministry in Berlin. With a short-distance reconnaissance plane he circled above the reservoirs, and on 18 May 1943 he took a series of photographs not known until recently. The "air raid alarm barometers", as the population called the silvery barrage balloons, were once more present after the disaster. When the balloons rose into the sky, an air raid alarm would follow. The balloon barrage chain was visible far and wide, till Neheim and Werl.

The sudden wide breach had caused a vast front wave during the night. Approximately 9,000cbm water at a speed of six metres per second shot down the valley. Water pipes leading to the vanished power station in front of the centre of the dam had been torn from their concrete anchoring in the ground. The figure of the air defence soldier Karl Schütte offers a scale for the size of the pipe.

Stunned, an air defence soldier is standing in front of the breach in the Möhne dam; a direct hit, an enormous hole, a great flood disaster. Could the disaster, the military fiasco at the Möhne dam, have been prevented? (Federal Archive Coblenz 1011/637/4192/23)

Police Constable (retired) Wilhelm Strotkamp was deployed as auxiliary policeman guarding the Möhne dam since 1942 and became eye witness to the explosive physics of a dam buster bomb. Below the dam he experienced five detonations. After the war, as the captain of a Möhne boat, he recounted the events to inquiring tourists time and again. The various bomb drops let him assume at first that the planes only wanted to destroy the torpedo nets to be able to approach the wall directly. Even during the first attack, the water foamed over the wall. With the second attack the power station exploded in a blinding flash. During their attacks the aircraft flew very low between the two towers. Bombers and Möhne air defence battled each other doggedly.

During the fifth attack there was a very different sounding, muffled explosion. Suddenly the ground on which he stood trembled and the whole wall vibrated like a running combined harvester. Similar to an earthquake the entire ground shook for a moment. In a matter of seconds the dam moved back and forth between the towers. Water streamed through the cracks in the masonry, and then an entire block of wall suddenly broke off in full width like a barn door opening wide. So it had been predicted by the inventor of the bomb, Barnes Wallis. One bomb with wall contact would suffice to initiate the collapse of the dam with the shock waves induced. From his hiding place at the northern slope Wilhelm Strotkamp ran up to the guard room and made his report. The guard on duty alerted the district administration in Soest. Like a giant waterfall the water masses tumbled through the breach into the valley. Soon dense fog obstructed the view as if in a laundry room. To this was added the thunder of the raging flood.

Netted chains with their buoys, protecting against a torpedo attack, had been torn from their anchoring in the lake by the flood wave. (Federal Archive 1011/637/4192/27)

This sensational photo of the destroyed Möhne dam with the draining lake went around the print media of the Allies, testament to their successful attack.

During the morning of 17 May 1943 at 7.30am, a single Spitfire, flying reconnaissance and piloted by Flight Officer Jerry Fray, took off from the RAF base in Benson towards the German reservoirs. At 9,000m altitude, with excellent flying weather and optimal visibility, he succeeded in taking a perfect series of shots of the target object, Möhne dam. Even as the Spitfire was still above Germany, the most inquisitive British Air Ministry called the image interpretation office in Medmenham to pass on the results of the raid immediately by telephone. In the film laboratory of the Benson airfield, the reconnaissance base, great excitement prevailed, after it had become known how important the film that they were developing was. From the airfield commander to the lab assistant, soon everybody gathered around a light table with the negatives. The crystal clear, brilliant negative of the Möhne dam caused great exaltation. The immediate call to the Air Ministry in London said: "There is a breach at the centre of the Möhne dam, seventy metres wide, water is draining from the reservoir, first class." After photographing the Mohne reservoir, the pilot flew to the Eder reservoir. He couldn't find it. He could only discern the floods in the Eder valley. Only by returning a day later could he capture photographs of the destroyed dam.

Shock waves of the exploding "Wallis bombs" had smashed in the copper roof of the north tower. The repair works had already begun when this photograph was taken. The artificial pine trees on and along the retaining wall could not fulfil their camouflage purpose.

The two centimetre anti-aircraft gun with Corporal Karl is ready for action again. A white kill ring is now adorning the barrel; in the background, the devastated Möhne valley.

the general say: 'It (torpedo?) will be dropped there.' 700–800 metres away, not from the Heve basin, as an accompanying civilian remarked, and then it runs against the Möhne road. What should be dropped there, the general did not say. I reported the conversation. It was copied into the log book.

On the night of 16 May 1943, I was on night watch when, at around midnight, the sirens began wailing at a distance. I went to the power station and helped my friend Clemens Köhler to read the meters. Outside the air defence began to fire. I said: 'Clemens, leave the power station and go up to the dam.' 'Well', he answered, 'that is not so bad, they shoot now and then.'

I walked along the retaining wall and around 00.20 waited for my relief by Wilhelm Stortkamp. Finally he came. I asked him why he came so late. 'Yes', he said, 'I have watched the spectacle of the planes at the lakeside.' I warned: 'Wilhelm, whatever you do, do not go into the tunnel inside the wall tonight, or you will drown when the water comes.' I went towards the road where there was fog like pea-soup after the first failed drops. At that moment another bomb fell and hit the torpedo net. The retentive cable roll uncoiled rapidly, it had probably not been fixed tightly enough. I wanted to sign off in the guardroom. Some colleagues stood below in the lake yard behind a thick terrace wall and watched the attack. Suddenly they ran into the guardroom and shouted: 'The wall has burst.' The water released by one of the explosions had washed over them and the terraces. With each explosion in the lake high air pressure arose. At one point I flew three metres across the guardroom and hit my head against a door. Fortunately I was wearing a steel helmet, because otherwise my skull would have been broken. Such an explosion I did not experience even in Verdun.

Out of breath, Wilhelm Strotkamp, who had stood guard below the retaining wall, reached the guardroom in which all the windows had shattered and no light was burning. Together we snatched the telephone which rang at that moment. The district administration Soest inquired what was happening at the Möhne. We reported the breach of the retaining wall and said: 'Here we cannot help ourselves; you have to raise the alarm down in the valley!' With that the responsibility was taken from us.

After the breach, it was impossible to see into the Mohne valley. Dense wafts of mist eliminated any visibility, only the thundering of the water could be heard which now brought death and destruction to the Möhne-Ruhr valley. As the sole eye witness my friend Wilhelm Strotkamp watched as the centre of the wall moved to and fro during the breaking, as during an earthquake, only to open wide like a barn door."

Walter Fischer, ninth grader from Soest, recalls: "fourteen grammar school students lay on the beds in the dormitory of the rowing club of the Soest Archi grammar school in Dellecke. A day of splendid freedom had passed. They had been out and about with the school's [foursome] rowing boats. Since many teachers had already been drafted into the army, supervision was missing that night in the rural hall of residence. The ninth graders simply could find no rest. On one of the beds a boxed gramophone played 'Lili Marlene'.

Seconds later this idyll was ruined, when a low rumbling announced the approach of a heavy aircraft. In May 1943 we knew the aerial war above our homeland, the rumbling of the bombers passing over at great height, the howling of falling bombs and the dull banging of the flak.

This, however, we did not know yet: like giant specimen of herons which during the day circle silently and elegantly over the Möhne Lake, this night four-motor bombers tore fast as arrows and with deafening noise over the peninsula between the Heve and Möhne basins, jumped over the last hills and trees and then chased at a height of a few metres across the mirror-smooth lake towards the dam. Each time when a bomber monster passed over the surface of the water, the suction of its propellers drove a veil of water fine as dust from the lake.

A fascinating sight in the backlight of the moon for fourteen ninth graders which seemed more like sport than war; the dam itself we could not see from Dellecke, as the pensinula with Dellecke House inserts itself in between. Each time a craft appeared, red and green strands drew close to it, the trails of ammunition of the two centimetre flak on the wall towers. When the tracer chains hit the plane, a bizarre pattern appeared on the lake.

Several times bombers flew against the retaining wall, firing full blast and trailing huge contrails of churning water, as if they wanted to land on the lake. Then behind the peninsula with Dellecke House, dazzling water fountains sprang up straight as posts, which were followed shortly after by a blast of detonation. At the fifth time there was a muffled, resounding detonation. We all had the same thought: the dam is hit. As fast as we could we ran from Dellecke to the retaining wall. A gap had been torn into the mural crown into which a large multi-family house could have been easily fitted. Calmly the water of the Möhne flowed through the breach in the dam, but thunder was sounding from the valley. The impact of the water mass made the dam road on top of the retaining wall tremble. At that moment I recalled the song to which we were listening when the cruel drama began: 'When the late mists are whirling, I will be standing by the lantern, as once Lili Marlene'. Now gloomy mists were whirling over the site of the disaster".

Second Wave against the Sorpe Dam

The second wave of Lancaster bombers which flew on the northern route to the Sorpe reservoir and took off before Gibson's main wave was not favoured by fortune. Separated by 200 kilometres, it passed over the Dutch coast almost at the same time as the first wave.

Munro's Lancaster AJ-W got into the fire of light anti-aircraft guns over the island of Texel, hereby the radio and board communication systems were taken out. Munro decided therefore to turn around ahead of schedule and landed at 0.26 in Scampton as the first to return from the operation, with the intact bomb on board despite the ban on bringing back an "Upkeep".

According to the statement by the air defence soldier Edmund Mantell, around 11pm the Lancaster AJ-K of pilot Byers was downed at the coast of Texel by the Sunday's shot of a turned down 10.5 centimetres anti-aircraft gun. Only four weeks later, much to the terror of some inhabitants of the island, the bomb exploded in the Waddenzee. Byer's Lancaster was the first casualty of Operation Chastise.

Also pilot Rice in his Lancaster AJ-H had to abort his mission prematurely. He flew so low over the island of Vlieland that he had to virtually jump over the sand dunes. On a south-eastern course above the sea, water suddenly crashed over his cockpit, accompanied by a hard blow. Instinctively he put the bomber into a steep climb, but the bouncing bomb had been torn from the suspension bracket during water contact. Water streamed through the bomb-free bay into the aircraft's fuselage. The tail gunner sat up to his neck in salt water. So Rice had to return to base, too, and had difficulties with the damaged machine during landing. Only 20 minutes after Munro's landing he could touch down, too.

The Lancaster AJ-E with the pilot Barlow flew over the point of interception with the route of the first wave near Rees at the Rhine and then dashed against the top of a high-voltage pole near Haldern-Herken. Barlow's bouncing bomb did not explode, as its time-delay fuse had not been activated and thus revealed its secret to the German air forces.

Johanna Effing describes the events of the plane's crash thus: "There was a loud bang. Thereupon we left the house's basement in Haldern-Herken and saw that the field in front of us was ablaze. A plane had flown from a westerly direction against the top of a high-voltage pole of a 100,000 volt line and crashed into the field. Fifty metres away from the crash site a large bomb had rolled out.

Already during the night a crowd of onlookers gathered despite the danger of exploding ammunition. Soon, Major Lehmann from Haldern also appeared and climbed onto the supposed large gasoline barrel. He said: 'I will notify the district commissioner that he does not need to send us gasoline chits any longer for the time of the war. That much fuel we have here in this tank.' When he learned later that he had stood on dynamite, allegedly he was still sick in retrospect.

All crew members of the aircraft had met their deaths and had been burnt beyond all recognition. Anti-aircraft positions and spotlights did not exist here; the plane had simply flown too low. The first detachment to stand guard at the crash site showed us the valuable finds such as wallets, gold rings, watches, and a large electric torch. On the latter, all sorties undertaken by its owner had been engraved, thirty-two in number. I clearly recall the name 'Palermo' and many other city names. From this sortie he did not return. The plane's crew had been around, said the soldiers who helped the next morning to collect the most minuscule scraps of the craft, probably to find out how the bomb had been attached to the plane.

The first pyrotechnical specialists could not defuse the bomb. We had to open windows and doors to avoid damage in case the bomb should explode during defusing. Then another squad of specialists came and defused the bomb.

In the morning after the defusing I went alone to the bomb. It was a dark black-green monstrosity. At one side the pyrotechnical specialists had removed a connection ring. More than twenty per cent of the total height of the explosive device was buried in the ground. After two days the bomb was driven off with a truck to the ammunition dismantling yard Kalkum near Düsseldorf. Political prisoners unearthed the bomb, pyrotechnical captain Heinz Schweizer then defused it. When the field was harvested, two depressions were still visible, created by the plane on impact.

The farmer **Josef Schlaghecke** who lives near the crash site of the Lancaster bomber recalls: "It was fifteen minutes to midnight, when the bomber crashed, snapped one high-voltage pole half off and compromised a second. The next morning a prison transport was driven to the unexploded bomb. During the meals the prisoners were allocated to different farms where they ate under supervision. During the meals speaking was not allowed. It was made plain to the farmers that the inmates were political prisoners. We considered these people to be a suicide command. An aunt on Borke's farm learned that allegedly a lawyer and a priest were among the prisoners."

Four of five planes of the second wave did not reach the Sorpe reservoir. Only the American McCarthy – he flew with his Lancaster AJ-T at full speed in the hope to make up for the delay caused by the changeover to the reserve plane – reached the Sorpe reservoir around 00.45 hours. In the vicinity of the lake mist prevailed, but immediately at the dam there was optimal visibility. During the approach over Langscheid difficulties ensued with the church tower of the location. McCarthy managed to climb down along a mountain ridge and to approach the dam in parallel flight. Nevertheless he could at first not find the prescribed ideal line to release the bomb. Finally he dropped his bouncing bomb without rotation and use of a spotlight altimeter exactly onto the centre of the dam. (The reserve plane did not yet have a spotlight altimeter.) After a short while a massive explosion shook the dam. In the moonlight some damage became visible, but the full extent was only provided by the cameras of the reconnaissance planes around noon in England. At 1am McCarthy passed over the Möhne reservoir on his way home, which already had proceeded to "wander" in the meantime. At 3.23am he landed in Scampton with a tire flattened by flak fire.

The machinist **Josef Ketting** reports: "Around midnight my wife woke me in the company flat of the Sorpe power station with the words: 'You have to get up now, there is a plane passing over repeatedly.' I had no idea and went outside where some colleagues stood in front of the power station. Via telephone they had received warning level three. Approaching planes from the Dutch border towards Hamm had been reported.

Just as I wanted to return to the house, a plane approached the dam from the direction of Langscheid. I saw how the craft flew low below the dam crest over the centre road, not 100 metres away from me. I recognised the English insignia, the rings. Quickly I ran into the house and ordered my wife to leave the power station with the boy and our valuables and to go to the basement of a company residence at the dam base below the inn Brinkschulte.

A short while later, again a plane appeared parallel to the dam and dropped an 'instrument' like an over-sized slurry tanker over the dam crest at the water side. After some seconds a column of water rose thunderously for 100 metres and tilted to the valley side of the Sorpe dam. At that moment I was still thinking: tomorrow morning you will go to the lake and gather the fish in a basket. The water column ran down the dam. I believed that the attack had been aimed at the power station. Meanwhile my boss had reached the power station, too.

About two hours later, another craft flew head-on from the water side towards the dam with the headlights switched on. It circled the Sorpe Lake twice and dropped its bomb with the second approach, which exploded shortly after. This aircraft I only saw from the power station, when it flew with its lights over the centre of the dam. Due to the air pressure all glass panes in the power station shattered, but the turbines continued to run at first. Stones from the dam's parapet flew as far as the equalising pond. As I later determined the hits were located below the water surface, the second probably higher up towards the road, causing deep indentations.

October attack on the Sorpe dam
This attack is often confused with that of the 17 May 1943.

On 15 October 1944 the 9th Squadron attacked the Sorpe dam. At 9.28am sixteen British combat planes of the Lancaster type dropped large-calibre bombs – 5.2 ton streamlined "Tallboys" – from a height of 4,000 to 5,000 metres.

Josef Kesting was present at the power station during this attack. He remembers: "I saw the bombers coming like a formation of cranes. The first six craft flew in a row with little spacing, slightly offset from each other. Accompanying fighter planes fired at the dam in low-level flight. Above us it pattered in the bushes under which I had sought refuge, as if a bag of peas had been spilled."

Werner Meschede, fifteen years old, had been deployed as an air defence aid at the Sorpe dam since 15 January 1944 and describes the attack thus: "I was a member of the forth train of the 1/892 air defence regiment. Our train lay together with the fifth train on the dam crest, and the fourth train was stationed in the first third. The weaponry per train consisted of three two centimetre quadruple mounts. On that Sunday, the air raid alarm sounded in the morning yet again. We trained our guns and searched the sky. Coming from Neheim, a heavy bomber formation approached the centre of the dam. As no chance of hitting them at that altitude existed for us, we followed the aircraft with the gun sight. Suddenly I saw how the bomb bays of the Lancasters were opened and bombs dropped out. In panic we jumped from the mount and took cover on the ground. In the same moment the Sorpe dam thundered and thudded. It seemed to shake and vibrate. My thought was 'in a moment you will drown in the water and mud of the Sorpe Lake'. After the massive explosions I stood up again and noticed that all my comrades had fled. A direct hit on the dam crest at the Langscheid side had annihilated the fifth train. There were several casualties. Because we had left the mounts, inquiries were made. Yet they remained without result. I have survived this attack, but will never forget the day. On the same day the Minister of Armament Speer came to the Sorpe dam to get a picture of the damage and the size of the bomb craters. The huge crater in the dam crest was covered with camouflage netting".
Some of the bombs dropped, as Josef Kesting can add, had long-delay fuses. At the centre road one of these bombs later claimed the lives of several people. Even as late as 1959, an unexploded "Tallboy" was recovered from the Sorpe Lake and defused.

When the situation had calmed down again, the party leaders came, the 'gentlemen of the brown colour'. From them I received the order to warn by telephone the houses below the dam which were endangered in the event of a disaster. These telephone numbers I knew by heart like the Lord's Prayer.

Immediately, the damage at the dam was provisionally repaired and, for this, huge amounts of bundled timber and brushwood were transported onto the dam. In case another attack should ensue, the gap should be plugged with this material and the leak be sealed up. (These objects presented the English aerial photograph interpreters with a riddle.) The Sorpe dam had held, although the reservoir was at its utmost capacity. However, the water level was then slightly lowered. I had to evacuate my company flat. Air defence soldiers moved in. We stayed for a few days with relatives in Hagen. They had already 'waited' for us on a bridge over the Ruhr below Hohensyburg to see who would arrive with the flood.

On my return journey to the Sorpe reservoir I wanted to buy a train ticket to Fröndenberg at the Hagen station. However, this was refused with the remark that the Sorpe dam had now broken, too. I could not believe this and telephoned via RWE to VEW to Arnsberg where I received confirmation that the Sorpe dam had not been broken. The 'Sorpe false alarm', which had caused a panic during the memorial service at the funeral of the Möhne victims, had travelled across the entire Ruhr valley."

Josef Brinkschulte remembers the attack on the Sorpe dam: "During the night of the 16/17 May only one guard was posted on the Sorpe dam as a precaution against sabotage. The guard detachment consisted of elderly gentlemen who took turns on duty. The first craft approached the dam in parallel flight without lights and relatively slowly. After the release of the bomb it circled once above the lake and then turned towards the north-east. Flares were not dropped near the dam.

The second craft flew at higher speed over the lakeside towards the centre of the dam. During the second approach it activated its headlights and illuminated the dam crest. An explosion followed, much heavier than that of two hours previously. All the roof tiles fell from the houses standing around 500 metres below the dam. In the immediate vicinity all windows shattered. The gigantic mushroom of water I can still see before my eyes today. The telephone lines went dead immediately. The anti-aircraft fire with the tracer ammunition in the direction of the Möhne reservoir was clearly visible after midnight. Shortly after 1am I heard the news from an official of the Ruhr Reservoir Society who had come to the Sorpe dam: 'The Möhne is running'."

Hidden Target Y: The Eder Dam

The five aircraft from the first wave did not meet any resistance on their flight to the Eder dam, but initially there were great difficulties in identifying the dam. Gibson reached the lake too far to the west. The many meanders of the reservoir made navigation difficult.

Also Shannon approached too far west at first and then made a feint attack on the rock face of a defunct stone quarry near Rehbach, a deceptively similar wall situation along the course taken. Shannon was just about to take another look at the "dam", when Gibson made contact over the radio and said: "I will drop a flare above the Eder dam which I have found here farther to the east. All aircraft shall come here." Soon the Lancasters circled in a left turn over the Waldeck castle, the Eder retaining wall and the settlement of Buhlen.

The difficulty for the three bomb-carrying Lancasters was to go down from 350 metres altitude through a ravine near the Waldeck castle, past the headland of the Hammerberg – slid protectively into the lake in front of the wall – to the height of attack, then to assault the retaining wall head-on flying horizontally. After the release of the bomb, the Lancaster had to be put immediately into a steep incline in order to avoid a collision with the mountains opposite the dam (Michelskopf).

Around 1.20am Gibson ordered the Lancaster AJ-L with the pilot Shannon to attack. Three times he tried in vain to reach the correct attack position. During the descent, altitude and angle of approach were not right. Consequently Gibson sent him into a holding pattern and ordered Maudslay to attack with Lancaster AJ-Z. After two failed attempts, he still hadn't found the right position and Gibson sent him, once again, into a holding pattern. Then it was Shannon's turn again. After one failed attempt his bombardier Les Sumpter released the first bouncing bomb at 1:37am. It made two jumps and detonated south of the retaining wall without result. The radio report "Goner 79 B" didn't reach Grantham until 2:06am.

Then Maudslay approached once more. During the second attempt Gibson saw how Maudslay's bombardier released the weapon too late; it hit the crest of the dam and the bomb exploded above it in a bright flash illuminating the entire upper Eder valley like daylight. This could happen, as Wallis had said, if the bouncing bomb ran against the dam with too much speed. Maudslay's Lancaster, however, was already in front of the explosion's flash, and Gibson tried to make radio contact with him, but failed. Some crew members recalled hearing a faint, unnatural, almost inhuman voice declaring tentatively "I believe I am okay.

Many were of the opinion at the time that Maudslay had crashed there due to the detonation of his own bouncing bomb. Yet he only fell victim to light anti-aircraft gunfire on his return in Emmerich-Netterden at 2:36am. The headquarters in Grantham noted at 1:56am "Goner 28 B": release, bouncing bomb jumped over the dam. At 1:57am Maudslay's operator made contact with operational command for the last time.

Then Gibson gave the order to the Lancaster AJ-N with the pilot Les Knight to deploy the last available bouncing bomb against the Eder dam. He finally managed to get into a good position of attack. The bouncing bomb jumped three times, hit the wall south of its centre and exploded. Gibson had approached in parallel flight at a distance of 500 metres from Knight and slightly higher. From an unparalleled vantage point, he watched the earthquake effect of the explosion shaking the base of the dam. Shortly after, the construction collapsed completely, leaving the impression of a gigantic fist having punched a hole through cardboard.

In the excitement Les Knight started to follow the floods, until Gibson urged him and the others to head home. At 1:54am Gibson's operator Hutchinson sent the code word "Dinghy" to England, the signal for success at the Eder dam. The operational command in Grantham requested repetition and confirmation of the report. Six minutes later the radio report from Les Knight's Lancaster followed, "Goner 710 B", "release, large breach in the Eder dam".

Now only the dangerous return flight had to be managed. Gibson said: "That was a fantastic show, let us all fly back home quickly."

At the headquarters of the 5th British Bomber Fleet in Grantham great excitement prevailed. Bomber Harris wanted to have a telephone connection established with the White House in Washington as quickly as possible in order to inform the chief of the RAF general staff, Sir Charles Portal, who was staying in the USA with a delegation and the Prime Minister Winston Churchill. After some failed attempts the line was established.

Sir Charles Portal, Air Chief Marshal, chief of the RAF, was in the process of dictating a letter by typewriter to Winston Churchill:

"Prime Minister, I understand that you wish to be further informed on "Upkeep", especially since the general staff has now decided to deploy the weapon immediately… It is necessary to carry out the attacks this week, when the position of the moon and the water level in the reservoirs promise the greatest possible chances of success. I would prefer to report the exact situation of the reservoirs *orally*. It is believed that the deployment of 'Upkeep' does not endanger the secrecy of 'Highball'."
Washington, 16 May 1943, C. Portal
(evening New York time).

By hand Sir Charles Portal added to the typed letter:

"Since dictating the above I have received a message from Harris by telephone saying 'Upkeep successful on two, possibly three, targets tonight' i.e. night of 16/17 May. Objectives were Möhne and Eder dams and one other."

Charles Portal informed Winston Churchill immediately, who made an important speech before the US Congress on the Capitol on 19 May 1943, in which he also mentioned the attacks on the dams.

During the early morning of 17 May 1943 the "Dams Raid" had not yet finished. At 2:10am the operational command asked the returning Gibson how many craft of the first wave were still available for an attack on the Sorpe dam. Gibson's answer: none. At 3:11am Maltby landed unscathed in Scampton on a predefined return course. A blip in his plans saw him evading light anti-aircraft fire on route to his destination. Martin was lucky too as, at 3:19am, the wheels of his Lancaster touched English ground again.

Shannon landed at 4.06am after a flight duration of six hours and twenty-nine minutes. Nine minutes later Gibson arrived, after a return flight over the draining Möhne Lake and through a known "hole" in the coastal defence near Egmont. The returning aircraft regarded the North Sea, as it appeared in view, as the best present in the world. At 4:20am, Les Knight's Lancaster also touched home ground in Scampton. "Dinghy" Young flew on return route number three. Close to Castricum-aan-Zee at the Dutch Channel coast, he was downed at 2.58am. Now, his dinghy, his saving grace on so many occasions over the Channel, remained empty.

Flying Reserve against Sorpe, Lister, Ennepe and Diemel Dams

Two and a half hours after the departure of the first and second waves, the five aircraft of the third wave (a mobile reserve) embarked on their combat course over Germany. They followed the course of the first wave on the southern route. Shortly before Ahlen the order to attack the Lister dam reached Otterley via his Lancaster AJ-C via radio. Immediately after this event, the plane got into heavy fire by two centimetre anti-aircraft guns north-east of Hamm-Heessen. Fred Tees who was intended as the front aerial gunner in the Lancaster had changed his place shortly before launch with the tail gunner Sgt. H. Strange, a change which would save his life during the crash of the plane. Fred Tees recalls: "The internal right motor was burning immediately, tall flames whipped up past my rear gunner station. The hydraulics failed, the turret could no longer be turned. From this height there was no escape even by parachute, especially since my chute was inside the fuselage and I could not fetch it. Shortly before the impact the pilot said over the on-board communication system; 'It is sad, boys, they have got us'." Then Tees' memories are blacked out. At the impact of the Lancaster at 2:35am the tail with the gun turret broke off and was hurled away from the immediate vicinity of the bomb exploding slightly later. By a miracle Fred Tees survived. Thirty-eight years later by his own free will, he put an end to his life.

The crash site of the Lancaster AJ-C is located in a forested area belonging to the Baron von Boeselager on Heessen territory north-east of the A-Road 63 between Harlinghauser and Herrensteiner Knapp. It is marked today by a cross and a commemorative stone, reminders of peace.

Friedrich Kleiböhmer experienced the crash: "I was sixteen years old at the time and went to bed around 10pm despite the air raid alarm. Around midnight the firing of light anti-aircraft weapons woke me up. From the window I watched as a plane flew at a distance of 1,000 metres from north to south, before being shot down with tracer ammunition. I thought: Have they gone completely crazy now and are firing on German planes? For at that time English and American planes did not fly so low. I went to bed again. After two hours the anti-aircraft firing commenced again. Now a four-motor craft approached from the south-east and turned west. It was under heavy fire, one motor was burning. After some seconds the bomber crashed at a distance at the edge of a forest. A detonation followed, then fire flared up, and the board ammunition exploded.

After around 30 seconds there was a really heavy explosion, accompanied by an orange flash. Shortly after, a shock wave, travelling 3,000 metres in distance, reached me at my window seat, pressing me back into the room. Now I thought: 'If you want to see something, you will have to leave immediately, later all will be cordoned off.'

I did not expect the crash site to be so far away. After one kilometre I passed my former school, the people sat in the basement and had not noticed anything. I went farther, met a schoolmate at the edge of a forest and asked him for the crash site of the bomber. He pointed towards the direction Bockum-Hövel. We were still talking when a figure came out of the forest. I said to my mate as a joke: 'This is a Tommy for sure.' The person approached, to a distance of five metres. When we addressed the man, he did not answer. Before I knew what was happening, my schoolmate had vanished inside the house.

My schoolmate recognised the man as English. He left the house through a back door to inform the police by telephone from a neighbour's house. Before leaving, my schoolmate called to me: 'Fritz, he is English.' So, I thought to myself, now you just walk up to the man pretending to be armed, and put your hand into your jacket pocket. With the left hand I waved him to me. Immediately the man raised his hands and said: 'British', not English.

I took him along. On route we passed the farmer whom I had warned previously. He gave me a hunting rifle with the remark, in case the Englishman tries any 'funny business' on the way. We walked through a lonely area, on the left I supported him, because I had noticed that he could not walk well. On my right shoulder the hunting rifle was resting. As we wandered along like this, I thought to myself: 'Just whistle the song 'We put our washing on the Siegfried Line'', and he immediately hummed along. When again an English bomber passed between Heessen and Ahlen, the Englishman gazed longingly after it. On the way he touched the rifle barrel once. I said to him: 'Keep your hands off' and he replied three times: 'Okay, okay, okay.'

We passed two farms where the lights were out. As I did not want to surprise the people at night with an Englishman, we walked on. At the next farm a girl sat at the window, whom I knew. I called: 'Elli, open up, I have an Englishman here who cannot walk any longer.' Inside the kitchen he sat down on a chair, he wore an aviator's outfit. In his hair there were a few dried leaves, and then I saw his wounds. His hands were severely burnt. On his face were two brown spots which were not so bad, however. His rib cage was hurting him. I assumed that he was hurtled from the craft against a tree during the explosion. I removed his jacket and gave him some water. Then the father of the girl came in and ranted: 'These are the blokes who are ruining everything for us.'

The Englishman took no notice of this and sat there totally exhausted. I searched his pockets in the hope of finding a pistol, revolver or cigarettes. He did not carry anything on him except a small sharp dagger. After half an hour a policeman arrived by taxi. I delivered the dagger to him. The policeman was immensely proud to be able to take an Englishman prisoner. He said to the taxi driver: 'Talk to him in Low German dialect to find out how many men were in the aircraft.' The Englishman said only one word: 'Seven'. That we could all understand. The policeman announced: 'Four are lying burnt near the plane, this is the fifth. Two must be still running around outside, arm yourselves and see to it that you catch them.' The Englishman got the shivers and trembled much. He was covered in blankets and driven off in the taxi.

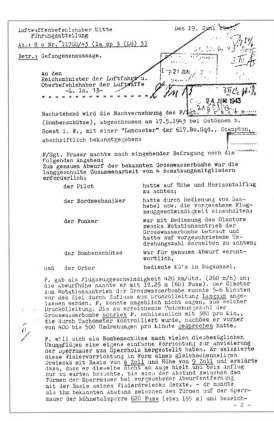

How well the German Air Force was informed of the dam buster raid is illustrated in this statement taken from the captured bombardier Fraser. He survived the attack on the Möhne dam and the crash of his Lancaster in Ostgönnen.

At the disposal site for explosive ordnance (Kalkum near Düsseldorf) the pyrotechnical specialist Captain Heinz Schweizer explains the operating method of the British rotational water bomb to high-ranking Nazi party leaders. In Haldern-Herken he had defused the precious find. Flight Lieutenant Barlow's Lancaster had smashed into a high-voltage pole there. Bombardier P/O A. Gillespie had probably not activated the self-destruction fuse of the weapon.

OKW-Bericht:

dnb. Aus dem Führerhauptquartier, 17. Mai.
s OKW. gibt bekannt: Aus dem Raum von
'elikije-Luki wird erfolgreiche eigene
ampftätigkeit gemeldet. In verschiedenen an-
ren Abschnitten der Ostfront brachen deutsche
oßtrupps überraschend in feindliche Stellun-
n ein, zerstörten zahlreiche Kampfstände und
achten Gefangene und Beute ein. Einzelne An-
iffe der Sowjets wurden teilweise im Zusam-
enwirken mit der Luftwaffe abgewiesen. Bei
r planmäßigen Bekämpfung des feindlichen
chschubs im südlichen und mittleren Abschnitt
r Ostfront wurden auch gestern wichtige Bahn-
fe und eine große Zahl von Transportzügen
er Art durch deutsche Kampfflugzeuge mit
rnichtender Wirkung bekämpft.
  Schwache britische Fliegerkräfte drangen in
r vergangenen Nacht in das Reichsgebiet ein
d warfen an einigen Orten eine geringe Zahl
n Sprengbomben. Es wurden zwei Talsper-
n beschädigt und durch den eintreten-
n Wassersturz schwere Verluste unter der
vilbevölkerung hervorgerufen. Acht der angrei-
den Flugzeuge wurden abgeschossen, neun
eitere feindliche Flugzeuge über den besetzten
estgebieten vernichtet, darunter eines durch
uppen des Heeres.
  Schnelle deutsche Kampfflugzeuge
ffen in der Nacht zum 17. Mai mehrere Stun-
n hindurch militärisch wichtige Einzelziele im
um von London mit Bomben schweren Kalibers
. Zwei eigene Flugzeuge kehrten von diesen
nsätzen nicht zurück. — Oberfeldwebel Kocick
ioß in einer Nacht vier sowjetische Bomben-
gzeuge ab.

Below: On 19 May 1943 England's Prime Minister Winston Churchill also touches upon the dam buster raid of the RAF in his historic fifty minute speech at Washington's Capitol. "The audacious mission will have extensive impact on the production of German military materials, but cost us eight of nineteen bombers deployed. The German armament machine, especially in the Ruhr area, will be widely shattered by this incomparable destruction." Churchill's speech was transmitted worldwide via short wave and received with remarkable clarity in England.

Above: On 18 May 1943 the Möhne dam receives a visit by highly decorated officers under the leadership of Colonel-General Hubert Weise (nickname: poison dwarf) to inspect the damage. The photo taken from the north tower shows the artificial pine trees at the parapet which did not fulfil their camouflaging purpose.

Below: An air defence soldier points to a bullet hole in his gun turret, made by a pilot firing from a Lancaster.

Around 4am I arrived at the crash site. From the wreckage many small blue flames still flared. The dead lay around; one was staked on a tree right through the belly. The parachutes which they carried on their backs had already partially caught fire. Air defence soldiers examined the debris, but nobody made an effort to drag the dead from the range of the fire."

Malte Schrader commanded an anti-aircraft installation in the Hamm area: "In May 1943 I led a 3.7cm anti-aircraft battery with several trains for the protection of the Hamm railway installations. My western train near Bockum-Hövel reported aircraft engine noise from the west. As there were no German planes in the airspace above Hamm, we received the order 'Weapons free!' from the superior duty station.

In the meantime, some enemy crafts had passed Hamm already in the north and had jumped over the Lippe valley. From my position I saw a four-motor aircraft flying at the lowest level across the railway facilities towards the south-east. We could not fight the plane, because we had to first tear off the safety barriers around the anti-aircraft guns which were supposed to prevent a firing on the neighbouring houses. It took some time before the gun barrels could be turned lower. After 2:30am the first train reported hits on an enemy bomber to me. Shortly after I saw a large fiery glow in the direction of Hamm-Heessen, with a delayed detonation echoing around. The plane had hurtled into a forested area near the Hamm-Münster road. I learned that a young Brit had survived the crash. Before I could inspect the crash site in the morning, I first had to redeploy a train of my battery to the Sorpe dam which had also been attacked during the night. As the Möhne and Ruhr valleys could not be passed, we drove across the bridge near Delecker and Arnsberg to the Sorpe dam.

Mid morning, back in Hamm, I also saw the imprisoned aviator who still was under shock and made a shy impression. During the inspection of the crash site I found a torn, bloody aeronautical chart from the Lancaster with the marked route from the end of the Datteln-Hamm canal to the Möhne Lake and farther to the Eder dam."

The Lancaster AJ-S with the pilot Burpee had taken off after Ottley and experienced the same fate. Burpee had lost the exact course, had flown too closely to the German night fighter airfield Gilze-Rijen and had crashed as the second plane of the reserve wave.

Radio operator **Herbert Scholl** saw the "spotlight kill": "On the airfield Gilze-Jijen there was based, at that time, Night Fighter Wing 2 and a Squadron of Night Fighter Wing 1. I flew as radio operator in a Ju 88 of a supplementary squadron E/NJG 2 which commanded six aircraft in May.

The squadron remained on the ground during the night to the 17 May, as nuisance attacks were evidently expected. The crews were grounded in readiness, and stood on the airfield waiting to see how the situation in the air would develop. As approaching enemy craft were reported, we listened to the night and heard as a plane approached the airfield from the west. The air defence positioned along the edges of the airfield did not fire.

I saw how suddenly a spotlight beam flared up and illuminated like daylight a four-motor aircraft flying at an altitude of just under twenty metres. The beam of the spotlight which was installed on a tower between our command post and the hangar caught the bomber in its almost horizontal approach, by which the pilot was probably blinded and pushed the craft even lower. The bomber got tree contact, tore a huge swath into a piece of forest and then crashed into an elongated, empty garage of the airbase defence. One hundred metres further and it would virtually have rammed the spotlight tower.

The plane burst into flames on impact, some seconds later a deafening explosion followed. The air pressure was so strong that the other air crews and I, who stood 700 to 800 metres away on the other side of the airbase, were nearly toppled over. In the light of dawn I saw the totally wrecked plane. Only the tail gunner station with the empennage had avoided complete destruction. This part had been torn off at the predetermined breaking point on impact. All crew members had been killed. The tail gunner did not show any visible injuries. He was very scantily clad, wore lace-up shoes with worn soles and thin scuffed uniform trousers. It could not be learned why the air defence at the airbase had not fired.

At 3am the Lancaster AJ-F with the pilot Ken Brown reached the Sorpe dam. In the wider surroundings, mist had risen in the meantime, from which the hilltops poked out of part. Brown undertook a flip around the dam during which he was impeded by the church tower of Langscheid. Contrary to the plan of attack, Brown approached the Sorpe dam head-on. His altimeter was exactly right, the bouncing bomb without rotation hit the dam almost at the same spot which McCarthy had marked two and half hours previously. At 3:14am yet again a huge column of water rose from the Sorpe Lake. Both bouncing bombs exploded at the Sorpe dam not with their water pressure fuses set to 9.1 metres – in that case they would have exploded without effect around twenty metres from the bank at the sloping dam – but with the programmed time-delay fuses. Nine minutes later the operator Hewstone sent the message: "Goner 78 C", release, "Upkeep" exploded in contact with the Sorpe dam, no visible breach."

On the return flight across the Möhne reservoir, Brown saw that the water had already drained significantly. Below the retaining wall a white inferno was raging. An anti-aircraft gun opened fire at the Möhne dam and duelled with the tail gunner. Near Hamm, Brown got into heavy flak fire once more and then again at the Channel coast. At 5:33am he landed in Scampton. Anti-aircraft projectiles had perforated the fuselage of the Lancaster. The last plane taking off for "Operation Chastise" was the Lancaster AJ-Y. Its pilot, Cyril Thorpe Anderson, got into heavy defensive fire north of the Ruhr area and ran into navigation difficulties near the Dülmen lakes. Fog shrouded the turning point, and the two frontal aircraft cannons of the Lancaster ceased to operate.

Anderson was supposed to attack the Diemel dam. However, as he had veered off course and did not find his position, at 3:10am he decided to abort the blind flight and turn back, especially as he could no longer reach the target during the dark. At 5:30am he landed in Scampton and brought back – as the second person – an intact bomb against regulations.

Mix-up: Ennepe and Bever Dam?

After the war there were differences of opinion amongst those in British aviation circles, and amongst war historians, as to whether the pilot William Townsend, flying Lancaster AJ-O, had attacked the Ennepe or the neighbouring Bever dam. Townsend and his navigator Howard claimed again and again to have attacked the Ennepe dam. Their description of the surroundings of the dam and the written statement given to the author about approach tactics prove them right. (Use of the headlight altimeter, time, location of the headland.) As a point of clarification, in British historical records, the Ennepe dam.

Townsend's Lancaster AJ-O attacked a dam as the second aircraft of the reserve wave and the last of "Operation Chastise". Veils of mist drifted across the water of the V-shaped Ennepe reservoir and the trees on the surrounding slopes.

The first difficulty: the attack chart showed an island in the lake before the retaining wall, yet in reality there was only a wooded headland. (In the Ennepe reservoir an island only appears during full capacity, otherwise it is an elongated headland.) The second difficulty was caused by the bouncing bomb which shook the Lancaster thoroughly, having no optimal balance, a gyroscopic effect. After three failed approaches, the aircraft gained the exact altitude above the lake with the headlights switched on. During the fourth approach the heavy bouncing bomb left the turbulent plane and after one bounce sank fifty metres in front of the retaining wall. The Lancaster AJ-O was exactly on course with 355 degrees and jumped the dam at a speed of 380kmh. Ten seconds later, at 3:37am (registered at the earthquake station Göttingen), a column of loamy water, 300 metres tall, rose from the Ennepe reservoir. Townsend veered onto a course home which led him past the Möhne reservoir once more. At 6:13am Townsend touched down his Lancaster AJ-O on the grass runway in Scampton. "Operation Chastise" had ended.

The war diary belonging to the High Command of the Wehrmacht from 16 May 1943 notes an attack on the Bever dam, and added a day later the air raids against the reservoirs (with several errors concerning the number of aircraft, the altitude, the weapons and the detection by devices). An attack did indeed occur during the night of the 16/17 May 1943 on the Bever dam, which had been built from 1935 to 1938 and regulates the flow of the Wupper. It had a predecessor, the "old Bever reservoir", the dam of which was constructed 1896-1898. The new Bever barrage has as its retaining construction a stone rubble dam with an internal seal of steel plating, 41.5 metres high.

At full capacity holding 23.7 million cubic metres of water, the old dam near Wefelsen lay invisible, eight metres below water level. At the beginning of the war, the German air forces had studied the effects of dynamite explosions of varying force with the aid of satchel charges at this decommissioned barrage of stone rubble. The old dam was damaged at the crest, but remained preserved as a whole. Only in 1959 was it demolished.

The earthwork of the Bever dam and the retaining wall of the Ennepe dam are ten kilometres apart in a direct line. Simultaneously with the attacks on the Möhne, Eder and Sorpe dams the diversionary attacks commenced, too. The daily British résumé of the night-time aerial operations from the 16/17 May 1943 notes the deployment of eighty-seven aircraft: laying mines before the Frisian Islands and before the western coast of France by fifty-five Lancaster and Wellington bombers. Four Wellingtons flew pamphlets to Orleans. Apart from the planes deployed against the reservoirs, the following Mosquitos were on a nuisance flight: three to Berlin, two to Cologne, two to Düsseldorf and two to Münster. One Mosquito which was supposed to bomb Berlin attacked Kiel.

The pilots reported drops of four 500-MC bombs each (224kg load) on the aforementioned cities. In the capital Berlin at 1:13am the 107th air raid alarm occurred. The situation report of the air defence office Düsseldorf registered on 16 May at 11:15pm air raid level twenty for the city's hospitals, and at 11:33pm the 496th air raid alarm. Several enemy approaches at the mouth of the Scheldt and near Amsterdam with a course of east-south-east; from 0:24 the start of the return flights from the areas of Arnsberg, Berlin, Hanover and Kassel is noted. At 3:27am the air defence diary documents the 497th air raid alarm in Düsseldorf with the second night-time alarm, at 4:11am the all-clear was given. On this May night, only two bombs were dropped onto Düsseldorf, one in the vicinity of the shooting ranges at Krönerweg in Unterrath (onto an open field), the second onto the airport grounds. Slight material damage was caused.

The Bever reservoir is situated thirty-five kilometres away from Düsseldorf, barely five minutes flight for a fast Mosquito. The duration was hardly longer for two Mosquitoes deployed in the airspace over Cologne. It is absolutely possible that a Mosquito dropped one of its four bombs into the Bever reservoir without reporting it during the debriefing after return. The Mosquito pilots stated that they dropped eight bombs on Düsseldorf. Furthermore they observed two fires in the city centre. These notes are in contrast to the air defence log of the city of Düsseldorf.

An eye witness provides proof of the attack by a two-motor aircraft on the Bever dam. Reservoir guard **Paul Keiser** saw the attack: "I was thirty-eight years old and was on home leave. I was familiar with planes, as I had seen many a downed aircraft with the Wehrmacht. During the evening of 16 May 1943 relatives from Cologne had come to visit to recover from the many alarms in the city here in the countryside. Due to the lively conversation it had become quite late. The kitchen clock showed 1am, when I heard aircraft engine noise outside.

I went out of the house and watched as an aircraft travelled in a westerly direction towards the dam in low-level flight. From my residence to the Bever dam the distance is only a few metres. So I remained on the road and heard, once more, engine noise approaching. From the east, from the direction of Halver, an unlit aircraft passed over me at the northern part of the Bever dam at an altitude of around fifty metres.

During the third approach it dropped a bomb into the lake, about 800 metres from the Bever dam. One hundred and fifty metres opposite the site of the explosion was the representative summer seat, House Uhlenhorst, belonging to the Düsseldorf district leader Florian who had inaugurated the new Bever reservoir on 14 June 1938. Two hundred and fifty metres in the direction of the flight, before the site of the explosion, the old damaged Bever dam was located underwater in the lake. The aircraft flew another circle and then veered towards Cologne. It was clearly recognisable as a two-motor craft, at the fuselage the English mark and large letters which I do not recall, however. I saw the explosion very clearly, too. A fiery glow, and water rose twenty metres high, not higher than the trees lining the shores, but in a manner so as to give the impression of fizz rising over the neck of a bottle of champagne. The bomb did not skip across the surface of the dam. On top of the dam no vibration could be felt, the explosion fizzled out in the water.

After years, when the reservoir was quite empty, I took a look at the site of the explosion. I discovered many rusty spots and found some splinters of distorted material, the size of walnut shells. When the bomb exploded, the aircraft was still halfway from the dam. None of the plane's lights were switched on. Outside, the moon shone so brightly that the pilot could see everything. My wife and a Mr Tacke approached from different windows of the house.

The next morning we took a boat and rowed to the site of the explosion, where we fished roaches and perches with a rake. Their air bladder had burst by the explosion. Many people from Hückeswagen came to collect whiting. The news travelled fast that there was food without stamps due to 'dynamite fishing'.

The next day I pickled a tall bucket full of fried fish in vinegar and took it along to my troop. On the train to Wilhelmshaven carrying the people on leave, there were many soldiers who were drinking Cognac from France or Vodka from Russia. Soon some were drunk. Then I opened my bucket, on which they pounced. In Bremen no fish was left in the bucket, they even drank the stock."

What was behind the mysterious bomb drop into the Bever reservoir can hardly be brought to light now. The old damaged "dam" as a bridge in the lake – if it was visible – with water in front and behind was certainly no target for a "dam buster" without "light altimeter". Apparently this was a "private diversionary attack" by a Mosquito pilot. Perhaps he had seen light in a house?

NO. 617 SQUADRON. NIGHT FLYING PROGRAMME 16. 5.43.

No.	Call Signs	A/C	Captain	F/Engr.	Navigator	W/Optr.	A/Bomber	Front Gunner	Rear Gunner	Remark
(1.		G	W/CDR. GIBSON	SGT. PULFORD	P/O TAERUM	F/LT. HUTCHISON	P/O SPAFFORD	F/SGT. DEERING	F/LT. TREVOR-ROPER	
(2.	J9P	M	F/LT. HOPGOOD	SGT. BRENNAN	F/O. EARNSHAW	SGT. MINCHIN	F/SGT. FRASER	P/O. GREGORY	P/O. BURCHER	MISSIN
(3.		P	F/LT. MARTIN	P/O. WHITTAKER	F/LT. LEGGO	F/O. CHAMBERS	F/LT. HAY	P/O. FOXLEE	F/SGT. SIMPSON	
(4.		A	S/LDR. YOUNG	SGT. HORSFALL	SGT. ROBERTS	SGT. NICHOLS	F/O. MacCAUSLAND	SGT. YEO	SGT. IBBOTSON	MISSIN
(5.	J9P	J	F/LT. MALTBY	SGT. HATTON	SGT. NICHOLSON	SGT. STONE	P/O. FORT	SGT. HILL	SGT. SIMMONDS	
(6.		L	F/LT. SHANNON	SGT. HENDERSON	F/O. WALKER	F/O. GOODALE	F/SGT. SUMPTER	SGT. JAGGER	P/O. BUCKLEY	
(7.		Z	S/LDR. MAUDSLAY	SGT. MARRIOTT	F/O. URQUHART	SGT. COTTAM	P/O. FULLER	F/O. TYTHERLEIGH	SGT. BURROWS	MISSIN
(8.	J9P	B	F/LT. ASTELL	SGT. KINNEAR	P/O WILE	SGT. GARSHOWITZ	F/O. HOPKINSON	SGT. GARBAS	SGT. BOLITHO	MISSIN
(9.		N	P/O. KNIGHT	SGT. GRAYSTON	F/O. HOBDAY	F/SGT. KELLOW	F/O. JOHNSON	SGT. SUTHERLAND	SGT. O'BRIEN	
(10.		W	F/LT. MUNRO	SGT. APPLEBY	F/O. RUMBLES	SGT. PIGEON	SGT. CLAY	SGT. HOWARTH	F/SGT. WEEKS	
(11.		T	F/LT. McCARTHY	SGT. RATCLIFFE	F/SGT. McLEAN	SGT. EATON	SGT. JOHNSON	SGT. BATSON	F/O. RODGER	
(12.	5CM	H	P/O. RICE	SGT. SMITH	F/O. MacFARLANE	SGT. GOWRIE	F/SGT. THRASHER	SGT. MAYNARD	SGT. BURNS	
(13.		K	SGT. BUYERS	SGT. TAYLOR	P/O. WARNER	SGT. WILKINSON	SGT. WHITAKER	SGT. JARVIE	SGT. McDOWELL	MISSI
(14.		E	F/LT. BARLOW	SGT. WHILLIS	P/O. BURGESS	F/O. WILLIAMS	P/O. GILLESPIE	P/O. GLINZ	SGT. LIDDELL	MISSI
(15.		C	P/O. OTLEY	SGT. MARSDEN	F/O. BARRETT	SGT. GUTERMAN	F/SGT. JOHNSON	SGT. TEES	SGT. STRANGE	MISSI
(16.	JBS	S	P/O. BURPEE	SGT. PEGLER	SGT. JAYE	P/O. WELLER	SGT. ARTHUR	SGT. LONG	F/SGT. BRADY	MISSI
(17.		O	F/SGT. TOWNSEND	SGT. POWELL	P/O. HOWARD	F/SGT. CHALMERS	SGT. FRANKLIN	SGT. WEBB	SGT. WILKINSON	
(18.		F	F/SGT. BROWN	SGT. FENERON	SGT. HEAL	SGT. HEWSTONE	SGT. OANCIA	SGT. ALLATSON	F/SGT. McDONALD	
(19.		Y	F/SGT. ANDERSON	SGT. PATERSON	SGT. NUGENT	SGT. BICKLE	SGT. GREEN	SGT. EWAN	SGT. BUCK	

The crews of the "Dams Raid" of 16/17 May 1943: bombardier Sergeant Tees and tail gunner Sergeant Strange switched their places before the launch.

Luftgaukommando VI
Führ.Gr. Ia op 3 (LS)

Münster, den 17.Mai
1943
Geheim!

Nr.700,II.Ang.

1.Nachtrag zum Lagebericht vom 17.Mai 1943
abgeschlossen um o630 Uhr.

1.) Fliegeralarm:

		Uhrzeit
LS-Wako Münster	Stadt Münster	2353-0345
	Warngr.West,Nordwest,	2337-0345
(Luftschutz-Warnkommando)	" Mitte,	2353-0345
	" Nord,	2356-0345
	" Ost,	oo12-o345
	Stadt Münster	0405-0428
	Warngr.Mitte,Ost,	0405-0428
	" West,	o403-0428
	" Nord,Nordwest,	0408-0428
LS-Wako Wuppertal	Stadt Wuppertal	2340-o124
	Warngr.Mitte,Süd,Nord,	2340-o124
	Stadt Wuppertal	o221-o4o7
	Warngr.Mitte,Süd,	o221-o4o7
	" Nord,	o212-o4o7
LS-Wako Bonn	Stadt Bonn	0009-0056
	Warngr.Mitte,	0009-0056
	" Süd,	0038-0049
LS-Wako M.-Gladbach	Stadt M.-Gladbach	2334-o118
	Warngr.Mitte Süd,	2334-o118
	" Nordwest,	2333-118
	Stadt M.-Gladbach	0206-0408
	Warngr.Mitte,Süd,	o2o6-o4o8
	" Nordwest,	o2o3-o4o8
LS-Wako Aachen	Stadt Aachen	2335-o1o2
	Warngr.Mitte,Ost,	2335-o1o2
	" Nord,	2329-o1o2
	" Süd,Südost,	0005-0032
	" Nord,	o2o8-o4o6
LS-Wako Dortmund	Stadt Dortmund	2336-139
	Warngr.Mitte,Nord,	
	Nordost, Süd,	2338-o139
	Stadt Dortmund	o155-o421
	Warngr.Mitte,Nord,Süd,	
	Nordost,	o155-o421
LS-Wako Düsseldorf	Stadt Düsseldorf	2332-o134
	Warngr.Mitte,Süd,	
	Nord,Nordwest,	2332-o134
	Stadt Düsseldorf	o327-o411
	Warngr.Mitte,Süd,	
	Nord,Nordwest,	o327-o411
LS-Wako Bochum	Stadt Bochum	2337-o136
	Warngr.Mitte,Süd,	2337-o136
	Stadt Bochum	o158-o415
	Warngr.Mitte,Süd,	o158-o415
LS-Wako Bielefeld	Stadt Bielefeld	oo16-o141
	Warngr.Mitte,	oo16-o141
	" Nord,	o2o4-o248
	" Mitte	o2o4-o3o4

LS-Wako Hagen	Stadt Hagen	2339-o411
	Warngr.Mitte,Ost,	
	Südost,	2339-o411
LS-Wako Wesel	Stadt Wesel	2338-o41o
	Warngr.Mitte,West,	
	Nord,	2338-o41o
LS-Wako Köln	Stadt Köln	2348-o15o
	Warngr.Mitte,West,	
	Ost,	2348-o15o
	" Ost	o324-o41o
LS-Wako Duisburg	Stadt Duisburg	2327-o15o
	Warngr.Mitte,West,	
	Nord,	o212-o412
	Stadt Duisburg	o212-o412
	Warngr.Mitte,West,	
	Nord,	2327-o15o
LS-Wako Recklinghausen	Stadt Recklinghausen	2336-o422
	Warngr.Mitte,West,	
	Nord,	2336-o422
LS-Wako Rheine	Stadt Rheine	2347-o430
	Warngr.Mitte,Nord,	2347-o43o
	" West,	2339-o43o
LS-Wako Arnsberg	Stadt Arnsberg	2341-o415
	Warngr.Nord,Ost,	
	Mitte,	2341-o413
LS-Wako Fulda	Stadt Fulda	kein Alarm
	Warngr.Nord-Ost,	
	Ost,	o122-o225
LS-Wako Kassel	Stadt Kassel	oo31-o3o8
	Warngr.Mitte,	oo31-o3o8
	" West,Nord,	oo19-o419
	" Ost,Süd-Ost,	o112-o3oo
	" Süd,	oo34-o312
	" Süd-West,	oo29-o339
LS-Wako Paderborn	Stadt Paderborn	oo16-o415
	Warngr.Mitte	oo16-o415
	" Ost,	oo3o-o253
	" West,	oo12-o415
LS-Wako Siegen	Stadt Siegen	ooo9-o445
	Warngr.Mitte,	ooo9-o445
	" Ost,	oo23-o425
	" Nord,	2348-o425

Unverändert.

Schadensfälle: Zur Möhnetalsperre:

Spermauer zwischen beiden Türmen auf ca.8om
Breite und etwa 15 m Tiefe durchschlagen.
Billigenbrücke gebrochen.
Straßen aufgerissen.
Neheim überflutet.
Häuser z.T.bis zum Tal von Himmelspforten weg-
gerissen.
Freiwillige Feuerwehr eingesetzt.

Air reports from the 16/17 May 1943 (incursion of the night bombers)

Reich Minister of the Interior Dr Wilhelm Frick, centre, inspects the breach in the Möhne dam. On his right, in a black uniform coat, the district president of Arnsberg Lothar Eickhoff. On his left the deputy district leader of South Westphalia Albert Hoffmann. Dr Frick was arrested in May 1945 by the Allies and accused of war crimes during the Nuremberg trials. He was sentenced to death and hanged in October 1946.

On the photo Johanna Effing shows the bouncing bomb found near Haldern–Herken. Ms Effing witnessed the crash of the Lancaster AJ-E of the second assault wave flown by Flight Lieutenant Barlow.

The dismantled water bomb in Kalkum which gave away its secrets, minus those relating to wall contact and water depth.

Debriefing of Gibson's crew after the attack on the dams, taken by RAF photographer Flying Officer Bellamy. Front left, with glasses, a man of the intelligence service, next to him the bombardier Pilot Officer Spafford and the Canadian navigator Pilot Officer Taerum. At the right, with teacup, tail gunner Flight Lieutenant Trevor-Roper with an aerial photograph of the Eder reservoir. "Bomber Harris" and Air Vice Marshal Cochrane, who organised the raid, are standing in the second row.

Reservoir guard Paul Keiser saw the attack of a two-motor aircraft on the Bever dam during the night of the 17 May 1943. The Mosquito flew without headlights and dropped a small bomb (X) onto the lake in front of the dam. After the war there were arguments about this attack amongst those in English aviation circles, as well as amongst historians. The Pilot Officer W.C. Townsend is supposed to have confused the Bever dam with the Ennepe dam, the actual target. Pilot Townsend could not find the island indicated on his Ennepe map, which turns into an elongated headland during low water level; proof that he had the right dam in his sights. Pilot Townsend flew along the headland and his bombardier released the bouncing bomb at 3.38am without hitting the wall. Reservoir guard Paul Keiser points to the approach of a two-motor aircraft on the Bever dam.

Many Questions from the Highest Authorities

Immediately after the return of the individual Lancasters, the debriefing of the pilots took place. Ten questions were posed to them. Some statements made in the first excitement later caused confusion. For example, Gibson claimed to have seen two holes in the Möhne dam. Also Shannon reported that he had bombed a three metre gap into the Eder dam. The flight engineer from Brown's Lancaster claims to have seen two adjacent breaches within the Möhne dam, the front aerial gunner claimed three.

Further questioning of other crew members could clear up those misapprehensions. The radio signals sent in the target region by the bombers were so strong that the radio officer could transmit them via amplifier to the control room at headquarters for analysis.

All of this enabled the Commanding Air Officer to answer all the questions posed by Gibson within one minute, whilst his aircraft flew up and down the valleys of the target area at an altitude of thirty metres. The balance sheet of eight lost Lancaster bombers showed the Commanding Air Marshal R.A. Cochrane that during similar future operations it would probably be better for the bombers to fly in at altitudes of 800 to 1,000 metres above ground and to go down at the appearance of night-time fighters.

At this height, a more favourable safety distance to machine gun fire and light anti-aircraft batteries would be kept, but they would still be low enough to make an attack by enemy night-time fighters difficult. The aircraft should receive better navigation aids for nocturnal low-level flight, as the pilots returning in the morning had considerable difficulties reading the maps. The valleys had filled with mist, the landmarks were difficult to recognise.

Protocol of the Debriefing of the "Dams Raid"

The statements of nine pilots were recorded immediately after the return from the sortie.

Special questioning of the pilots after the attack
1. What did you see of the target during the attack?
2. From what distance did you see the target first?
3. a) How many jumps and of what height did the "Upkeep" weapon achieve?
   b) Had the "Upkeep" weapon been put into rotation?
4. Description of the explosion, with specific regard to the behaviour of the water, the height of the water column …
5. Description of the damage to the target.
6. How many approaches did you make?
7. Were you impeded by another plane during the attack?
8. Which control method was employed, and was it effective?
9. What effect did the deployment of one hundred per cent tracer ammunition have?
   a) On the enemy?
   b) On our own aerial gunners?
10. Personal report of the pilot (criticism and commentary).

Answers in response to the special questioning

Lancaster AJ-G W/CDR. Gibson

Möhne dam target GO 939

Time of attack 00.28h

1. We saw the whole "thing".
2. From a distance of five to seven kilometres.
3. a) Three jumps.
   b) 500 rotations.
4. An enormous water column.
5. There were two holes in the wall.
6. One.
7. No.
8. Frequency-modulation radio communication was perfect.
9. a) Very good effect against the German anti-aircraft guns.
   b) No confusion or blinding.
10. The river below the Möhne dam showed a multiple increase of its usual size along a distance of five kilometres.

Lancaster AJ-P F/LT. Martin

Möhne dam target GO 939

Time of attack 00.38h

1. Smoke of a preceding explosion inside the power station obscured the target.
2. From a distance of two kilometres a tower of the wall could be detected. The other tower was still shrouded by the smoke of the preceding explosion.
3. a) Were not observed.
   b) 480 rotations.
4. The water column rose higher than the smoke, an exact height could not be determined.
5. No visible damage occurred. This aircraft attacked as the third.
6. One.
7. No.
8. Frequency-modulation radio communication was good.
9. Good from the aerial gunners' viewpoint.
10. A very good trip. Against numerous spotlights and light anti-aircraft positions north of the Ruhr area the aerial gunners had their work cut out. The tail gunner obliterated two spotlights. The front aerial gunner fired on further anti-aircraft positions and spotlights. Navigation and map reading were first-class. The attack leader had a great idea by splitting the assaulting fire and drawing it from the target onto himself. The whole crew did their work well.

Lancaster AJ-J F/LT. Maltby
Möhne dam target GO 939
Time of attack 00.49h

1. Everything was clearly visible, including the wall towers. It would have been easier to attack against the moon instead of approaching from it.
2. From 700 metres we saw the towers.
3. a) Three jumps, the height could not be determined.
   b) Rotation yes.
4. We saw the water rise, but were hindered from close observation by tracer projectiles.
5. We saw a breach in the middle of the wall before our attack, and then we approached and made "contact" with the retaining wall.
6. One.
7. No, no hindrance by a plane.
8. The frequency-modulation radio communication was very good.
9. a) Not known.
   b) No difficulties, a good aid for aiming.
10. The frequency-modulation communication was excellent. During two attacks a second Lancaster joined the approach in parallel flight and fired on the gun positions at the northern side of the Möhne dam. The flight routes were good, free of air defence and map reading was easy.

Comment on the attack of the target GO 934 Eder dam: the first and third bomb hit the dam, while the second bomb jumped the target. Definitely a large hole was punched into the dam. Vast masses of water were observed running out of the Eder Lake.

Lancaster AJ-L F/LT Shannon
Eder dam target GO 934
Time of attack; 01.39h

1. The target was completely visible. The moonlight was good, but it would have been better if it had come head-on during the approach.
2. From a five kilometre distance.
3. a) Two jumps.
   b) Running in rotation.
4. We saw a vast column of water, more than 300 metres tall, roughly a minute after the attack.
5. We made a hole of three metres width at the eastern side of the Eder dam. We saw as the second Lancaster overshot the target.
6. Three approaches.
7. No.
8. We were led by frequency-modulation communication by Lancaster "No. 1".
9. a) Not known
   b) A bit of "magical light", but the aerial gunners love it like that.

10. The attack plan worked perfectly. The routes were extraordinarily good. In Coesfeld a train was fired upon.

Lancaster AJ-N P/O. Knight
Eder dam target 934
Time of attack: 01.52h
  1. We saw everything very clearly. The moon was at starboard.
  2. From 1,600 metres distance.
  3. a) Three jumps, it was not possible to estimate the height of the bouncing bomb.
     b) Rotation yes.
  4. A water column of almost 300 metres height rose at the southern side of the wall. The explosion obstructed the view of the wall contact of the bomb.
  5. Torrential water streamed through the breach and caused a flood wave of ten metres height which was observed for 1,000 metres down the valley.
  6. Two approaches.
  7. No.
  8. The quality of the frequency-modulation communication was very good.
  9. There was no air defence at the Eder reservoir. On route the one hundred per cent tracer ammunition blinded the aerial gunners slightly, and intimidated the German gunners and operators of the spotlights.
  10. The planned flight route was excellent. Radio reports of aircraft ahead with flak warnings were very useful. The attack was carried out head-on, as calculated beforehand. It turned out that we could very easily regain a height of 350 metres after the release of the weapon. Satisfaction about the fact that the operation was carried out successfully.

Lancaster AJ-F F/LT. McCarthy
Sorpe dam target GO 960
Time of attack: 00.46h
  1. The Sorpe dam was clearly visible. The moon was at starboard during the approach on the dam.
  2. From a distance of eight kilometre, the target could be seen.
  3. The bouncing bomb was not put into rotation; the release was carried out conventionally, parallel to the dam.
  4. First, a semi-circular wave of the diameter of the dam's width showed itself from which a water column rose almost 300 metres high.
  5. The crest of the dam burst along a width of eight to ten metres.
  6. Ten approaches were flown.
  7. No. None, we attacked alone and independently.
  8. We received by radio the positions of anti-aircraft weapons and spotlights. At the Sorpe dam no air defence was in place.
  9. The pilot was not so keen on the ammunition with one hundred per cent tracer.

10. It cannot be said whether a large breach has occurred in the Sorpe dam, but the attack seemed to have gone forward successfully. The approach route was easy to find. On the return route the landmarks were not found due to a faulty compass. So we took the approach route back and chased across the Zuiderzee.

Lancaster AJ-F F/SGT. Brown
Sorpe dam target GO 960
Time of attack: 03.14h
 1. The target was clearly visible. The moon was at starboard during approach.
 2. From 500 metres distance
 3. a) normal bomb release
    b) without rotation
 4. The bomb dropped three to four metres away from the dam crest, slightly from the centre of the dam towards the south.
 5. After the explosion a semi-circular wave ran against the dam, from which a column of water of almost 300 metres height arose.
 6. Ten circles and approaches were made.
 7. There was no hindrance through other planes, as we were alone.
 8. No lead by radio communication. We attacked independently and alone.
 9. The firing of one hundred per cent tracer blinded very much. Mixed on-board ammunition would have been preferable. Yet it seems that a considerable effect on the accuracy of the spotlights was achieved (disruption).
10. The flight route was good. The attack on the Sorpe dam seems to have been successful. The difficulty during the attack was in the mountainous terrain and trees on both sides of the dam. During the return flight we took a look at the Möhne dam. The flight engineer saw two large breaches closely together between the towers. Water streamed through both. Each breach was approximately a quarter of the space between the two towers. The water streamed through both gaps, and shot far out before it fell down in two mighty streams. The valley seemed to be quite filled with water. The front aerial gunner reports a third breach in the Möhne retaining wall beyond the northern tower at the end of the dam. This breach was half the size of the others, here water streamed out, too.

Lancaster AJ-O F/SGT. Townsend
Ennepe dam target GO 935
Time of attack: 03.37h
 1. We recognised the target by the contours of the landscape and flew in the twilight of the moon which was reflected on mist and water.
 2. From 1,200 metres distance.
 3. a) One jump was made by the bouncing bomb. The explosion occurred thirty seconds after the release.
    b) The bouncing bomb was put into rotation.
 4. There was a high column of dirt and water. A circular wave hit the dam afterwards.

5. There was no sign of damage.
6. Three approaches were made.
7. No hindrance by other planes.
8. No method of leading.
9. a) One hundred per cent tracer ammunition had a deterring effect on the German anti-aircraft positions.
    b) There were no difficulties from blinding or jamming.
10. The island drawn on the target map in the middle of the lake in front of the dam was actually linked to a narrow headland. We made three trial approaches, circled several times and had difficulties with drifting mist and blinding moon. (Confusing gleaming moonlight?) If the timing is considered, it was too late, as we were still over Germany at dawn. We flew the aircraft back with 240mph on the same route, and that seemed to surprise (to confuse) the defence. We had a view of the Möhne reservoir during the outbound flight and could not find it for some time. We discovered a sheet of water of almost twelve kilometres in length which partly reached a width of six kilometres in the valleys, with the dam at its centre. Roofs of houses poked out of the torrential flood.

Lancaster AJ-Y F/SGT. Anderson
There are no answers to questions 1 to 8.
9. One hundred per cent tracer ammunition was very satisfactory, there was no blinding, and an unbroken line of fire was very helpful and evidently terrified the enemy.
10. We were not able to find the lake near Dülmen serving as a landmark for orientation. Mist in the valleys made identification difficult. Around five minutes before Dülmen we

Group photo of the 617th Squadron after the "Dams Raid". Fifty-six aviators did not return from the sortie. In the centre of the first row sits Wing Commander Guy Gibson. He received the highest British decoration for valour, the Victoria Cross, for the successful attack on the German reservoirs. The British Crown honoured Flight Lieutenant J.H. Maltby, Flight Lieutenant D.J. Shannon, Flight Lieutenant H.B. Martin, Flight Lieutenant J.C. McCarthy and Pilot Officer L.G. Knight with the Distinguished Service Order. Ten aviators received the Distinguished Flying Cross and Bar. In total thirty-four aviators received different decorations.

were driven off-course by spotlights. Also we were not able to fire at the spotlights at that moment, as we had jamming in the frontal guns. When we realised that the target could no longer be reached in time, we turned around at 03.10h and went on course towards home with the bouncing bomb aboard.

English Radio Reports

The radio communication between the base and the Lancasters ran via short wave and was recorded at headquarters of the 5th British Bomber Fleet in Grantham. Shortly before launch Wing Commander Gibson changed the code names XYZ for the Möhne, Eder and Sorpe dams to ABC, as the training targets – the reservoirs in Great Britain – had been called. (Coding scheme – see "encrypted radio reports with 'tulip' and mermaid'".)

Time	Lancaster or Base	Report
00.11	G	Flak warning in the area six kilometres north of Haltern
00.12	Base	Repetition of the flak warning at full force by HQ
00.28	G	Gibson reports
00.37	G	Drop 68 A (Möhne dam)
00.38	F	Martin reports
00.46	T	McCarthy reports
00.49	J	Maltby reports
00.50	A	Drop 78 A (Möhne dam)
00.53	P	Drop 58 A (Möhne dam)
00.55	J	Drop 78 A (Möhne dam)
00.56	G	NIGGER, destruction Möhne dam
00.57	Base	NIGGER, repetition of this report with full force by HQ Lancaster G (Gibson) answered "correct"
01.45	Base	Flak warning to the third wave: flak six kilometres north of Haltern
01.50	L	Shannon reports
01.51	G	Radio report B (Eder dam)
01.52	N	Knight reports
01.53	G	Radio report B (Eder dam)
01.54	G	DINGHY, destruction Eder dam
01.55	Base	Repetition of this report with full force by HQ Lancaster G (Gibson) answered "correct"
01.57	Z	Drop 28 B (Eder dam)
02.00	N	Drop 710 B (Eder dam)
02.06	L	Drop 79 B (Eder dam)
02.10	Base	To Lancaster G. How many planes of the first wave are still available for the Sorpe dam?
02.11	G	No aircraft
02.19	Base	Headquarters (HQ) calls each individual aircraft of the third wave
02.21	O	answers

02.22	Base	To O "Gilbert". Attack last resort targets as discussed
02.22	F	answers
02.24	Base	To F DINGHY
02.25	F	Report received
02.25	Base	To O "Gilbert". Attack last resort targets as discussed
02.26	O	Report received
02.26	Base	To Y
02.28	Y	Carry out mission
	Base	To Y DINGHY
	Y	Report received
	Base	To C
02.30	C	Carry out mission
02.31	Base	To C "Gilbert". Attack last resort targets as discussed
	C	Report received
02.32	Base	To S DINGHY
02.33	Base	To S DINGHY
02.57	L	Drop 79 B (repetition radio report from 02.06h)
03.00	T	Drop 79 C (Sorpe dam)
03.14	F	Brown reports
03.23	F	Drop 78 C (Sorpe dam)
03.37	O	Townsend reports
04.11	O	Drop 58 E (Ennepe dam)
04.23	Y	Return to base without success

British Aerial Photographs in the Interpretation of the Military

On 17 May 1943 three reconnaissance flights of Spitfire and Mosquito planes led across the target areas section by section. The imaging flight no. D/578 took place at 9am over the Möhne dam, the largest part of the reservoir and sections of the Möhne and Ruhr valleys. The images at a scale of 1:9800 are of excellent quality. Also the Sorpe Lake with dam and equalising basin were captured. This reconnaissance flight did not lead across the Eder dam, but across large areas of the lake, the pumped-storage power station, the hydroelectric plant Affoldern and flooded valleys up to ten kilometres downriver. The flight D/581 at 10.45am showed the upper and principal part of the Möhne Lake as well as flooded areas twenty-five kilometres below the Eder Lake at a scale of 1:10300. Also the reconnaissance flight D/585 in the afternoon at 4.30pm delivered no photographs from the Eder dam. Only three kilometres of the Eder valley in the Affoldern area were photographed. The floods show without a doubt that the Eder dam had broken, too.

Extent of damage in the valleys of Möhne and Ruhr
The breach in the crest of the dam of the Möhne barrage between the two towers was roughly seventy-five metres long and tapered to fifty metres at the base. Although the main water pressure had already lessened at the time of the shot, a strong torrent still flowed through the hole in the wall. At 9am the upper Möhne Lake was already void of water, while the

Möhne-Ruhr valley, aerial photographs 18 May 1943, river length c.120 kilometres

"State secret"; stamped in red, is the longest German aerial image from the war which stretches in twenty-two composite photographs from the emptied Möhne reservoir along the Möhne-Ruhr valley until the Essen area, the Möhne disaster in context, in total and at a glance. The light grey strip of water in the image documents the trail of destruction over 120 kilometres of river. On 18 May 1943 the aerial district photo service in Münster commissioned Lieutenant Colonel von Groote with the photographic aerial reconnaissance. From 11am, thirty-four hours after the beginning of the catastrophe, the shutter of a large format camera clicked inside a plane at 1,600m altitude. Each image, at the scale 1:8000, shows brilliantly sharp the finest details of the valleys when enlarged. The valleys have turned into a new "Urstrom" land. The British competition worked faster and delivered pictorial documents to the RAF military already on 17 May. The white lines between the partial images are the result of an inexact montage.

← Direction of flow

On the right is the broken Möhne dam, starting point of the disaster. The power station Möhne Lake in front of the retaining wall with 120,000kVA output has sunk without trace. With the exception of a transformer found 100m from its original site, all heavy machines have vanished. The southern subsidiary power station was so heavily damaged that it could not resume operations.

NIEDERENSE

HIMMELPFORTEN

BRANDHOLZ

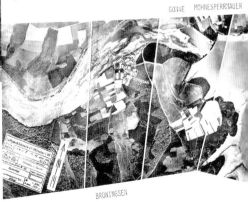

GÖNNE   MÖHNESPERRMAUER

BRONINGSEN

Two bents in the Möhne valley south of Niederense; here the small village of Himmelpforten with its almost 700 year old monastic church "Porta Coeli" was situated at the centre of the valley. After the flood waters had receded, a field of rubble remained. The Mohne bed was full of pebbles and gravel. It had to be rebuilt right from the dam to the outlet into the Ruhr.

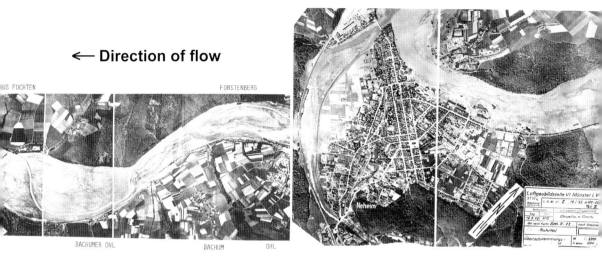

← Direction of flow

US FOCHTEN · FORSTENBERG · Neheim · BACHUMER OHL · BACHUM · OHL

Picture sequence of the Ruhr valley between the Neheim district Ohl and Füchten House; in front of the severely damaged bridge over the Ruhr near Füchten House, mighty alley trees have withstood the water pressure. Below Neheim, "Im Ohl", pebble banks have formed, several 100,000m³ thick, blocking the Möhne valley. They have impeded the drainage and are the reason why extensive parts of the lower Möhne valley are still under water.

The Ruhr valley between Warmen and Wickede; in this section of the valley the flood wave destroyed railway tracks, bridges, and hydroelectric and other power stations. Over large stretches it swept away the topsoil from the valley floor and covered fields and any spaces it could penetrate with mud and rubble.

Above Echthausen the infiltration basins of the water works Echthausen are filled with mud in the bend of the Ruhr. The weir installations of the water works Soest in Wickede, the United Steel Works in Wickede and the community power plant in Wickede are destroyed. Twenty-two kilometres downriver from the Möhne reservoir, a section of the railway bridge at Wickede is found in the Ruhr bed.

MEN · WARMEN · Warmen · Wickede · Echthausen

The Ruhr valley from Fröndenberg till Delliwg (left); the elongated basins for drinking water production near Fröndenberg are clearly visible. The damage on water management seemed to be immense at first, for the Möhne reservoir formed the backbone of the water supply of the entire Westphalian industrial area east of the Rhine with around four and a half million people.

To the right of centre on this image, the town of Fröndenberg; the British long-distance reconnaissance planes were particularly interested in this part of the Ruhr valley.

← **Direction of flow**

The trail of the deadly flood near Rheinen and Geisecke; in the Ruhr valley between Dellwig and Rheinen, primarily the water works of the city of Dortmund are affected. 74,500m² of infiltration basins and 690,000m² of infiltration meadows are silted up. Workforces of the Organisation Todt and of the National Labour Service and employees of the works cleared the grounds and installations.

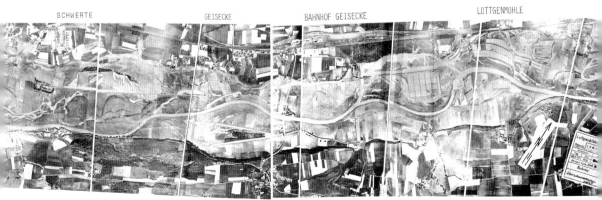

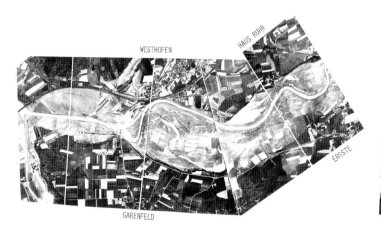

At the centre of the image, Westhofen; on the left the Lenne meets the Ruhr. Shortly thereafter begins the Hengstey Lake, across which a four-track railway bridge is running whose foundations have suffered damage from scouring.

Between Schwerte and Wandhofen; urban districts of Schwerte are under water. In the Ruhr valley, sections of the railway line to Ergste are destroyed over a 200m stretch.

← Direction of flow

On the top right the Hengstey Lake begins. The island in the lake is clearly visible. At the centre of the image (top) the pump storage power station can be discerned, situated sixty kilometres downriver of the Möhne reservoir.

At the inlet to the Harkort Lake the Herdecke railway viaduct leads over the Ruhr into the town. The missing wall section of the construction is clearly visible. On the left the Ruhr valley twines around the town of Wetter.

This aerial photograph shows the impact of the flood on the Bommern area. The village is at the centre of the image south of the Ruhr. On the other side of the valley, in Witten, the factories Union Bernhardsglück and parts of the United Steel Works are under water, plus eight residential barracks of the workers. The water works near Witten are flooded. Two hundred people were made homeless as a result.

Ruhr valley between Dahlhausen and Stiepel; here the traces of the passing water wall are showing everywhere, too. One-hundred-and-seventy-eight infiltration basins, including the primary sedimentation basins of all water works in the Ruhr valley with a total area of 1,000,000m², have to be cleared of pebbles and mud. The Organisation Todt cleaned 8,000,000m².

The Ruhr valley between Stiepel (top left) and Herbede (right) south of the river; opposite Stiepel, near Kemnade, the railway tracks are under water. After the arrival of the police radio reports in Herbede, the houses in the Ruhr valley were vacated.

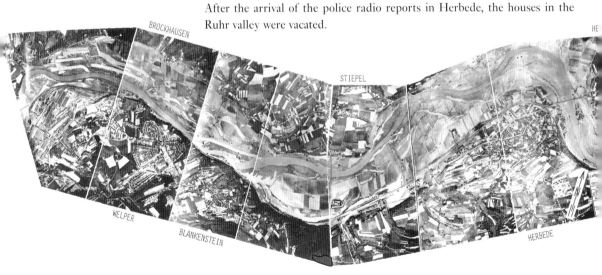

← **Direction of flow**

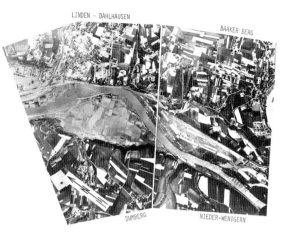

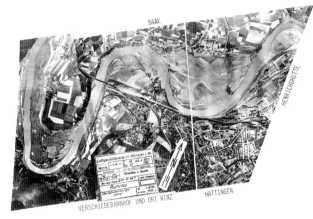

On the top left of the image, large parts of the settlement in Linden-Dahlhausen are under water. Below Baldeney Lake near Essen, some 120 kilometres downriver of the Möhne reservoir, the highest water level gradually sank below the known high-water record of the Katherine flood in 1890.

The Ruhr bend near Hattingen; the railway bridge and the road bridge across the river remained standing (middle section, top left and right). In the proximity of the bridges the Bochum fireman Camillo Fischer took (strictly forbidden) photographs of the flood in front of the Friedrichshütte with a film camera. The shunting station Winz serving the work seems to be undamaged, but it is almost entirely under water.

⟵ **Direction of flow**

Near Kupferdreh, this series of photographs of the German short-distance reconnaissance plane ends. However, the floods ran on to Duisburg-Ruhrort into the Rhine whose water level rose 1.5m. This extraordinary series elucidates the total extent of the Möhne disaster and makes visible the damage amounting to millions.

⟵ **Direction of flow**

The water works Gelsenkirchen in Altendorf-Steele, with thirty-two infiltration basins and 242,000m² of surface, is totally silted up. Urban districts of Steele are under water.

Direction of flow ⟶

Wameler basin was full. The deluge had completely carried off the power station in front of the Möhne dam.

The photographic coverage of the disaster zone until Duisburg showed seventy-two square kilometres of land under water. Of eleven square kilometres no photographic material was yet at hand on 17 May 1943. The entire area of the flooded valleys of Möhne and Ruhr amounted to eighty-three square kilometres. The width of the flood varied from the Möhne dam until the river's confluence with the Ruhr by 400 metres. From this spot onwards the flood widens to 1,000 metres, in parts even to five kilometres. Parts of the settlement of Günne have been completely swept away. The narrow-gauge railway line between the Möhne dam and Neheim is underwashed in many places or has completely vanished. The situation was similar along the German State Railway line between Neheim and Fröndenberg. In Bösperde the floods ascended the valley of the little Hönne River.

Excellent aerial pictures were likewise delivered by the reconnaissance flight D/599 on 19 May 1943: sixty-five kilometres of the Ruhr valley from Schwerte till Kupferdreh, around five kilometres south of Steele with a small part of Hattingen were in evidence. The photographic flight no. D/604 showed the Ruhr valley from Kupferdreh up until a spot south of Rellinghausen in medium quality. Also the area from Werden to Mintard, the centre of Mülheim, and the entire harbour area of Duisburg were captured. Between Schwerte and Hattingen there were sizeable floods, which had in part already retreated.

Upriver of Schwerte the floods had not gone down so much, many houses and factories were still under water. In the river valleys of the Ruhr around Mülheim and Duisburg few built-up areas were under water. Flood water only protruded onto lower-lying pockets and open meadows. Many bridges over the Ruhr were destroyed, railway lines and shunting stations flooded.

The most significant destruction was the breakage of the railway viaduct near Herdecke which bore a principal line between Dortmund and Hagen. The massive damage to the railway network made extensive repair works necessary. The rebuilding of railway embankments and the cleaning of silted-up tracks resulted in a huge demand for manpower and material.

The traffic relocation in the Ruhr area had to be considerable and would inevitably lead to traffic jams and congestions on alternative routes via Duisburg and Düsseldorf. Also the Wuppertal area was affected in part, as most of its direct northern connections to Mülheim, Essen, Bochum and Dortmund were disrupted.

The cut through the Schwerte-Fröndenberg railway line as one of the three principal eastern railway routes meant the temporary disruption of this line for the Ruhr area. The two remaining eastern principal connections from the Ruhr area via Hamm and Soest now had to bear the main brunt of railway traffic. The destruction of the railway bridge in Wickede/Ruhr on the main line Kassel – Ruhr area remained hidden from air reconnaissance.

Damage due to the break of the Eder dam
On 18 May 1943 a reconnaissance plane of the 542nd squadron was able to photograph the breach in the Eder dam at 10.15am. It thus confirmed the successful night-time operation.

The water in the Eder Lake had largely drained away; the water level had dropped to twenty-five metres below the crest of the dam. The two power stations Hemfurth I and II at the foot of the wall seemed intact from the outside. The course of the Eder River had changed, and the banks had vanished except for a fifty metre section at the northern power station. The transformers of the substation of the pumped-storage plant Waldeck I appeared to be much silted up and were partly washed away on the northern side. The settlement of Affoldern lay completely isolated amidst the dirty floods. Many bridges over the Eder had disappeared, railway embankments had broken away. Scattered farms and villages poked out from the floods, railway lines, roads and bridges were submerged. Hangars, barracks, ammunition depots and the runway of the Fritzlar airfield stood under water.

Below the Eder dam the water had flooded more than fifty square kilometres of land to widths of 500 to 1,500 metres up to twenty-five kilometres downriver. There a lake of three kilometres width and nine kilometres length had formed. The floods then narrowed to a width of 1,600 metres on a stretch of five kilometres. From this point until Kassel the width of the river varied for twenty-three kilometres from 200 to 300m and sometimes even to 1,000 metres.

The flooded area in Kassel was 6.5 kilometres long and often up to 1,600 metres wide. Below the town the water had not extended so far, but thirteen kilometres further, it yet again reached widths in excess of 1,000 metres.

Damage at the Sorpe dam
Eight hours after the first attack against the Sorpe dam the first aerial photographs of target "C" were taken at 9am. A stretch at the crest of the dam, sixty-five metres in length, had been damaged. An unknown, elevated and rectangular body, approximately twice as high as the parapet of the dam with a size of eight by thirteen metres stood on top of the dam crest, and blocked the road there, where most of the devastation had taken place. According to the statement by Josef Kesting this was a quick aid made of faggots and fascines to seal it. A loam-coloured semi-circle of seventy metres diameter at the valley side of the dam attested to overspilling water. Two thirds of the water in the equalising pond was polluted by dirt. At times water also spilled over the overflow weir, a sign that the lake was filled to its maximum. At the time of the imaging the turbines did not work.

A second series of images of the Sorpe dam was made fifty-seven and a half hours after the attack. The photographs show a working platform at the damaged area. Debris had been removed, the unknown object on top of the dam crest had become smaller and changed its shape, and one turbine was working again. The slight discolouration of the water in the equalising basin had dissolved. At the water's edge in the centre of the dam, a discolouration of the water revealed that debris and rubble had been thrown into the lake to make space for a working platform. The photographs demonstrated the start of repair works for the protection of the concrete core inside the Sorpe dam which was now secured by a chain of nineteen barrage balloons. Aerial shots of the Ennepe and Lister dams showed no damage.

"Nigger" and "Dinghy" Prompt Exultation in England

The first official news of the spectacular night-time operation was announced by the Air Minister Sir Archibald Sinclair, when he spoke the next day during celebrations held in aid of Norwegian independence at the Royal Albert Hall. King Haakon VII of Norway and the crown prince were present.

After the disclosure of the manner of attack, which – as he said – "is the spearhead of our war machinery", the minister added, "our praise belongs to the confident and determined commander-in-chief Air Marshal Harris. Further to the staff who planned the details of the attack and to those outstanding and daringly talented crews who have delivered a severe blow to the Germans last night. It is a decisive success for the allied forces and, by extension, the freedom and independence of Norway."

Air Marshal Sir Arthur Harris sent this encrypted telegram to the strategist of the attack, Air Vice Marshal R. A. Cochrane, of the 5th British Bomber Group: "Please convey to all involved my warmest congratulations on the successful, brilliant deed of last night. To the crews I would say that their thoroughness and their willpower during training, and their aptitude and spirit of perseverance during the attack will forever be an inspiration for the RAF and a shining example. With this notable operation we have won a surprise victory in the battle for the Ruhr. This effect will last, until Nazi Germany is swept away by the floods of a final catastrophe."

Prime Minister Winston Churchill in Washington received this personal encrypted telegram from Air Minister Sir Archibald Sinclair:

"17 May 1943, Aerial photographs confirm the success of 'Upkeep':

- In the Möhne dam a breach of more than seventy metres width, power station vanished, extensive floods in the Ruhr valley;
- Eder dam not photographed yet, but the Eder valley is under water, the Eder Lake has drained;
- the surprise attack was a complete success, the weapon worked wonderfully – we lost eight of nineteen Lancaster bombers deployed;
- Wing Commander Gibson led the operation via frequency-modulation communication and returned undamaged."

The British Air Ministry in Whitehall sent this congratulatory telegram to bomber Command headquarters on 17 May 1943 at 11.50pm:

"To the chief of Bomber Command from the Air Ministry: the War Cabinet has commissioned me to convey to you and to all who participated in the preparation and execution of last night's aerial war operation, especially Wing Commander Gibson and his wing, its congratulations on the splendid success achieved.

This attack, pushed through despite great resistance within our own ranks, is a legacy without precedent of the tactical resources and energy of those who planned

it, furthermore of the audacity and the perseverance of the flight crews and of the superiority of British technology and workmanship. The war cabinet confirms with satisfaction the damage that has been done to the German armament industry.
Sir Archibald Sinclair"

Barnes Wallis received a flood of congratulations, among them also a letter from Guy Gibson:

"My dear Mister Wallis, now that the floods are slightly receding and the excitement is calming down (wait for the Sorpe!), I have finally found time to write a few lines to you. My apologies, I am not a great writer of letters, but I wish to say the following: the weapon which you have delivered to us works like a dream, and you deserve the gratitude of the civilised world. All my pilots and I are proud that we have gotten the opportunity to participate in this last great experiment which provides proof to substantiate your theories. And now I believe you have earned a holiday.
Yours sincerely, Guy Gibson"

With this letter Sir Archibald Sinclair from the Air Ministry suggests that the King of England, George VI, confer the Victoria Cross on Guy Gibson:

"22 May 1943. Most subserviently presented by Your Majesty's most obedient and most respectful servant that it may please Your Majesty most graciously to confer the 'Victoria Cross' on the serving Wing Commander Guy Penrose Gibson, reserve of the Air Force officers, 617th Squadron of the Bomber Command, for the following reasons:
    This officer has been deployed as a night-time pilot ever since the beginning of the war. He quickly gained a reputation as an excellent operational aviator.
    In addition to the fact that he had the largest possible share of all normal operations, he flew alone on his own initiative and, during his nights of rest, attacks on such heavily defended targets as the German battleship Tirpitz in Wilhelmshaven.
    When his time in bomber deployment was over, he applied for further deployment with the night fighter unit instead of taking on bureaucratic duties.
    In the course of his other combat missions he shot down at least three enemy bombers and contributed much to the deployment of new night fighter units. After a short training period Guy Gibson once more volunteered for deployment and returned to the night-time bombers. Both as a fighter pilot and as a squadron leader he achieved unique successful results. His personal bravery knew no limits.
    Berlin, Cologne, Gdansk, Gdingen, Le Creusot, Milan, Nuremberg and Stuttgart were among the targets he attacked day and night. After the conclusion of his third campaign, Wing Commander Gibson urged with every determination to receive permission to remain in a combat unit.
    He was chosen to command a squadron for a special operation. Under his exemplary leadership his squadron has now executed one of the most devastating attacks of the

war, the busting of the Möhne and Eder dams. The task was fraught with difficulty and danger. Wing Commander Gibson personally led the initial attack against the Möhne dam. He released his bomb with the greatest accuracy by descending to a few meters above the surface of the water and thereby had to suffer the full force of the air defence. Afterwards he circled for forty minutes at a very low altitude and drew the enemy fire onto himself to secure an approach as unrestricted as possible for the next bombers which attacked the dam one after another.

Wing Commander Gibson has flown more than 170 sorties, with more than 600 hours of flight. In his entire combat career, which was extended on his own wish without exception, he has demonstrated leadership qualities, determination, courage and bravery to the peak of perfection.

Wing Commander Gibson then led the remainder of his bomber squadron to the Eder dam. Here he repeated his tactics with complete disregard for his own safety and once more drew the enemy fire onto himself so that also the mission against the Eder dam could be completed successfully."

(Sir Archibald Sinclair's suggestion contains a factual error: there was no air defence at the Eder dam.)

King George VI granted the request. On 22 June 1943 the great day came for thirty-four members of the "Dam Buster" squadron. In Buckingham Palace decorations were conferred on deserving aviators. They were surprised that not the king, but the queen did the honours. For the first time since the reign of Queen Victoria, a queen conferred decorations again. King George VI of England was at that time on a tour of inspection in North Africa.

In the throne room Wing Commander Guy Gibson, as the first in line, received his Victoria Cross from the hand of Queen Elizabeth. With this Gibson was the highest decorated aviator of the RAF in the Second World War at that time. After Gibson, thirty-three further men of the squadron received their decorations. The three survivors of the Lancaster crashes in Germany did not receive any honours after the war.

The demolition of the German dams made headlines in the English, Canadian, Australian, South African and US press with a flood of reports and commentaries which counted the event among the most important in the course of the war so far, but which sometimes took liberties with the truth. On 18 May 1943 the foreign press fell all over itself: "A group of nineteen Lancaster bombers has written history…" Also the newsreels of the war opponents dedicated more extensive reports to the nocturnal operations against the reservoirs in Germany. Even Mrs Gibson gave a film interview.

Royal Visit with the Dam Busters

Press report, release for 8.30am on 28 May 1943:

All Lancaster crews that returned from the attack on the German reservoirs were presented today to King George VI and the Queen by Wing Commander Guy Gibson V.C., D.S.O. plus bar, and D.F.C. plus bar. The reception began in front of Gibson's Lancaster in which he had led the attack. The Majesties spoke with each officer of the squadron, and the Queen inspected women of the W.A.A.F. (staff assistants of the RAF) on the airfield. Many of them had assisted in the preparations for the attack.

Together with Air Marshal Sir Arthur Harris, Air Vice Marshal R. A. Cochrane who commanded the group, Group Captain J.N.H Whitworth, airfield commander in Scampton, Mr. Barnes Wallis, scientific advisor, and many officers who had flown in the attack, the Majesties took lunch in the officers mess.

After coffee the King congratulated Flight Lieutenant Shannon from Australia in particular for his mission at the Eder. For him a double honour, his decoration with D.S.O. and his twenty-first birthday.

The King and the Queen were shown complete models of the reservoirs which the crews were able to study before the attack. Torpedo nets, retaining walls and power stations were well-modelled, and Gibson explained the plan of attack.

Through a stereo viewer the majesties examined the flooding areas in the valleys. Power stations and railway tracks were shown before and after the breaking of the dams up to twenty-five kilometres downriver, in addition Kassel under water with the floodplains, and how the floods cut their way through the industrial areas of the town. Before one picture the King remained standing for a particularly long time, it showed the Herdecke railway viaduct with the railway tracks hanging free from pillar to pillar over the Ruhr valley.

Two designs for a new squadron armorial were presented to the king by Wing Commander Gibson. Both templates were created at the Scampton airfield. One showed the cutting of a chain at Europe's fetters with the motto: "Change the map", the second, a dam broken in its centre with the maxim: "Apres moi le deluge". No decision was made, and the King suggested seeking the specialist judgement of the Chester Herald.

THE SONG OF THE RUHR

On 18 May 1943 the "floodgates" of the British and American popular press were opened. A flood of reports and commentaries counted the event among the most important in the course of the war so far. They took some liberties with the truth, though. The Daily Herald: "The RAF demolished the dams with mines. Millions of tons of flood water are thundering through the Ruhr valley this morning". The New York Times: "The RAF demolished two giant dams in the Reich. Electrical power for the Ruhr area is cut off, the traffic brought to a standstill, and the floods are spreading death and ruin." The Daily Mirror wrote in reference to the Hitler quote that English towns should be struck by the lightning bolt of the German Air Force: "The Germans are now struck by the bolt of the flood", the Daily Herald: "The German floods sweep over the armament cities, turbulence in the Ruhr area", the Daily Express: "Kassel an island". Even caricatures dealt with the disaster; "The song of the Ruhr" in the Punch magazine; the Daily Express with a pocket cartoon referencing the victorious German submarines. The Daily Telegraph published this propaganda bogus report: "Light signals to the dam busters, five men shot in Neheim, a large number of foreign labourers arrested." In Germany a veil of silence was cast over the dam disasters. There was only a two-line note in the daily army report: "… two dams [without names] were damaged."

27 May 1943: Royal visit with the dam busters at the operational airfield Scampton; King George VI of England at the centre, on the left Guy Gibson, on the right the airfield commander Group Captain Withworth.

After Guy Gibson had described the attacks to the King with the aid of the reservoir models, the latter showed great interest in the large-format pictures taken by the aerial reconnaissance. Almost in three dimensions the King views the flood damage in the river valleys through a stereoscope. He was particularly pleased with the destroyed railway viaduct of Herdecke. At the front of the table, the model of the Sorpe reservoir is visible.

During Their Majesties' visit to the airfield at Scampton, two designs for an emblem of the 617th Squadron are presented to the King, here in front of the Möhne reservoir model.

First: cutting of a chain attached to a map of Europe, the motto; "Change the map". Second: three lightning bolts over a broken dam, motto: "après moi le deluge". The King was amused by the use of the altered quote by Madame Pompadour. A heraldist was commissioned, the suggestion approved, and until today it is the emblem of the 617th Squadron of the Royal Air Force. The press were not admitted into Scampton on the occasion of the Royal visit. An RAF photographer took the historic pictures, and the cameraman of the "Movietone News" newsreel filmed a two-minute report on the Royal visit.

Wing Commander Gibson signs a large format photograph of the destroyed Möhne dam as a present for Barnes Wallis.

After lunch in the officers' mess, as the conclusion of the Royal visit at Scampton, this group image with King George VI and Queen Elizabeth, later the 'Queen Mother', was taken. Hideen behind the King, Barnes Wallis is standing, left of the majesties: Air Vice Marshal R. Cochrane, on the right airfield commander Withworth and Wing Commander Gibson.

The "Water Front" Breaks, Death and Dismay in the Möhne and Ruhr Valleys

Günne and Himmelpforten

Vast masses of water shot from the torn Möhne dam into the valley and with a thunderous roar overran several buildings within a minute, the shooting club hall and three hydroelectric power stations in the community of Günne. Here there were already thirty casualties, some of whom were swept as far as Fröndenberg. The enormous torrent – in the narrow sections of the Möhne valley up to twelve metres high – raced through the peaceful landscape, squashing everything standing in its way, towards unsuspecting villages and towns. The thundering of the water echoed nightmarishly from the wooded mountainous slopes.

Karl-Heinz Dohle from Niederense experienced the ruin of the cloister of Himmelpforten in Niederense: "I stood in the garden with my father. We observed the large birds of doom as they passed over the place towards the dam at a very low height and were fired upon with tracer ammunition. After some detonations a thundering and rushing came from the east. Internal unrest and curiosity drove us to 'Köster's Shore', a hill above the cloister complex of Himmelpforten. Through the valley a breaker seethed like the Niagara Falls unleashed towards the Baroque church 'Porta Coeli', a most beautiful treasure of art which devout Cistercian nuns had erected more than 700 years ago for the glory of God as their 'gate to heaven'. Immediately the buildings of the estate and the nave were submerged, only the short church tower still peeped from the foamy floods. For roughly ten minutes, the top of the tower resisted the thunderous surging. Then it tipped to the west and vanished with a last muffled ringing of the bell. It was a spooky feeling to have the forces of water so close in our sight this moonlit night. Uprooted trees drifted on the waves.

The next morning I saw the devastating results of the disaster. Himmelpforten had been eradicated. The priest of the church, Joseph Berkenkopf, found death in the air-raid shelter. Railway tracks of the narrow-gauge line had slung themselves like corkscrews around individual trees along the road to Günne. Trees completely stripped of their bark by flotsam and jetsam looked like white ghosts."

Niederense

Elisabeth Lingenhöfer recalls: I had only been living some two weeks in a half-timbered house close to the Mohne river in Niederense. In fact, I had only just put the curtains up. That Sunday evening we had cycled to Neheim to the cinema to see one of the first films in colour, 'The Golden City, in the Apollo theatre. In this film somebody met his death in the marsh. When we were back at home, I wanted to write a letter to my husband who was in the army. My sister-in-law said: 'Let us rather go to bed'.

Yet at that moment heavy planes thundered over the village. Shots and explosions echoed from a distance. I fetched my three children from their beds and at first ran into the basement with them. Suddenly we heard a dull roar and breaking noises. We left the basement immediately, which shortly after filled with foaming water. Around the house a raging lake had formed through which I could perhaps have run by myself, but never with the three children. So inside the house we raced upstairs to the first floor and tried to get help from the neighbours by calling out from the window, a futile effort. The water rose higher and higher, therefore we ran up to the second floor and from there to the attic. Here the water rose, too. The children cried and clung to me, other residents of the house prayed. I began to remove the roof tiles and climbed through battens onto the roof, women passed the children to me. Up to the gable of the roof I threw away the tiles and uncovered the battens. So the other residents climbed onto the roof, too.

With the children in front of me, I sat on top of the crest. How we managed that seems like a miracle to me today. The house creaked and groaned in all its joints, and it started to sway. Wooden trunks pierced the half-timbered walls. I clung desperately to the roof in the hopes of floating away on it with the children, if the roof tore off.

The lightning rod had been extremely stretched. On the flood a small half-timbered house drifted towards Neheim. Behind one of the windows a burning candle was standing on the table in one of the rooms, casting a weird light. Again and again timber from the lumber mill crashed against the house, dead cows floated past the roof.

Then planes with lights circled at a rather low height. At first we thought that we would be rescued. But when they started to fire, we cowered on the roof in the 'brightness' of the night so that the planes could not detect us. During the deluge on top of the roof I remembered the film time and again, which we had seen some hours before. 'Now it is over, now we will all vanish into the marsh'. Finally the water started to fall. I put my youngest daughter to sleep in a wash tub in the attic. Due to the excitement I got a bilious attack and had to lie down myself.

The descent from the crest down to the attic was worse than the ascent. The entire staircase was missing. My little daughter woke up and was hungry. Around morning the water level dropped. Firemen and neighbours got us down from the roof by ladders, on which we had to endure for over seven hours. Masses of sludge had laid waste to the apartments, yet we kept our lives. The water had risen to a height surpassing eight metres and all the furniture had floated away through the doors and windows. To begin with, we were taken care of and help was offered from those who lived in the houses on higher ground in Steetsberg.

Never again in my life will I reside in a valley below a dam. The fear does not leave me, it remains. I do not want to experience that again."

Neheim-Hüsten
Private disaster warning did not work.

Norbert Kampmann, a tobacconist from Neheim, had his shop on 6 Main Street in the proximity of the church of St John the Baptist. Shortly after 1am he received a call from his brother-in-law Westhof who was living in Niederense on the Steetsberg. With a nervous voice he reported: "The Möhne reservoir is coming, raise the alarm and get to safety!" Immediately Mr. Kampmann ran to the police station opposite and reported his call to the policeman on duty. "That is not true", the latter answered, "we would know this by now,

This British aerial photo shows the emptied Möhne Lake with the bridge of Delecke standing on "stilts". In front of the breach in the Möhne dam the remaining water of the lake is collecting which had to be drained before rebuilding.

In a pub down-river of the dam, Adolf Nolle, the regulator, documented the highest water level and stopped at 0.50. All the furnishings in the house were swept away, only the clock remained hanging on the wall. Despite repeated repairs the clock stopped time and again at 0.50. Proudly the master baker Adolf Nölle shows the familiar regulator, sole souvenir from the former pub.

In Niedernse in the Möhne valley the small village Himmelpforten was located with its historically important monastic church "Porta Coeli". Erected 700 years ago from greywacke from the Möhne valley, for a long time it served the Cistercian order. For centuries, church and convent had weathered the storms of numerous wars, lootings, pillaging and manifold other calamities, until the Niederense church fell victim to the flood disaster of the night of 16th to 17th May 1943. The high festivity of the Baroque dominates the internal space. Treasures of art adorned the walls and altars. Wooden statues, some of which could be dated as far back as the Gothic period, were swept to the Schwerte area by the flood waters, from where they were later recovered.

Shortly after the war the treasury of the church with the liturgical objects and the Sunday collection of 67.75 Reich marks were excavated from the rubble.

we would have received an official call in that case." The police station in Neheim received other private calls with the tip that the Möhne dam had broken. The callers were rebuffed brusquely with the words: "This fairytale has now been told so many times, stop it already". The receiver was slammed down.

So valuable time was wasted for an improvised warning of the endangered lower-lying town districts, where people stayed in the air-raid shelters and did not realise the new danger looming over them. Then, when the official report of the breaking of the dam by the Arnsberg administration reached Neheim, it was too late for this warning. Water alarm plans with escape routes and acoustic signals for the endangered villages and towns were only drawn up after the disaster.

Ferdi Dröge, eye witness in Neheim: "I was sixteen at the time and apprenticed at a plumbing and installations firm on Möhne Street in Neheim. Every night, if there was an air raid alarm, I had to go with two suitcases in the company of the boss' wife to the air raid shelter of the neighbouring lamp shop Hillebrand. My boss had to be on call for the fire brigade during alarm. Already on the street we saw the tracer projectiles rising from the area of the Möhne reservoir and immediately thought of an attack, but nobody had counted on such consequences. In the company's air raid shelter 150 to 200 people from the neighbourhood were gathered already. The air raid shelter of the firm where I was apprenticed did not seem secure enough to the house's residents, as it only had a wooden ceiling. The air raid shelter of the Hillebrand firm had no special features, but everyone had their accustomed place. We sat with several 'cheerful wenches' on planks and beer barrels and were playing cards as usual.

After fifteen to twenty minutes a man (Johannes Kessler) ran in and called agitatedly: 'The Möhne is broken!' With this he meant the dam, which was immediately clear to us. I thought to myself: 'The water is draining, go the short way to the small Möhne bridge and see if the river is now twice as deep, up to the chest perhaps'. The air raid shelter emptied quickly. On the way to the bridge I suddenly heard terrible cries, behind me loud calling began to emit from the people who had come from the shelter. The cries down from the valley came from the area of the camp for female Russian prisoners. These women and girls I had seen daily from the window of the workshop, for hundreds of Ukrainians and Poles went to work in the town's factories.

All at once I saw a wave, like a black high-rise, approaching in several steps, full of trees, timber and animals. The wall of water, black as coal, heading towards me was at least twelve metres tall, within it parts of barracks stacked on top of each other intertwined with screaming people, and within whirling timber fragments scattered small lights were spinning which extinguished in foam. The distance from the vanguard of the flood to me was 200 metres at the most.

I ran back to Möhne Street as fast as I had ever run in my life before. Almost at the same time the flood in the valley rushed past me into the transformer station of the United Power Utilities. A short circuit illuminated the valley with a terrible lightning bolt. Then the water also advanced through Möhne Street, and I ran with other people up the ascending Peace Street. Half way up we halted and watched the tragedy in the valley, the crashing, swooshing, cracking and the death screams. The first huge wave had a stepped profile. One water wall followed the next, in such manner the flood advanced through the valley. Before the Totenberg, the houses rotated and vanished in the floods. I saw as a squashed barrack, on which people were visible like spectres in the aqueous vapour, collided with the building of the Brökelmann Company and shattered. The screams died.

When the water had drained the next morning, the Möhne valley showed itself to be mown down. Hundreds of dead Russian women and girls lay strewn between the debris, morass, wardrobes, suitcases and possessions, a picture of misery. After half a year, when the mill race was cleared out, the workmen found further corpses of female Russian forced labourers.

On the streets along the disaster zone the Red Cross had set up field kitchens. Nurses distributed food and sandwiches to those affected by the flood, until they could provide for themselves again. They railed against the British bombers. On the quiet people griped and whispered about the meagre air defence at the Möhne dam. They had wondered already before the disaster where the barrage balloons along the retaining wall had gone, why the number of anti-aircraft batteries had been reduced and why the lake was so full. The fact that only a few, light minuscule guns stood on top of the towers and the dam, had spread like wildfire around Neheim already before the attack. Official statements from the administration or the party did not come forth later."

Willy Kaufmann, eye witness in Neheim: "There was an air raid alarm. From the houses on the Wiedenberg where I was living I saw peculiar mushrooms of smoke rising above the forest on the horizon of the Möhne reservoir. After some time neighbours heard a swooshing and a rolling, like the sound of trains, but did not ascribe any importance to it. Suddenly a tumultuous screaming echoed through the night, for us a signal that something terrible must have happened. I had the strong feeling, especially since I had seen the mushrooms of smoke: 'That is the Möhne reservoir which is approaching, it has flattened the Russian camp between Möhne river and mill race.' I said to my wife: 'Fetch a cushion and the little boy; I will fetch the air raid luggage from the basement and the light pack with the valuables which we always take along in the event of an alarm.'

Outside the racket became louder and louder, the rushing stronger and stronger. When I left the basement, I already had water around my feet. Then I ran quickly up the ascending street. I called to my wife: 'Further up, further up.' I saw as the houses of our neighbourhood collapsed with a cracking sound, just like a dentist, prying out a tooth.

We had to hold back one neighbour, because he wanted to go back inside his collapsing house to save his relatives. Fortunately these had fled up the Totenberg by a different route via Werler Street, but which he had not noticed in the general chaos. Also the French prisoners of war from the Peoples' Hall, now completely destroyed, had fled to this ascending road. The sound of the water could be heard at least a quarter of an hour before it reached the town of Neheim. I watched, as the high-voltage poles in the Möhne valley snapped and vanished while emitting lightning bolts. Between the houses two motor boats from the Möhne Lake came rushing, which had survived the fall through the breach. Within the whirls they swam along almost elegantly. Sometimes, it seemed as if they would shatter upon the next house still standing, but they veered off at the last moment and continued to float upon the stream, until they stranded somewhere.

Our house remained standing, the staircase was missing, and the water stood twenty centimetres above the window tops on the ground floor. An entire roof top came floating towards us, and we thought it would tear away one of the remaining houses, but then it settled on the ground after all. I had known the Russian camp doctor Dr. Mihailowa, she spoke perfect German and was in charge of the medical care for the foreigners working for the Kaiser Company. She perished in the floods together with her children, but a niece of hers survived the disaster. Many Russian girls spoke German which they had learned at school."

Hermann Kaiser, eye witness in Neheim, son of the well-known light fixture manufacturer Heinz Kaiser from Neheim, reports of his rescue: "On principle we only went down to the air raid shelter when we received the alarm from our company's headquarters. Like every larger company in Neheim it was directly connected by telephone to an air raid warning centre in Dortmund. When it was reported from there that enemy aircraft approached the Neheim area, there was still enough time to go to the shelter.

Before midnight we were woken and went down to the basement which lay for three quarters below the ground, as was customary. The shelter itself was located in the centre of the house and was thus protected by additional walls. Planks and supporting pillars secured the ceiling. My sisters were ten, fifteen and almost twenty years old, I was thirteen. Camp beds were kept at the ready, in an effort to reduce the disruption to our sleep as much as possible.

My parents had travelled to Stolberg in the Rhineland on the occasion of Mother's Day to visit grandmother. With us in the shelter were the maid and our Russian cook Anna who lived next door in the play and ironing cellar, a light and airy room with large windows. Anna was with us from the first day the Russians came to Neheim. At first she came in the morning and left again in the evening. But my mother got her way when father finally allowed her to stay in the house with us. As a very good cook she often prepared Russian dishes for us. For this purpose two milk sheep were obtained. We had noticed on several occasions that she was very homesick and very sad about the death of her husband in the Soviet Navy. His photograph stood on her bedside table.

Many a night she wept and opened a window; she did the same on the night before the catastrophe. On Saturday she had said to us that she would not be able to hold on for much longer, something would happen. The night watchman of the Kaiser Company passed our house on his round at 10pm and found her crying piteously. He asked her for the reason. She answered: 'Tonight I will be united with my husband…' This we were told later by the night watchman.

The detonations of the bombs at the Mohne could be heard all the way over in Neheim. Once the sound of the planes overpassing the town had abated, our cook Anna went to her room and locked herself in. She always went to bed early. At that moment the telephone rang upstairs. Our maid went upstairs, but came back immediately and said: 'Outside something is happening, I think incendiary bombs are falling, it patters and crackles so.' Suddenly our driver and gardener Josef Greis stormed into the basement and shouted: 'Out, out! Everyone out immediately!' At first we did not realise what had happened. He also knocked loudly at the door of the Russian and called, yet she did not open the door. Perhaps she was frightened by the noise and the events around the house. Mr. Greis tried everything to get her out of the house.

At first I only thought of the incendiary bombs and swooped for my little briefcase in which there was underwear and a shirt. Headless we ran from the house. I held the briefcase above my head, assuming something would come from 'above'. Our house was situated directly in the Möhne valley at the mill race. In front of it, in the bright moonlight, I saw something silver gurgling on the ground. I still thought of exploding incendiary bombs. Then we ran uphill between our factories, towards Ring Street where hundreds of people found safety.

Along the way the water was already lapping on the railway tracks of the Ruhr-Lippe narrow-gauge line. Mr Greis rescued us, since my parents were away. He lived less than a hundred metres apart from us. During the air raid alarm he checked if we went to the air raid shelter. We owe him our lives. If my parents had been at home – my father did not go down to the basement on principle, he just remained in bed – my mother would have first had to wake him upstairs and we would have waited obediently in the basement and thus lost precious time for the flight.

The flood wave came very quickly, in a matter of minutes. I know of a young woman who was in the service of the Bahnschulte family and who lost her parents, although they had left the basement only ten metres behind her. She managed to escape with her life, but her parents drowned behind her on the street.

I ran with my siblings to the highest point on the Neheim Head. Fear had driven us so far uphill. On the Ring Street people were saying: 'Stop running, come inside our house.'

The next morning my eldest sister went to relatives in town to fetch clothes for us, for we all had ran away only in our pyjamas, nightgowns or dressing gowns. At home nothing was left. From a height I saw the water masses, wide as the Mississippi, heave through the Möhne valley with the sound of twenty-five express trains in the night. Our cook Anna was found the next morning drowned in the laundry room, into which she had been swept from her bedroom. Nothing indicated an attempt to flee.

My father, Heinz Kaiser, was a passionate stamp collector. He possessed a collection, not very valuable in monetary terms, but nonetheless holding some nice pieces from his youth. They were his pride and joy. Father had a premonition that something would happen during the aerial war or that the enemy would capture the town. So he had packed his collection in wooden boxes, enclosed it in water-repellent material, then wrapped all of it in oil paper, then locked it into hand-made steel containers, sealed them and virtually walled everything up in our basement. Nobody thought of a water disaster, otherwise its occurrence would not have been such a surprise.

My father had believed his collection to be safe from the war, due to the manner in which he had protected it. But, as our house had been undermined by the water, the three containers were naturally swept away. They also contained Father's most private papers and part of my

P136 top: On 13 May 1943 a British
reconnaissance plane coming from the
Möhne reservoir captured these marginal
areas of the town of Neheim in a series of
aerial photographs. The photo shows the
barracks for the forced labourers between
the rivers Möhne and Obergraben on
a kind of island below the Wiedenberg,
further the "French barracks" at the
Möhne road below the Neheim cemetery.
Here the memorial service for the German
victims of the flood was held on 20 May.

Five days after the British aerial photographs
were taken, the death valley of the Möhne was
photographed by a German reconnaissance plane
for documentary purposes. Between the wooded
Wiedenberg at the top and the Möhne road at
the bottom the valley is flooded (broad grey strip
of water). All barracks apart from one "French
barrack" on slightly higher ground have shattered
and drifted away.

Group photo with foreign labourers during
clearance work in a camp of the light fixture
wholesale company Wilhelm Kaiser; four first
names can still be recalled, from left: Vera, Anna,
Kallja, Shura. Vera did not return to her Ukrainian
homeland. She had fallen in love with an Italian.

This barrack for French prisoners of war withstood the Möhne floods. André Guillon from Poitiers in France survived the night of death here. The German guards had immediately decided to open the doors to the barracks and camp. All the lodgings of the forced labourers swept away looked similar.

Records created by camp commander Werner Kittler, documenting the night of the disaster.

Hagen, den 19. Mai 1943

Werner K i t t l e r
    Lagerführer
        der
Wohn-u.Verpflegungslager-Gemeinschaft
    e.G.m.b.H.

N e h e i m - H ü s t e n 1

An den
Vorstand der Wohn-und Verpflegungs-
lager - Gemeinschaft e.G.m.b.H.,
N e h e i m - H ü s t e n 1.

B e z u g : ohne
B e t r . : Bericht über den Luftangriff in der Nacht vom 16.
            zum 17.Mai 1943 und der damit verbundenen Beschä-
            digung des Staudammes der Möhne - Talsperre.

In fraglicher Nacht wurde um 23,35 Uhr Luftalarm gegeben. Ich habe
die Wachleute - Wachmann Stuppert - Brune - und Roberts - zusammen-
gerufen und Anweisung gegeben, sämtliche Lagerbewohner zu wecken.

Wie sich der Angriff verstärkte, gab ich Anweisung, da Vollmond
war, daß sich die Lagerbewohner vor den Baracken aufhalten sollten.
Kurz vor 0,30 Uhr wurde eine Bombe geworfen und setzte die Abwehr
in verstärktem Maße ein. Ich beobachtete, daß die Abwehr aus der
Luft stark beschossen wurde. Um 1,05 Uhr hörte ich ein Rauschen und
machte meine Wachleute darauf aufmerksam, daß es Wasser sein könne.
Man sagte mir jedoch, daß dies ein Zug sein müsse.Nachdem dieses
Rauschen jedoch nicht aufhörte und sich noch mehr verstärkte, hatte
ich das Gefühl, daß die Sperrmauer getroffen sein müsse.Daraufhin
habe ich den Wachleuten Anweisung gegeben,daß sich die Lagerbewohner
über die Möhne in den gegenüberliegenden Wiedenberg retten sollten.
Ich selbst bin zur Möhne gelaufen, habe den dort stehenden Stachel-
drahtzaun umgerissen um den anstürmenden Lagerbewohnern die Möglich-
keit zum Überlaufen zu geben.Daraufhin bin ich (1.15 Uhr) zum Fern-
sprecher gerannt, um die Polizei davon zu verständigen,daß der
Staudamm getroffen sein müsse. Ich bekam jedoch durch Besetzzeichen
keinen Anschluß.

Wie ich das Büro verlassen wollte, weckte der Apparat(1,20 Uhr)
und bin ich nochmals zurückgelaufen und meldete sich der Elektriker-
meister Josef Erlenkamp. Als ich den Hörer abnahm, hörte ich schon
die ersten Baracken der Fa. Gebr. Kaiser zusammenbrechen.Ich gab
noch durch, daß der Staudamm gebrochen sei und bin dann durch die
Küche zu einer vor dem Arztzimmer stehenden Straßenwalze gelaufen
und habe mich dort festgehalten. Im selben Moment kam die Sturzflut
an. Durch das Gewicht der Walze fluteten die Barackenteile über mich
hinweg.Nach kurzer Zeit merkte ich,daß die Walze keinen Grund mehr

hatte, sich in Bewegung setzte und vor die Fabrikmauer der Fa.Honsel
gedrückt wurde. Die Wassermassen und die schwere Dampfwalze drückten
die Mauer ein.Ich weiß nur noch,daß die Mauer auf mich herabstürzte
und auß ich daneben bewußtlos geworden sein. Wach wurde ich durch die
Explosion des Kraftwerkes der Stadt Neheim-Hüsten. Ich fand mich auf
einem Barackendach wieder. Als ich das volle Bewußtsein wiedererlangt
hatte, merkte ich, daß ich mit dem Barackendach in die Strömung trieb.
Daraufhin bin ich ins Wasser gesprungen und von einem Barackenteil zum
anderen gesprungen. Bei dieser Gelegenheit habe ich vier im Wasser lie-
gende Ostarbeiterinnen auf eine Baracke gezogen.Ich hörte von dem
Dach der Fa. Brökelmann, Jäger & Busse Rufe und sah dort einen Mann, der
mir die Wegrichtung zu der außenliegenden Feuerleiter wies. Mit diesen
vier Ostarbeiterinnen habe ich mich zu der Feuerleiter hingearbeitet
und bin so gerettet worden.

Nachdem uns die Nachtwache der Fa. B.J.B. mit trockenen Kleidungsstücken
versorgt hatte, ist der Wachmann Karl Engelhardt wieder ins Wasser gesprungen und hat mit noch einigen Kameraden zwölf Ostarbeiterinnen vom
Tode des Ertrinkens gerettet.

Wie ich am an-deren Tage feststellen konnte, sind aus dem Wiedenberg
a. 450 bis 500 Ostarbeiterinnen durch Schlauchboote nach Neheim ge-
.chafft worden.

Der Geschäftsführer der Wohn-u.Verpflegungslager-Gemeinschaft - Herr
Paul Kühne - hatte inzwischen eine Schule beschlagnahmt und die geret-
teten Ostarbeiterinnen dort untergebracht.Herr Kühne hat weiterhin für
Verpflegung und Kleidungsstücke gesorgt. Außerdem hat er ein dringendes
Telegramm an den Reichsminister für Bewaffnung und Munition, Außenstelle
Köln, aufgegeben und um Anlieferung von Eßbestecken,Tellern,Tassen und
Decken gebeten.
Herr Obering. P f e i h l der Außenstelle Köln war bereits gegen 11 Uhr
in Neheim und brachte im Personenwagen 750 Messer, Gabeln und Löffel mit.
Ein Lastzug mit den übrigen angeforderten Gegenständen war bereits auf
dem Wege von Köln nach Neheim.
Ich selbst habe dafür gesorgt, daß die Schule bezw. der Saal des Gilden-
hauses mit Stroh zum Schlafen beliefert wurde. Ebenso habe ich mich um
die Heranschaffung des warmen Essens bemüht.
Durch den Fg. Roland der DAF-Kreisawaltung Arnsberg wurde mir bekanntge-
geben, daß ein weiterer Mitarbeiter in der Betreuung und dem Arbeits-
'insatz der geretteten Ostarbeiterinnen für Herrn Kühne und mich nicht
  rwünscht sei. Daraufhin habe ich mich mit bei dem Vorstandsmitglied
Herrn Dipl.Wirt.-Ingenieur B u s s e jr. gemeldet und diesen von der
Anweisung des Pg. Roland unterrichtet.Gleichzeitig habe ich gebeten,
für einige Tage zu meiner Familie fahren zu können,um mich von den über-
standenen Strapazen zu erholen.
Diese Angaben sind von mir gemacht nach bestem Wissen und Gewissen.
Blatt 2 weist meine persönlichen verlorengegangenen Wertgegenstände
auf.

                                        Heil Hitler!
                                        [signature]
                                        Lagerführer

Verteiler:
Wohn-u.Verpflegungslager-Gemeinschaft Neheim-Hüsten
Polizei-Verwaltung z.Hd.des Herrn Bürgermeister Löffler
DAF - Kreiswaltung z.Hd.des Pg. Stiller
Wirtschaftsamt Neheim - Hüsten

In the centre of this image lies the submerged camp barracks that once existed along the banks of the river Mohne, usually only 10 metres wide.

Around 6.50, a citizen of Neheim photographed the brown flood within the town, already receding.

In the background of the rubble field the parish church of St John the Baptist, in which hundreds of dead were laid out for identification.

The landscape below the Fürstenberg at the conflux of the Ruhr and Möhne; the receded water mass has left behind a vast field of rubble. Below it, many missing persons were still suspected to rest.

Wehrmacht soldiers are searching for dead people among the debris at the edges of the valley in Neheim.

Twenty minutes after the breaking of the Möhne dam, ten metre high flood waters reached the unsuspecting town of Neheim, where many citizens were sitting in the basements due to the ongoing air raid alarm and thus drowned. Some still managed to flee: they climbed from floor to floor, squeezed through skylights, and hung onto chimneys in the face of death.

This truss was transported almost undamaged by the flood down the Möhne valley.

View of the Neheim valley of death: at the top left, the wooded Wiedenberg above the barracks; hundreds of Russian women could flee hereto on command of the camp director Kittler. The guard, Robert, a war-disabled veteran, had opened the wire fence towards the river Möhne. He himself drowned during the rescue. With the approach of the water the camp gate, usually closed for the night, was immediately opened.

On Werler Street people are standing among their rescued possessions. The wide Möhne divides the town into two halves.

mother's jewellery. Two steel boxes were found again, one below Voßwinkel Station, the other between Echthausen and Wickede. The third has remained lost until today. Perhaps it is lying trapped inside the vast amounts of rubble in the Möhne-Ruhr valley."

André Guillon, former French prisoner of war from Poitiers, experienced the Möhne tragedy in Neheim as follows: "At that time I worked at the F.W. Brökelmann Company, an aluminium work. Initially we found shelter in a cellar below the kitchen, which later served as a shelter for the workforce during air raid alarms, due to the fact that, after 1943, yet more and more bombers showed up. German, French, Belgian and Dutch went willingly into this shelter. Everyone could decide for himself, whether he wanted to remain in the factory during an air raid alarm, go to the shelter, onto Werler Street, or to find protection outside. The Reich was lacking in soldiers and thus had reduced the guards. We were totally free inside the factory and lived in a barrack, approximately two kilometres from the Brökelmann Company, near Möhne Street towards the Möhne reservoir.

In the night of terror we heard at first the noise of aircraft and then the peculiar sound of an express train. After a cry of alarm, all 100 prisoners of war rushed towards the door of the guard on duty. The German guards had immediately decided to open the doors to the barrack and the stores. Very quickly the water rushed into the barrack. The last two to escape were, by sheer luck, a comrade and I. As the barrack door opened to the outside, we had great difficulty opening it against the pressure of the water. Many comrades fled onto the roof of the barrack, others swam ashore. Only one fellow countryman drowned. A neighbouring barrack with perhaps ninety Russian women pitched and tossed for a moment like an ark on top of the waves spraying up, splintered and sank. I thought that the dam had broken in two sections, for one first wave nine metres tall approached Neheim, then a second of six metres.

All the people who had gone into the air raid shelter of F.W. Brökelmann Aluminium found death in the waters. The door of this shelter was neither locked nor blocked. I remember that the door opened on the inside. The many people who had visited the shelter during the night shift, went inside voluntarily and were pushed back by the water. Later nobody mentioned that workers were pushed inside the shelter at the sounding of the air raid alarm, either. The next morning we had to report, facing the factory. The Germans went looking for the victims alone. I then went into the cellar pumped dry and saw my dead comrades hanging stuck between the heating pipes and the ceiling whereto they had fled in their need for air. I found nobody who had seen the drama inside this shelter. Roughly sixty corpses lay in a row opposite the factory without coffins. Later, they were driven away. Where they went, I did not learn. I helped to restore the riverbed of the Möhne with a shovel, during which we found corpses time and again, mainly Russian women.

After the catastrophe, the Germans allowed us to send for civilian clothes from France, and we could move freely inside the town of Neheim. That was not possible before the disaster. After the tragedy we no longer had any guards. From 1944 onwards I worked with the master butcher Heinrich Menge in Neheim-Hüstern. I have good memories from my stay with him until 24th April 1945, when I went home after my liberation." – "I would be happy if you could send him my regards", André Guillon writes to the author.

Scandal at the Funeral of the Reservoir Victims in Neheim

Clergyman Joseph Hellmann writes a report: "Our parish church of St John the Baptist was set up as morgue, the benches in the nave pushed to the sides to make space for 200 coffins. Soon soldiers ordered here from elsewhere brought the corpses. Men, women and children, from infant to dotard, were laid out inside the church to be identified. For many this deed was possible with the aid of notebooks, identification, rings and other objects found. Some corpses, disfigured by water and injuries, had to be registered as unknown. It was terrible to look at the dead, as they lay there partly with clenched hands and faces distorted with fear. Some of the dead had peaceful expressions, as if they were sleeping. Some even held a cross or a rosary in their hands and had thus passed into eternity. Relatives came to see their dearly departed one more time.

More than 400 foreign female workers have been buried in mass graves. The French, among them a Catholic priest who had had the cure of souls here for the French, the Belgians, the Dutch and our Germans, were buried either in mass or family graves."

The first funeral of the German deceased took place on Thursday, 20 May 1943. The memorial service was held by **Dr. Friedrich Rintelen**, general vicar from Paderborn. On 24 May 1943 he sent this letter of complaint to the Reich Minister of the Interior in Berlin, Dr Frick, and demanded clarification about the scandalous, staged events during the funeral of the flood victims of the town of Neheim:

"The signatory feels obliged to notify you about the following events:

1. In the town of Neheim which is very badly affected by the destruction of the Möhne dam, the Catholic parish church was allocated for the laying out of the corpses. The entirely plain, frequently make-shift coffins were to the largest part adorned with a simple wooden cross. At the behest of authorities unbeknown to me all crosses were removed one day. The deeply Catholic population in Neheim, especially the relatives of the drowned, were extremely embittered by this. They gave their outrage such a vociferous expression that the crosses reappeared.

2. During the negotiations about the interments of the victims, initially the suggestion was made that the memorial service of the state and the party should take place during the morning of 20 May at the cemetery. In the afternoon, the liturgical functions of both Christian denominations were supposed to be carried out. Finally it was agreed to have the memorial service of the state at 10am and after that the church service at the graves themselves. Around quarter to twelve the state ceremony was supposed to finish. I myself wanted to carry out the liturgical service as the representative of the Arch Bishop of Paderborn. With the participating clergymen I went to the cemetery in time, so as not to have the bereaved waiting unnecessarily. At our arrival the national songs were being sung as the concluding act.

3. After the formations of the party had left the cemetery and the coffins had been carried to the mass graves, the large group of bereaved gathered around the mass

graves. I began with the reading of a brief gospel. Just as I had finished the last sentence, the sirens sounded and gave the air raid alarm. With three sentences I concluded the service. At the same moment a truck with some young lads raced along the street in front of the cemetery. The lads shouted: 'Water, the Sorpe dam!' and indicated by their waving that the population ought to flee up the slope of the cemetery into the mountains. With a cry of terror the nervous, overwrought and frightened crowd of many hundreds of people scattered in a blink of an eye, up the slope of the cemetery and vanished into the neighbouring woods or ran home to the children and the sick. As the cemetery is on fairly high grounds and as the local clergy told me that the cemetery could not be endangered by the waters of the Sorpe, at first I remained beside the grave so as not to increase the unrest. Shortly afterwards the sirens sounded once more, but did not give the all-clear (then perhaps the faithful could have gathered around the graves again), but the signal for an air raid. We then left the cemetery and went into the town in which a terrible panic had taken hold. For example, people stormed the hospital and shouted that the water was coming, and the sick ought to be carried up to the attic. In large crowds the people fled to the mountains. Those remaining behind, however, told us on the street that this was only a practice alarm. That had been announced by loudspeaker, too. In my understandable outrage I went immediately to the town hall in the company of the local clergyman to ascertain whether this had indeed been a practice alarm, just at the moment when the Christian service was about to start. In the town hall I met the district commissioner of Arnsberg who told me that it was not a practice alarm, but that a heightened state of alert had been announced before the regular alarm was sounded. At my request to ascertain who had ordered the alarm, he called the warning centre by telephone. At the same moment the door was opened. In the utmost state of excitement the district president of Arnsberg entered the room with the words: 'What an outrageous scandal!' Thereupon he saw us clergymen. We were introduced by the district commissioner. I told him why I was at the town hall, whereupon the district president said to me that a relay by car had come and reported the breach in the dam of the Sorpe reservoir, subsequently the alarm had followed, and by the ringing of the bells the general panic had been enhanced. There was no doubt, however, that the Sorpe dam was sound. At my objection that alarm was not permitted to be sounded without an official instruction, the district president replied that this could not be said in such a case. I would probably have acted the same as the individual with the duty of operating the alarm. The explanations given to me satisfied me very little. That the district president and the district commissioner were very outraged about the events they did not tell me outright, but I could surmise it from all of this nevertheless. After my return to Paderborn, I received a report from a local clergyman, via telephone. He told me that he had previously received notification that a call, by an unknown person, had been made to the district administration in Arnsberg, reporting a breach in the Sorpe reservoir. From the district office in Arnsberg a telephone report was made to Neheim. At the same time a relay by car had arrived there and brought the same message. Consequently the alarm was sounded. At the moment when I left the parsonage in Neheim around 2.30pm, a senior lieutenant of the uniformed police arrived at the parsonage to explain that in future all bell ringing had to cease, because the panic in Neheim had been caused by the ringing of the church bells. My remark to this: at the beginning of the Christian service the sexton rang the knells for three minutes on instructions by the local clergyman. Then the alarm sounded, and the news spread through Neheim that the Sorpe dam had broken. Somebody rushed towards the sexton with the command that he ought to ring the alarm with all the bells, which the sexton naturally did. When an unchecked report of alarm is made, the authorities in charge must make the decision whether or not to activate the sirens. A simple sexton must be excused if he gave into the demands of incessant ringing, in all the general excitement. Moreover it is the most unreasonable thing, in the event of danger by water, to force the people into the shelters during an air raid alarm. The ban on ringing bells was now justified, after the fact, by the local police. Now, the ringing of bells should only be undertaken in the event of a break of the Sorpe dam.

In the interest of state authority I considered it necessary to report the events in Neheim. I ask you, Mr Reich Minister, to instigate an immediate, thorough investigation so that the guilty are met with strict punishment if need be. I express the hope that you will also order a revocation of the ban on bell ringing.
Signed Rintelen, general vicar"

The written answer of the Reich Ministry of the Interior: the events have been investigated. Nobody was at fault! In future the general vicar ought not to hassle the highest state authorities with such petitions, but address himself to lower-level authorities.

Signatory declares under oath: "On Thursday, 20 May 1943, I was in the parish church to assist sexton Wilmes with his duties. Suddenly – it might have been around 11am – the siren on top of the town hall sounded the signal of an air raid danger. Then PC Kurz, Neheim, came rushing through the main portal of the church and declared that all bells should be rung at once, as the Sorpe dam had been hit by the enemy. I hurried as quickly as possible to the sexton in the vestry and reported the order. Thereupon the sexton rang all the bells. This he would not have done, if he hadn't been ordered to do so. Later PC Rösen, resident of Neheim, 4 Sonnenufer, told me that he was on duty in Hüsten during the time the siren was sounding in Neheim. In Hüsten (although Neheim and Hüsten form one town) the siren had not been activated.
Neheim-Hüsten 1, 21 June 1943,
signed Josef Wiegelmann"

Pastor Joseph Hellmann of the parish of St John the Baptist fought a futile paper war with the authorities in order to have the ringing ban revoked until the surrender by Germany. On the very day that disaster struck, he began drawing up lists of the Mohne victims. Number

The villa of the Neheim light fixture factory owner Kaiser is standing in the Möhne valley, torn apart by the water masses. Josef Greis, the family's gardener and driver, was able to save Kaiser's children at the last moment. Kaiser and his wife were away. Anna, the Russian cook of the family, had not wanted to leave the house out of fear, and died as a result. The clearing work has commenced. Morass, mud, debris and rubble pervade the Möhne valley. Metre-high layers of pebbles and gravel have left behind a vast field of rubble.

At the narrowest part of the valley between Neheim and Niedernse, flood markings on tree trunks show a record water level of fifteen metres. In the Neheim valley of death the flood had cleanly razed off dozens of houses at their foundations and swept them away. Pioneers created a means to cross the Möhne by military rubber crafts as an interim measure. Shortly afterwards a 100m long footbridge was built below the Wiedenberg. Thousands of workers from the organisations Todt, Wehrmacht and various others, were on duty in the weeks following the attack, in order to clear away the debris and resume order. The Mohne and Ruhr had to be guided back into their former riverbeds.

This car was carried by the flood to the back of the houses in Vom-Stein Street in Neheim in the backwater area of the Ruhr. Between the houses and the car lies the flooded railway line serving the Ruhr area – Kassel. A four metre-high mark is clearly discernible on the outside walls of these houses, indicating the water level, and providing a stark reminder of the raid.

At the rubber boat stop Werler Street "national comrades" are waiting for a lift.

From the Wiedenberg, female citizens look in disbelief at the water masses in the valley.

A drinking water cart on Möhne Street in Neheim. Members of the Hitler Youth assist in the task of filling up buckets with water, for use in the homes of the citizens of Neheim.

20 May 1943: The public memorial service for the German dead, recovered thus far, occurred at 10am in Neheim cemetery. Along the fifty-three, Nazi formations have taken up position. During the service, a false alarm reporting the breaking of the Sorpe dam caused a panic.

sixty-eight was Otto Stöffgen, born in Riga, cook from the Russian camp. On 27 May 1943 the list of the missing still counted thirty-four to forty citizens of Neheim. On 29 May he buried the 120th German in the Neheim cemetery. On 3 January 1944 the official list of the dead named 153 German persons; forty-six men, eighty-eight women and nineteen children.

The Camp of the Foreign Female Workers, 800 Dead behind Barbed Wire

Since the beginning of the war, on the orders of the Reich Ministry of Labour, the labour bureaus and factory inspectorates methodically trawled companies of all branches for men to be drafted. After the complete exhaustion of all reserves this was followed by the close-down of companies not relevant for the war effort, an efficient merging of factories, the employment of women and the rise of the weekly working hours to sixty in the industry. When these possibilities were exhausted to fill the gaps in industry, mining and agriculture and, in the midst of a continually worsening war situation, with increased numbers of air raids and food shortages, the mass assignment of foreign workers inevitably came about.

Millions of prisoners of war and "foreign workers", the latter mostly drafted against their will, were brought to the Reich and its sphere of influence. As the number of civilian voluntary foreign workers was insufficient, from 1942 onwards detachments of snatchers in the east rounded up people as "labour booty" for deportation as labourers to the Nazi state. The transportation of deported people forced into labour was organised by the German National Railway. The labour bureaus took over the distribution, and the factory inspectorates guarded the camps of the "foreign workers", as they were then called.

After the withdrawal of the German workforce, the armaments companies reported their demand in labour to the labour bureau in charge. Thereupon the labour bureaus assigned foreign workers to the firms, whose accommodation the latter had to take care of. Thus until the early summer of 1943, with the aid of the labour bureau in Soest, more than 1,200 female foreign workers from the Ukraine and Poland reached the "Residential and Provisioning Camp Registered Limited Company" of the Neheim armaments industry on the Möhne meadows.

The supervision of the accommodation of the foreign workforce for the duration of the war was governed in Neheim-Hüsten by the factory inspectorate Soest. State police headquarters were responsible for offences or crimes by foreign workers (sabotage, arson, disinclination to work, strike and sexual offences). The maintenance of the camp was subject to the German Labour Front (the compulsory successor organisation of the unions in the Nazi state).

In accordance with Section 12 of the Regulation on Conditions of Employment of the Eastern Workforce (Reich Law Gazette, 2 July 1942), the forced labourers had income and council taxes subtracted from their wages by the revenue office in Arnsberg.

In May 1988 rumours circulated in Neheim about the night of the disaster in the camp of the forced workers. Thereupon the author looked for further eye witnesses, also in the Soviet Union.

On 12 July 1990 the "Ukraine Pravda" published his announcement under the heading "Tragedy at the Lake": "During the war a labour camp with deported women from the Ukraine was situated in Neheim-Hüsten. On the night of the 16/17 May 1943 a tragedy took place in the camp near the Möhne Lake. British bombers destroyed the dam, the water rushed out, and more than 700 Ukrainian women found death. Many were able to save themselves. Who survived this terrible night?

Please write to Helmuth Euler, 4760 Werl, Steinerstraße 22-24, Federal Republic of Germany."

On 18 July 1990 Ms **Darja Michajlowna Moros** from the Ukraine wrote a letter to the author:

"Dear Helmuth Euler,
In the paper "Ukraine Pravda" I read the notice 'Tragedy at the Lake' in which you describe the event taking place on 17 May 1943 in Neheim-Hülsten below the Möhne Lake, and I decided to respond.

I was at that labour camp and worked in the 'Kleki' factory. I remember that we were woken by an alarm during the night. Such alarms were numerous and we were utterly fed up with them. Therefore we rose only grudgingly. Yet this night the alarm saved our lives. We ran as we were from the barracks. There were many of us.

Not all of us fitted through the gate. The camp was surrounded by a tall barbed wire fence. The tragedy would have claimed even more victims, if we had not been saved by a guard. He was called Robert, but I cannot recall his last name. I only know that he was very old and limping on one leg. He cut through the wire with some pliers, created passages for us, and we ran through them. He hurried us along: 'Quickly, quickly'; more quickly up the mountain where the water could not reach. Ten women of my home country were living with me in one of the barracks and all survived, and now they are living in different places.

Mr. Robert saved our lives. When the huge wave came, he could not save himself and drowned. The water approached very quickly and swept the fleeing off their feet. Whoever fell over drowned on the spot and all of this by night.

In the morning, instead of the barracks, a huge lake with many drowned floating atop was found. For a week they were fishing corpses from the water and drove them to mass graves beyond the town. On the mountain behind the river Möhne we stayed until the morning, drenched, half naked, and freezing. Then we survivors were led to a farmer (Plesser) who fed us. Everybody received a piece of bread and a jug of milk. Afterwards they sent us to work in the same factories again."

A second letter:

"Much time has passed and much is forgotten, especially the names of people and places and dates. My fellow country-women and I were brought to Germany in June

On 18 July 1990 Ms Darja
Michajlowna Moros from
Kamenetz-Podolskij in the
Ukraine, a former forced
labourer, got in touch with
the author by letter which
was followed by further
correspondence.

The remains of the toilet installations of the Russian camp in Neheim
were still visible thirty years after the war.

1942 from my home village Gruschka, Staroushinski jaron, in the Khmelnitz region
of the Ukraine.

The deportations were carried out by force. We were stuffed into boxcars; these
were tightly locked and driven away. In a German town (Soest) they let us out. Staff
managers waited for us to select workers for their factories. I got into one of the groups,
and they drove us into a camp. In the confines of the camp there were many barracks,
in each, the workers of one factory were living.

It was forbidden to make contact with residents of other barracks. We merely knew
two guards who monitored us in shifts and accompanied us to work and back. One was
called Robert, and the second was called Josek who was an old man unfit for military
service. For a walk to town ten girls went in the company of a guard, but these were rare
occasions. Primarily we had to work.

I did not know the camp doctor Dr. Mihailowa or the camp supervisor Werner
Kittler. Many of the women in the camp did not come from the Ukraine. For example,
I personally knew two Polish women, Christina and Tatjana. Many girls came from
the Poltawa region. I often spoke about this topic at home with my fellow sufferers in

Neheim. This photograph, which I sent home during the war, was made in a studio in Neheim. In which, I can no longer say exactly. Now I have sent it to you, back to Germany again. We very rarely received letters from home in the camp, mainly postcards. Twice a month we were allowed to write.

We were not fed in the camp, but in the factory. The food was very bad; we received a kilogram of bread per week and in addition a turnip soup daily. That was all. We were living half starved and subsisted on waste from the German kitchen, for example vegetable trimmings which we cooked and ate in secret. During the entire time of our stay in Germany we lived in this manner.

After the flood we lived, at first, in a different barrack, which was subsequently burnt down during an air raid. We then lived on a basement of the 'Kleki' factory. Soon, we sensed that the time for returning home was drawing near. We were very glad about our liberation by the Americans; they gave us their field rations.

We still remained some days in the factory without working. Trucks brought us to the city of Magdeburg which had been liberated by Soviet soldiers. There a first check was made. We were asked who had come voluntarily to Germany and who by force. I had come to Germany by force.

From Magdeburg a train went to Bresk. Here a second check, as to whether we were volunteers or forced labourers, was carried out. In August 1945 I reached my home village. The 'volunteers' in the Neheim camp had several privileges in comparison to us. They worked in the kitchen or in professions like German women. All those times when we were hungry, they received different food. They also received better clothes. They did not have other advantages."

On 26 May 1943 the factory inspectorate Soest stated in a letter to the district president of Arnsberg: "The extensive camp for the eastern workforce of the Neheim companies, which had been erected at the cost of one million Reichsmark according to the managers, has disappeared.

Further it has to be pointed out that the question had been addressed several times during inquiries at the companies as to whether the labour camp did not lie in the flooding area of the Möhne. The spot for the camp was doubtlessly disadvantageously chosen, moreover since this resulted in long commutes for a part of the Neheim companies, and the drainage of the terrain and the long access routes created many difficulties. I assume that the idea of a communal camp is not taken up again, as for many other reasons the conditions were unpleasant. Complaints about insufficient food and lack of supervision of the eastern workers were lodged repeatedly, as well as complaints of the difficulties arising from the fact that the eastern workers were drawn from different companies, and therefore comparisons were made of their work and treatment in relation to each other.

Happy End with German-Russian Wedding

Erika Hoffmeister tells of her parents: "My mother Elena was born in Tomsk in Siberia. From her fourth year she lived in former Stalino in the Ukraine. In April 1942 she was deported for forced labour in Germany. Actually she herself did not need to go, but she volunteered for her older sister who had two children. So then she came with another sister to the camp in Neheim. My father met her in the camp on the Möhne meadows where he worked as a guard. Several times he had to collect her, when she 'had done a bunk' out of homesickness, together with her girlfriends, once even reaching Oeventrop. My father always took care that she did not receive any punishment. He fell in love with Elena, but relationships with the forced workers were strictly prohibited. So they met in secret.

My father's sister helped to organise visits to the hairdresser. Elena was served as a deaf-mute so as not to betray herself. My mother spoke only a few German words, my father only little Russian. They even went to the cinema together, in the middle of the war. As a passionate film-lover Elena later learned her German in the cinema. During her time in the camp she saw some films three times. She also did a bit of shopping in town in the company of my aunt who spoke on her behalf. During Sunday walks, my father has regaled me with tales of his experiences with my mother in the camp. He even showed me where the barrack stood in which my mother lived.

The foundations and the concrete frames of the toilets were still visible for decades after the war. That night my father Karl Josef Stüppardt heard a strange, terrible detonation. Thereupon he walked with his shepherd dog along the camp fence by the river Möhne towards the reservoir to investigate the matter. A little later he had the feeling as if a storm was rising, but immediately had the idea that the Möhne dam might have been hit. He quickly ran to the closest barracks, unlocked them and called: 'Everybody out, the Möhne dam is hit, the water is coming!' Many of the women in the barracks didn't believe his warning. They said: 'This is not true', and remained in bed.

Many also ran, naturally, towards the Möhne Street gate. The water followed at their heels. Farther they ran up an ascending road. My mother fled through the opened camp gate in her underskirt with her coat thrown over. Near the Hillebrand firm, the water had caught up with them. The surviving forced workers were at first housed in the guildhall and later brought to a camp behind the main station. My father continued to keep in touch with his Elena. As a punishment for supporting foreign workers, he was imprisoned by the Neheim police.

However, after the war, a happy ending awaited the former camp guard Karl Josef Stuppardt and the forced labourer Elena. Their wedding took place on 16 June 1945 in the parish church of St. John the Baptist. One of the first post-war weddings in town, perhaps the first German-Russian wedding in Germany. My mother wore the wedding dress of her sister-in-law with a long trail. In the very crowded church a choir of former Russian prisoners of war sang in the organ loft. My mother was of Russian-Orthodox faith. Her identity card showed the wrong date of birth, as she had given the authorities an earlier date at her arrival in Germany, perhaps to get more money or a larger food ration with an older age."

Elena Wolkowa, photographed on 31 May 1942 in front of the "Residential and Provisioning Camp Ltd", is carrying a German neighbour's child. After her liberation by the Americans in 1945 she married the former camp guard Karl Josef Stüppardt in the crowded parish church of St John the Baptist, one of the first post-war weddings in Neheim.

The political spring enabled the author to publish an announcement in the "Ukranian Pravda" in 1990 looking for eye witnesses of the fateful night in the camp. Several women described their rescue from the floods in letters.

Death notices in the local newspapers did not always state all victims. On 27 May 1943 in the Mendener Zeitung, an unknown person had published a large announcement on the death of a fifteen person family who never existed, at great risk to him or herself. The bogus announcement was supposed to expose the cover-up of the consequences of the disaster by the regime, a form of resistance in the local press.

Some identified foreign victims of the Möhne have been conveyed to their home countries after the war. The photo shows the grave of an unidentified Frenchman.

Wir verloren durch ein tragisches Geschick am 17. Mai 1943 unsere Lieben durch einen gemeinsamen Tod, unsere liebe Mutter

Frau Erna Krothaus
verw. Gottlob geb. von Witthauer
geb. am 2. 1. 1900 zu Ulm

und unsere lieben Geschwister

Ingrid
geb. 25. 11. 1923

Ewald
geb. 25. 12. 1928

Egon
geb. 13. 2. 1930

Ernst
geb. 4. 8. 1933

Josefa-Maria
geb. 14. 12. 1935

Heinrich
geb. 24. 12. 1937

sowie unsere liebe Urgroßmutter

Frau Anna-Maria Krothaus
geb. von Keudel
geb. am 4. 12. 1849
auf Gut Keudelstein a. d. Werra

Dies zeigen an

Regina und Renate Krothaus

Mit ihnen sind im Tode vereint mein unvergeßlicher Mann

Dr. med. Egon Krothaus
geb. 1. 2. 1903 zu Lübeck
und unsere lieben Kinder

Hermann-Josef
geb. 1. 3. 1934

Maria-Therese
geb. 16. 8. 1935

Angelika und Sigismund
geb. 24. 12. 1938

Agnes
geb. 8. 11. 40

In tiefer Trauer

Frau Regina Krothaus
verw. Weil geb. von Witthauer

Mit ihnen starb unsere liebe Mutter

Frau Witwe Erna von Witthauer
geb. Börner
geb. 2. 11. 1896

In tiefer Trauer

Peter von Witthauer
Werner von Witthauer
z. Zt. im Felde

Haus Hermannsruh über Stockum Möhne, Menden Kr. Iserlohn, Fulda und Ulm, den 27. Mai 1943

Beisetzung und Seelenamt haben stattgefunden.

Minister of Propaganda Joseph Goebbels used a false English report as an opportunity to stir up hatred against the Jews in six regional newspapers in whose distribution area the disasters could not be concealed.

Entire families from Neheim were eradicated by the water; a mass grave for 479 unknown forced female labourers from the Soviet Union and Poland. In front of the destroyed industrial enterprises a Russian woman is looking for her possessions in the morass.

"Sometimes the camp on the Möhne meadows was visited by 'bigwigs'", tells **Karl Josef Stüppardt**. "Then the girls had to primp the camp especially. It is astonishing how the Ukrainians had smartened up the camp with their modest means. During the camp visit they had to wave flowers. Then better food was served, too.

One time the Soviet general Wlassow, captured by the Germans, visited the camp, probably for propaganda purposes. At the beginning of 1945 he formed two divisions of a 'Russian Liberation Army' from Soviet prisoners of war for Hitler's Germany. In May 1945 Wlassow and his soldiers became American prisoners. The Americans handed Wlassow and his troops over to the Soviet Union; he himself was executed in Moscow on 1 August 1945."

Eye Witness Reports from the Flooded Areas Wickede–Fröndenberg – Schwerte

Hermann Kerstholt reports:

"In the middle of May I was in a military hospital in Arnsberg and was on weekend leave in Wickede. On Mother's Day I visited my mother-in-law in Echthausen with my oldest children. She was living on slightly higher ground in the village. I was staying over night, when I was woken by a strong tremor. The half-timbered house was quaking at the seams, it seemed to lift up.

I stood up and met my sister-in-law in the hallway. 'Hermann, what is going on, the planes are circling so low?', she said. 'Yes, I hear that, too.' An uncanny unrest came over me, and I went to the window where I had a wide view over the nocturnal Ruhr valley. After perhaps thirty minutes I heard strange noises. I believed that the planes had hit a train in the valley. The sound like draining water became much louder. Then I saw a grey wall heaving down through the valley, a foaming flood upon which floated parts of barracks with people on top who signalled with lamps or lanterns. Fixed lights moved, sometimes lights flared up which went out again, just like a match being struck and thrown away.

When I saw the floating rafts, barracks from Neheim, I immediately thought of my relatives who were sheltered further down the valley in a well-appointed air raid shelter that they always utilised during air raids. Then I ran quickly into the village of Echthausen, to Major Rasche, an uncle of mine who had a telephone. I called Wickede and prompted them to vacate the shelter and to flee to safety from the flood. I then wanted to run immediately from Echthausen to Wickede. That was impossible, since all bridges were destroyed and the Ruhr valley was filled to the brim with raging water. I went over the mountains along the edge of the forest to Wickede, here the Ruhr bridge to Menden was missing. Water as far as the eye could perceive, not a soul could be seen. So I returned to Echthausen, full of unease, and was preoccupied with the question of whether my relatives had been able to save themselves. The telephone line to Wickede was dead but, thankfully, my relatives lived."

In the area of the Wickede/ Ruhr railway station the force of the water has pushed locomotive no. 44215 – weighing several tons – together with its coal cars from the tracks. The station is strewn with heavy scouring. Tracks have partly shifted across hundreds of metres. On the main line Ruhr area – Kassel, at several sections between Wickede and Neheim, the railway embankment was torn open and swept away.

A picture of devastation: railway tracks lie on top of toppled-over wagons. Uprooted trees, undermined roads, and chunks of debris from torn houses show themselves at many unrecognisable spots in the settlement of Wickede. The 2nd A Company of the 1st Battalion of railway pioneers from Fürstenwalde near Berlin, whose training period was nearing its end, was deployed to West Germany on 22 May 1943. At the airbase Werl they learned their mission target: reconstruction of the railway bridge of Wickede. On 24 May 1943 at 5am, trucks of the National Railway brought the 'construction soldiers' to the disaster zone.

Severe damage to the destroyed railway bridge of Wickede over the Ruhr and the Obergraben affected one of the main supply lines to the Ruhr area/eastern front. It was imperative to make it passable again as soon as possible. Stone abutments torn apart and bent iron girders were a difficult challenge impeding the early efforts of the reconstruction teams, especially since many tasks had to be carried out by hand.

The primordial force of the water has torn the bridge apart, the tracks lead nowhere. The mighty pillar had burst and required removal by controlled detonations.

Sixteen-year-olds from the National Labour Service level the railway embankment in Wickede.

Pioneers carry tree trunks weighing several tons to the railway bridge in 'centipede fashion'.

Bleak images surpassing all the anticipations of the railway pioneers deployed; unfettered floods have swept away much, as they went along, and have washed up the jetsam and flotsam at obstacles and shores. On 7 June midday the railway pioneers had restored one track of the bridge. A "high commission" has arrived for inspection.

The "juggernaut N", two heavy locomotives for freight trains of the construction series 50, drove slowly over the bridge once, and then once again, very fast, as a load test. The instruments measured considerably less than the permissible limit. One hour later the first passenger train rolled over the repaired construction.

Karl Brockmeier describes his experience:

"An alarm had woken us suddenly, and after some time it became spooky outside. We called our neighbours named Quenter, but received no reply. Later we learned that they had already left the house after a warning by telephone. I ran downstairs and opened the front door, and the flood waters gushed in. Carrying our baby in my arms we ran up into the attic. From the skylight I saw the floods. In dire need I climbed onto the workshop's roof of the adjoining Quenter firm and looked for help anywhere I could. Then the dramatic rescue came about. My daughter – she was twelve years old at the time – had found a long rope on the street. She took it along to school, for the teacher was supposed to find its owner. The teacher returned the rope to my daughter and said that she ought to hold it in custody. This rope was to become our saviour. In our fear I tied the rope around the chimney and threw the other end towards the window of our neighbour Rennebaum. There they quickly attached it, and then I slid across the rope to the Rennebaums like a 'tightrope artist', my daughter in front of me, three metres above the turbulent waters.

My wife was waiting in the attic, while I attempted to get help at the Rennebaums. But then the chimney collapsed, and the entire Quenter house was torn away by the masses of water. The roof drifted towards a house of the 'Iron and Steel' company and came to rest on its roof. My wife and baby had drifted off on the roof beams. Falling roof tiles had caused injuries to my wife, and her spattered blood had marked the infant in such a way that we feared for his life.

After six hours my wife and the baby were rescued from their plight. With two mismatched boots found in the mud, I was the first person to enter the Henke house. There I found the mother and her four children lying dead in the morass. Mr. Bauer stood at the corner of Ring Street and Main Street and grumbled about the mess the leader was making for us. This was reported to the Gestapo who fetched him for interrogation. Some days later a major alarm was sounded again. It was put out that the Sorpe dam had been hit. Fortunately, this was a false alarm.

After about eight days we went looking for our things. We found the sewing machine in a hedge by the chain factory Koch. I continued to search, a futile enterprise. At my return the sewing machine had already disappeared. At the Arndt inn we received food. We saw the many casualties of the flood. After some time I got back my communion photograph. It had floated all the way to Frondenberg and is the only thing remaining from our household. It was taken in 1913."

Hanna-Maria Kampschulte swam ten kilometres in the deadly flood from Wickede to Fröndenberg. She reports in a film interview:

"I was sixteen years old at that time and was living with my mother, grandmother and two brothers in Wickede on Ring Street. Father was in the army. We children had returned to bed after the air raid alarm and the detonations – one with a palpable shock wave – and were counting on the all-clear. Yet Mother found no rest, she ran from one window to the next and listened into the night. Around twenty to two she woke us with the words: 'Outside it is gusting so terribly, it has become so misty, although it is the full moon. Get up quickly; they have probably hit the Möhne dam!' I ran to the window and saw the water streaming around all corners of the house, like a huge grey wyvern. I screamed: 'Water, water!', and woke my brother and Granny who, at eighty-two years old, did not understand.

We climbed up to the attic. Mother brought little Udo there and I returned with her once more to fetch some things from the wardrobes. During the second attempt the water had already reached the upper floor and streamed through the windows like a torrent. All five of us huddled up in the attic, little Udo wept bitterly, as he was so tired and did not understand what was happening to him. Below us the terrifying, roaring water was drowned out by cried for help. Mother placed Udo on her lap, held him tightly and said to us: 'Now all of us together have to die, we will all drown, nobody can help us!' My brother Willi looked out of the skylight and shouted that Meier's house next door had already vanished (father, mother, and five little children). I dragged him away from the window and saw, at that moment, the tall pear tree belonging to the Gerdes' opposite, tearing the entire front of their house away.

For some time the house stood there, cut in half from the roof to the water level. In the light of burning candles the inhabitants were hunched on the floor and praying. Then an enormous wave approached, and all fell on top of each other. As in a nightmare, the large house and all the people in it sank into the water. We took hold of each other, prayed, wept and cried. Then a slight jerk occurred and we began to sink. Almost imperceptibly our feet started to touch water. My mother said: 'Hannchen, you are able to swim. Willi shall try it, too, perhaps you can save yourselves. What shall Papa do without us?!' The floor pressed us towards the roof construction and wedged us in. I reached above my head and felt battens and roof tiles. With a last effort I broke through some tiles and was able to push my head through, regaining some air.

For a while the roof floated along with the water. I climbed on top and pulled some clothes through the hole in the hope that somebody would have clung to them. I removed further tiles, but nobody was visible.

The roof that had been my life raft splintered bit by bit until it finally broke into pieces and sank. A floor drifting by became my next raft. Around me were doors, furniture, barrels and boxes, floating alongside the bellowing and dead cattle that had fallen victim to the flood. When my floor fell apart, I grabbed a door and climbed onto it. Suddenly I heard shouts for help in the mist. I called: 'Who is there?' It was our neighbour Franz Lohage who had his mother and a Miss Neurath with him. They drifted away in different directions.

Then I was heading for a weir, fell into a swirl of two to three metres depth and lost my door in the process. I floundered around, there was no escape. With all the rubble drifting towards me a broken telegraph pole headed for me. I tried to grab it, but it turned and was difficult to grasp. Nevertheless I managed to escape the swirl with the turning timber.

A wardrobe, a bedstead and again a door were my next saviours. With the door I drifted down the Löhn towards a row of houses. I saw lights in the windows and people who stretched their arms towards me to help. I bumped with my door into the first house of the settlement, it started to veer off and I with it, then I collided with another house; again and again and again. There simply was no rescue. The people at the windows above me even tried to throw me a rope, but without success. Then I drifted over a railway embankment out of the main flow into calmer waters and got caught in a row of truncated willows standing along a road near Fröndenberg.

I had become quite hoarse from all the shouting. I climbed into a willow tree. In front of me the clutter stacked up higher and higher, I even saw a living cow. During the entire night it tried incessantly to climb up to me, during which process it managed to touch my feet with its tongue. When it moved, the trees creaked and groaned and slanted more and more. I was afraid that they would not withstand the pressure and that I would fall into the water once more. I took off some of my clothes to be more mobile for a renewed plunge into the water and to cover my feet so that the cow could not reach them.

Covered in dirt and mud I was freezing miserably. I was totally exhausted and almost incapable of calling for help. Nobody answered. Gradually it became calmer, it began to dawn. The water started to fall, day was breaking. I thought I heard voices from afar, and I called for help once more. From the shore people shouted encouragements. As soon as the water had fallen a little further, they wanted to fetch me. Roughly around 8am I saw a man up to his shoulders in water cautiously approaching my 'tree of life'. He gathered me into his strong arms and carried me ashore. The man was from Frohnhausen and on leave; he later died in the war. I was brought to a farmer, where I was washed, given dry clothes and put to bed to warm up properly. Yet I could not fall asleep after my experience and looked at the place of my rescue once more.

On the railway embankment the collected drowned were lying, horribly disfigured. Amongst them were some of our neighbours. The corpses were transported to the hospital yard in Fröndenberg to be cleaned and identified. At noon I heard of three further people rescued in my neighbourhood and went to them. We embraced each other and, in spite of everything, we were glad to see each other again.

In the afternoon we drove with a horse carriage to Wickede. Where our houses had been standing, a huge field of rubble remained, only mud and dirt. I went to the house of my aunt and uncle. When I entered, they thought they were seeing a ghost. In my black clothes I must have seemed like an apparition. The clothes came from the farmer's grandmother, as everything else had not fit.

The next day my father arrived on leave and it was a sad reunion, for I was the only thing left to him. With borrowed bicycles we travelled to Fröndenberg to look for our family members and to identify them.

Grandma, Mother and Udo had already been found. They were lying amongst the long rows of dead inside the morgue and in the courtyard of the hospital. Simple coffins of pinewood were at hand. Mother was put inside a coffin with Udo in her arms,

Grandma into the next. We did not find our Willi. It is likely that my father identified him with the help of a photograph, but his corpse had meanwhile been interred with the anonymous dead in Fröndenberg. Father wanted to convey him to Wickede with the other dead family members. He drove with some colleagues to the exhumation at the Fröndenberg cemetery. Unfortunately only the photographs of the anonymous dead and their coffins were marked with the same numbers, but not the graves themselves. My father opened four graves without finding Willi and gave up the search."

Disaster Zone Fröndenberg

Helene Schulte writes to her brother in Berlin about the mood in Fröndenberg:

30 May 1943
"Dear Adolf!
     Although I am not at all in the mood to speak of the events in any way, I want to give you a short report, since you asked for it. (Eight closely typed pages!)
     I still cannot get over the fact that the state is capable of acting so carelessly. Experts must have recognised the danger and been able to calculate how high the water would rise, and could have trained the population accordingly. The flood waters hit us two hours after the breach in the Mohne dam. What could have been achieved in those hours? So many people and cattle didn't have to die and so many things could have been saved. A sense of responsibility and organisation are everything.
     Now we are sitting here in our rubble, having barely escaped with our lives, and cannot stand the smell of decay. The Sorpe dam has developed gashes, too, and might one day 'favour' us as well. So we sit on powder kegs, awaking with a start at the sound of a call or quick running. Now and again the siren fails, then men cycle through the streets, blow horns and shout 'air raid alarm'. Sometimes we just hear the horns, then I think of water, and that the blower does not dare to enter the danger zone. These warnings are nerve-wrecking, especially at night. During the first weeks the frustration was compounded by the fact that some people still had basements full of water. Many of these people gave the impression of startled deer, streaming towards the air raid shelters of houses on higher ground.
     During the night of terror, around 2.45am, we heard the honking of the Technical Emergency Help or fire brigade in the far distance. At the same time we heard a noise like freight trains being shunted. Then the events happened very fast, it was actually a matter of seconds. From the direction of the Ruhr we heard shouts: 'Back, the water is coming!'
     The water did not rise from the basement as during high floods, but rushed at breakneck speed through the street and broke into the houses with an elemental force. It took a moment until the basement had filled up, from which we had managed to fetch some oil paintings and a child, arriving on the upper floors half drenched. Then

The road bridge of the Reich Road from Wickede to Menden is totally destroyed, as is the long-distance gas pipeline that supported it. The Organisation Todt built a provisional wooden bridge next to the destroyed one. Dirk Zuider, together with his entire Dutch construction company and conscripted specialists, came to Wickede and they have stayed there to this day.

Dutch, French and Belgian workers participated in the project. Their lodgings were at the school and the neighbouring construction barracks on Church Street. The Belgian Bik Seegers worked as a cook for the personnel of the Organisation Todt who received army provisions. On Seegers' birthday, 31 July 1943, the emergency bridge was completed. The reward was a feast for the company's personnel. The pioneers had already built a footbridge over the Ruhr some weeks earlier.

The centre of destruction in Wickede/ Ruhr; here the water wheel rolled through the settlement and left behind chaos at the corner of Main Street and Ring Street where a memorial to the community's flood victims is standing today.

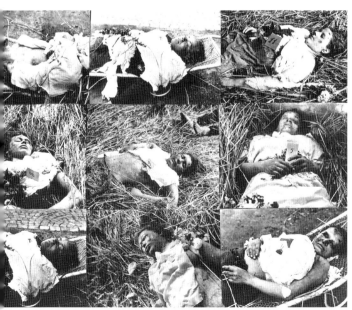

The identification of the flood victims showed itself to be extremely difficult in Wickede/ Ruhr, as some of them were washed up from as far as Günne and Neheim. Even in the Essen area corpses were recovered. Severe injuries and staining complicated the measures of identification. After the corpses had been washed, unidentified persons received a number tag and were photographed. A file with fingerprints, find spot, personal description and objects found provided information. Among the dead were many female forced labourers. Some of the dead were adorned with spring flowers, a last gesture before the unknown women found their final resting place in a mass grave far from home.

A soldier on leave together with some children looks at the destroyed weir of the Fröndenberg power station in Wickede/ Ruhr. The front line had now extended, encroaching upon areas that had once seemed safe.

After a grand memorial ceremony on WuRAG Square for the "flood victims" of the community, as they will be called from now on, the funeral procession is moving towards the cemetery, accompanied by delegations of the party, the Wehrmacht and the support organisations and by relatives. Seventy-nine coffins decorated with fir sprigs were driven to the cemetery at the foot of the mountain next to the parish church of St Anthony. Including the dead found later, the community counted 118 drowned persons, the highest number of victims in relation to the population. (Insert) Lance Corporal Rudolf Hillebrand received two telegrams in short succession while deployed with the German Africa Corps. After receiving the death notice, it took him fourteen days to make the return trip from Tunis to his destroyed family home.

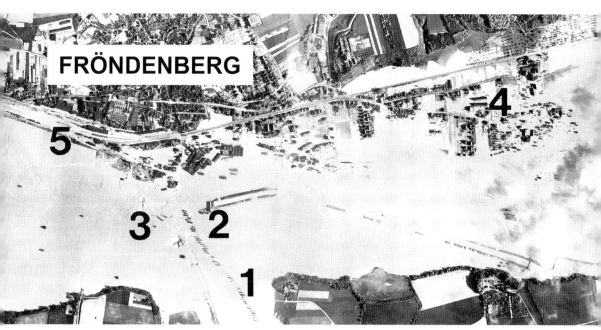

FRÖNDENBERG

5

4

3 2

1

Fröndenberg; this sensational British aerial photograph from the morning of 17 May 1943 went around the world's press at the time. "The German floods engulf the armament industry, the rivers continue to rise! Turbulence in the Ruhr area while the devastation is spreading." **1** – undermined roads; **2** – a stranded power station; **3** – a destroyed railway bridge; **4** – flooded streets; and **5** – flooded grounds of the railway station. The Ruhr valley, the light grey strip across the centre of the image, is completely under water.

Parish church and houses are reflected in the waters on Fröndenberg's squares and streets.

The railway bridge of Fröndenberg–Menden lies fifty metres away from its pillars. Almost one hundred kilometres of meadow, field, path and road in low-lying parts of the Ruhr valley were devastated. Depending on the location, sewage and water works were inoperative for varying lengths of time.

In the area of the railway station a signal post is reflected in the flood waters.

The torn railway bridge Fröndenberg–Menden

As the damage to the foundations of the bridge was too severe, the Organisation Todt decided to build a one-track permanent auxiliary bridge across the Ruhr. A National Railway service train is transporting the heavy T-beams for the bridge.

The road bridge from Fröndenberg to Menden, in the foreground, was swept away by the flood waters, as was the neighbouring railway bridge.

In this picture, the empty pillars of the two-track railway bridge on the Menden line are standing in the riverbed of the Ruhr. On the opposite bank, people are waiting for an opportunity to cross the river in rubber crafts.

Fröndenberg: the mud is scraped off the streets. The daily routine returns, life goes on. Housewives clean their vandalised homes; washing is drying on lines spanned across the street.

In Halingen near Fröndenberg women are gathering their household belongings. Chairs, beds, tables, mattresses and doors are lying ready for collection.

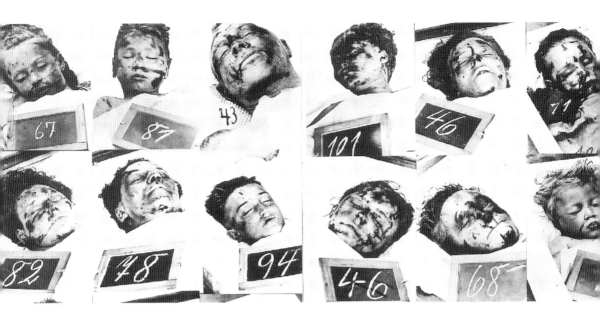

In Frondenberg, more than 160 unidentified dead were numbered with blackboards. After having been fingerprinted and photographed, the corpses were interred in the cemetery.

The grand memorial ceremony for the drowned of the town of Fröndenberg on Saturday, 22 May 1943, at the war memorial below the cemetery. The coffins were placed on low carts below flags and standards of the Third Reich. Representatives of the districts tried to turn the suffering of the people affected into feelings of hatred and revenge in their speeches. Mass funerals were a welcome opportunity for those in power to make propaganda speeches on the subject of perseverance.

Uwaha!

Wody uzywaty tilky perewarenoji, bo w protywnim wypadku mozna dislaty zaraslywu chorobu.

L'eau doit être cuite!

SEUCHENGEFAHR!

Wasser darf nur abgekocht genossen werden!

Warning posters in several languages informed all persons, including prisoners of war and forced labourers, of the danger of epidemics.

Seventeen-year-old Gunter Swolana leads brown Belgian gelding 'Siegfried' to safety. During the approach of the nocturnal flood wave, the animal stood tethered in a stable. In the rapidly rising flood waters, the horse broke loose in deadly terror and escaped via the tall piles of straw that were stored inside the stable. Unfazed by the seriousness of the situation, two boys are bathing in the Möhne-Ruhr flood on Hellpoth Street.

Trapped by the flood caused by their allied friends, French prisoners of war are sitting on the roof of their lodgings, a pub named, appropriately, "In the Water Kingdom".

the electrical light failed. Fortunately we had a candle at hand which we placed on the stairs to the attic and which offered us some emergency illumination. Due to the rising water we had to assume that the entire house would be seized by the flood and that we would not survive the night.

Those who haven't seen it cannot imagine this roaring, raging monster. Because the moon was shining, everything could be seen clearly. With a dynamo torch I peered down the stairs again and again to see whether the water would reach us soon. Just before the first floor, six centimetres below the ceiling, was the highest mark. We were sitting drenched and exhausted on the ransacked floor by a small candle flame and were glad that the water did not rise further. We shared cognac from a travelling flask, even the child got some, for it was frozen through and through. Then we blew out the candle and lay down by the window. We still had to worry, as our house was protruding from its row and everything approaching crashed against it: parts of bridges, fences, walls of weekend cottages with doors and windows, halves of cattle pens etc. Every time we thought that the house would collapse, it persisted. More than 160 corpses washed up in Fröndenberg. For the most part they could be identified by relatives. Twenty-six could not be recognised and were interred in Fröndenberg, after they had been photographed.

The disaster wasn't felt to such an extent here as in the narrower valleys upriver. The affected area represents a picture of devastation, with gardens eroded, trees uprooted and mountains of unimaginable stuff washed up.

Two thousand military men are here, furthermore Labour Service, storm troopers from the 'Feldherrnhalle' unit and 800 men of the Organisation Todt. National Socialist Women's League, League of German Girls and girls' schools from Unna, Hamm and Iserlohn reported here to help in the households. The soldiers on permanent duty in the bombarded cities have no longer any sympathy for individual fates. They said that they had seen much in Essen, Dortmund etc, but that water was worse than fire.

My fingers were bloody and inflamed from searching in the mud of the basement floor for possessions and papers. Our files floated about in the cellar and have, for the most part, been destroyed by the waters. The bank-savings books were later found by chance in a meadow. We didn't have any clean drinking water until Friday evening. For all that time, we were sitting in dirt and muddy water. In the morning I spat into my hands and rubbed my face.

Due to the lack of water, terrible sanitary conditions arose. To this was added the emotional pressure, the horror of a devastated dwelling, hunger, thirst, no opportunity to cook, no light, no dishes and most of all no good news. Only Johanna came. Hot coffee was driven through the streets, but not through ours so close to the Ruhr. At my complaint a car came with coffee. Meanwhile there were handouts, but what good is asparagus if you cannot cook it. Only two soldiers, one from Cologne with his dialect and dry humour and one from Detmold, managed to lift my shattered spirit somewhat. They were so willing and understanding.

Yet the worst occurred during the time of clearance, I nearly had a heart attack. We had just folded the muddy clothing from the cellar, when the following happened:

around noon the soldiers were away for lunch, when a shout echoed through the streets: 'Flood! Clear all houses and up to the Sümberg!' My brain could not process this. All the helpers fled with lightning speed, only a nice young girl persevered and carried the dirty clothes upstairs for me so that they would not float away again.

I did not care; I was really tired of life. Monitors checking the houses led me out by force. It was said that the Sorpe had broken. After an hour, it was said, we could return. But this turned out to be a false alarm.

Can you imagine something like this? To chuck such a bomb into the population whose nerves are already stretched to breaking point? The false alarm came from Neheim. There they had agreed that at a future reservoir disaster (Sorpe) the bells would be ringing. (For us, this would have been futile by the way as our lovely bells, with their beautiful chime, had already been spared, finding their way into the armaments furnace during World War I.) Incidentally we could have had a culinary feast of fish, for fish were scattered throughout the apartment in abundance.

Now I have probably told you enough and will conclude. I have made a copy of this letter which in the future I will hand to anyone who wishes to know about these events. I do not want to speak of them again.

I borrowed the typewriter from the administration for today. It cannot be spared for longer. You do not have to think that I exaggerated anything, on the contrary it cannot be described how terrible everything has been. Downstairs it is worse than in a den of thieves, but upstairs we have a brilliant view, from the bedroom we can see as far as Schwitten, because all the trees have been swept away.

Fondest regards, Your Helene"

Elfriede Pitzer reports from Schwerte:

"We were on full alert for almost the entire night. At some point the volunteer fire brigade under Chief Kathol moved into Mill Street. Apparently an alarm had been triggered at the fire station. They spoke of flooding, but nothing more detailed could be learned. My mother, Auguste Grewe, asked the fire chief again, but he soothed her with the words: 'Grandma, it's not so bad, if flooding should come here, we will help.'

Despite the soothing words my mother had me dress my paralysed sister Hanna who was sleeping in the back room of the lower apartment and bring her upstairs. A fireman helped with the transport. When we wanted to return downstairs, already on the stairs we were surprised by the inrushing flood. One fireman who was standing in front of our house could see the flood wave approaching Haber's, on lower Mill Street. He ran, head over heels, up the stairs of our house without closing the door behind him. This happened at the same moment that we sat Hanna down at a table in my flat.

I only saw the other fireman up in the attic. I believed that my mother had run upstairs, too, but she was not among the refugees. Therefore, she must still be in her apartment. As a result of the open door, the water entered the lower floor with enormous force, making it impossible for my mother to reach the safety of the stairs.

The Technical Emergency Service rescued us later with a tub docking at the back window of the upper apartment. When the water began to fall, my mother was recovered dead in the back room of the lower flat. My mother, Auguste Grewe, had become a victim of this senseless tragedy at the age of seventy-eight."

About her recovery **Walter Schuhmacher** says: "With a tub we reached the back side of the Grewe house, the current was pushing. In the stable corner we provisionally moored the boat and looked through the window of the ground floor apartment. In the room a bed was floating around which we poked with our paddles. Suddenly a hand came out from under the bed frame. After it was certain to us that the woman could no longer be alive, we tied a rope around her hand and with the boat pulled the departed to the shore."

The Viaduct of Herdecke Collapses

Ulrich Hake, at that time a man in the Reich Labour Service on his return to his unit in Lippstadt:

"As scheduled, the passenger train number 1435 departed on 17 May 1943 at 1.30pm from Platform 5 of Hagen Main Station towards Dortmund South. I was sitting in a Prussian compartment with many doors and looked through the window, when the train drove in a wide curve onto the Herdecke railway viaduct at around twenty kilometres per hour. Suddenly a pillar collapsed, the tracks sagged down with a swing. I tore open the door and jumped down the embankment rolling from the moving train. A female conductor had also jumped off the train which almost simultaneously came to a halt. Passengers had pulled the emergency break. So the train stopped on the first third of the viaduct. The railway staff let the passengers of the first car alight, and they slowly returned to the beginning of the bridge following the train.

For about an hour the train was standing in this position, while the staff conferred what to do. Finally the engine very slowly pushed the waggons back onto the tracks, so that the still vibrating viaduct was not exposed to further tremors. After we had gotten on board again, the reverse journey continued towards Hagen Main Station. By detours I reached my destination Lippstadt and got into trouble with my superior due to the delay. Today I still experience a feeling of unrest when I travel over the Herdecke railway viaduct."

Wilhelm Duhme, on the move as a linesman:

"Due to the pressure of the flood waters the viaduct was vibrating. I was just approaching the next breaking point on my inspection round, when a pillar collapsed. So I ran towards the passenger train approaching from Hagen which at that moment had stopped on the viaduct. Probably the train driver had the order to go slowly and had seen the collapse of the viaduct."

On 19 May 1943 a British reconnaissance plane managed to take this picture of the destroyed railway viaduct of Herdecke, fifty-six kilometres downriver of the Möhne reservoir. King George VI looked at this picture through a stereoscope with particular interest. Through spatial impact and perspective, the railway tracks casting their shadow, swinging freely from pillar to pillar, probably conveyed a strong impression of the force of the disaster in the Ruhr valley.

The viaduct was inaugurated in 1879 on the Hagen–Dortmund South line. It was 31.5m tall and 314m long, and it had eleven freestanding pillars and two tracks. The 120 million cubic metres of drained Möhne water toppled over the fifth pillar, including its arch.

On 17 May 1943, the driver of passenger train no. 1435 had this view of the two-track Herdecke viaduct. The train had left the Hagen main station for Dortmund South on schedule at 1.30pm. A disaster almost occurred on this spot. Shortly before the yawning void, the train was brought to a halt.

Lower Ruhr Valley

Near Hirsel in the Ruhr valley, the one-track railway line has been destroyed.

One hundred kilometres downriver of the Möhne reservoir, the flood still possessed the enormous strength to topple this locomotive of a freight train off the tracks.

At a distance of 135km from the origin of the disaster, the Möhne floods destroyed the Obergraben dam at the Kahlenberg power station in Mühlheim/ Ruhr (4,500kW output). With the force and rapidity of a natural disaster the floods befell the landscapes and populations in the valleys of Möhne, Ruhr, Eder and Fulda during the night of 17 May 1943. A balance sheet of the total damage amounting to hundreds of millions of Reich mark has never been drawn up. In most cases, state compensations were never paid out.

Lotte Buerstätte, schoolgirl, on the train:

"The train, already travelling at walking speed, was overcrowded, and I remember it as being very long. We schoolgirls did not know what had happened during the night. The fellow passengers seemed very restless, and all at once we saw an overwhelming, horrific view outside: a vast tumult of water, raging, gurgling, filled with trees, roofs and animals. Then an exclamation in the compartment; through the window we saw the bulk of a pillar crashing into this tumultuous flood. Foam sprayed upwards, the train stood still, and we jumped out of the compartment and ran, ran and ran along the embankment towards the front of the viaduct."

Gertrud Caspari, travelling to Dortmund:

"The train stopped with a jerk. Excited voices called from car to car: 'Viaduct collapsed'. Almost fifty years later I only remember that I said to myself: 'My god, we have been lucky.' The compartment in which I was travelling stood at a spot where shrubs obscured the view of the viaduct."

The Deluge Races through the Eder Valley

One hour after the breaking of the Möhne dam the Eder dam experienced the same fate, and the night of terror and horror also began in the Eder valley.

Werner Salz described the night of the disaster at the Eder dam in a filmed statement:

"In May 1943 I was working as a shop fitter at the power stations Hemfurth I and Hemfurth II situated directly below the retaining wall. As it was customary at that time, the older village youths went for walks of a Sunday evening. When we returned across the dam around 11.30pm, we met people who had taken part in an air raid assembly in House Bergmann in Hemfurth. There it still had been explained to the inquiring citizens that it was impossible to destroy the dam lying nestled between the mountains. The Eder Lake was full to capacity. When the wind drove the waves against the wall, they overspilled into the valley. At home I soon retired for the night.

At around 1am, an air raid alarm woke me with a start. Immediately after, planes were circling over Hemfurth like never before. I stood up and went up a hill near our house. Four-motor planes flew so low between the mountains that we could see the crews in the cockpits by the light of the moon. The engine noise must have actually warned the population: tonight the Eder dam is at stake. A bomber approached the retaining wall again and again with upturned headlights. That did not bode well.

Around 1.30am the first heavy bomb was dropped into the reservoir. With the third explosion there was a ringing inside the ground. I felt a jerk travelling through the road, for me a sign that the dam had been hit. Immediately after, the rushing of the water commenced. I only thought: 'Now our power station is gone.'

I then immediately ran to the village of Hemfurth. Houses near the Eder had already been enclosed by the water. People were running for their lives, many were looking for their families. I then ran back to the retaining wall to see how large the breach in the dam was; an enormous hole, thundering masses of water, a catastrophe. I worried about my colleagues, for the night shift was maintained by four people. Did they drown? At dawn, when it gradually became light, it could be observed that two men on the rooftop of the switch room of the power station Hemfurth I sent light signals. A machinist had escaped via the stairway of the power station. In the morning the other two colleagues were brought down from the switch room's rooftop with ladders.

The fourth, the machinist Jakob Kurtz of Geismar, was missing. Probably he fled into the basement and was swept away by the penetrating water. His corpse wasn't found until August, when excavation work was carried out at the turbine exit channel of Hemfurth I and he was discovered beneath the rubble."

Emma Becker in a conversation in front of a film camera:

"I had visited an air raid assembly in House Bergmann that evening. The air defence director assured us emphatically: 'The dam will never be hit,' and: 'Who leaves the shelter during the alarm is a traitor to the fatherland.' So I was sitting in the air raid shelter of my neighbour Kohl with my two children, together with women and children from the neighbourhood, as always during an air raid alarm.

Suddenly Mr. Kohl who had stayed outside shouted: 'Everybody: quickly leave the basement, up the mountain near Beckers, it is rushing, the dam has been hit!' All nineteen of us raced from the basement. I held my boy's hand. Behind the house I was missing my daughter Waltraud. 'She has run upstairs inside the house', the boy said.

I ran back to the house and dragged her after myself like a sack. Then I saw as the first wave of water, about six metres tall and white as snow, approached across the playing field. We ran up the hill behind our house. A pasture fence blocked our way. We lifted the children over it and pulled and tore at the wire, while the flood caught up with us. What a miracle, suddenly the fence parted, we were saved. People called: 'Lie down, planes are coming really low, they are shooting!' We continued running, wet to the bone. The Bergmanns opened their door for us, so we could warm ourselves."

Private Telephone Warnings Help to Save Human Lives

The mayor of Hemfurth, **Wilhelm Ochse**, had heard the heavy detonations.

When the rushing of water started in the valley, he had the presence of mind to call the post office in Affoldern from his private telephone, but did not get a connection at first. Thereupon he called his relative, the master painter Heck in Affoldern, and gave a disaster warning. Heinz, the son of the family, and his friend Heinz Sölzer, cycled through the village to raise the alarm.

Eder Lake dam

The merchant Fritz Fisseler served as an armoured infantryman in the Wehrmacht. He was on leave in Nieder-Werbe, when the Eder dam was bombed. The event alarmed the scared villagers, especially since they saw the water level of the lake dropping noticeably. Fritz Fisseler mounted his motorbike, a 980cm Fichtel and Sachs model, and drove along the nine kilometres of lakeside road to the dam, equipped with his 6.5 by 11 centimetres folding camera. Still unimpeded by road blocks, he took this crystal clear picture of the dam breach. Due to the excitement stirred up by this dramatic sight he forgot to wind up the film for further shots and thus ruined the other negatives by double exposure. Fearing police investigations, Fisseler had the film privately developed by acquaintances.

Only thirty-two hours after the attack on the Eder dam, a long-distance reconnaissance plane of the 592nd Squadron managed to document the breach in the Eder barrage during imaging flight no. 590. The breach in the curved dam is clearly visible due to the shadow it is casting.

During the attack, the approach of the Lancaster bombers led across the wooded tip of the Hammerberg in the foreground. The water level in the Eder Lake has dropped considerably, the loamy banks and the rock formations of the Hammerberg have appeared. At the top, next to the dam, lies the village of Hemfurth. The Eder valley is completely flooded by water.

On 16 May 1943 at 8am the lake level showed a height of 244.96 metres above sea level. This corresponded to a capacity of 200.2 million cubic metres of water. The water level was four centimetres below overspill.

On 17 May 1943 at 9am the level was at 234.6m above sea level: seven hours after the breaking of the dam the water in the Eder Lake had fallen by 10.4 metres and 106 million cubic metres were still held by the lake. At 10.55am another twelve million tons of water had streamed through the gap, and the capacity amounted to 94.5 million cubic metres. Around 5pm there were just 72.4 million cubic metres of water left. On 19 May 1943 roughly 40 million cubic metres of water were dammed up in front of the breach.

On 17 May 1943, Anton Riedinger photographed the broken Eder dam from a Fieseler Storch plane, thus beating the British recon competition. Admittedly he could take his pictures at low-level flight, while the British had to deploy their Spitfire reconnaissance planes at 9,000m altitude. Thundering and foaming, the water rushed into the valley, bringing death and ruin to the quiet Eder valley.

The force of the falling water created a gouge of ten metres depth in the bedrock in front of the dam. Some of the closing units for emergency release were damaged by the second hit on the north side. The water is escaping in torrents of spray.

View from the Michelskopf to the flooded Eder valley; despite the few cameras in private possession, lack of film and a total ban on the photography of war damage, a few amateurs managed to get close to the origin of the catastrophe. Today we are grateful to these, mostly anonymous, photographers, for their illustrative documents, revealing the horrible and miserable truths that those in power wanted to keep hidden. The attack was planned amidst the greatest secrecy in England, and the disasters declared a 'secret Reich matter' in Germany. After the brief mention in the report of the High Command of the Armed Forces on the "damage to two reservoirs", veritable inspection tours of the disaster zones commenced.

The damaged sites were blocked off by the police. The cameras and films of curious onlookers were confiscated, and their owners interrogated. In the local press notices like the following were published: "Onlookers are not permitted access; unnecessary trips to the Eder valley are strictly forbidden." On 19 May 1943, Colonel of the SS Karl Burk, commander of the SS anti-aircraft training and reserve regiment Arolsen, had complained to the general headquarters in Kassel about too many curious onlookers who were impeding the rescue measures. The SS commander had arrived in the early morning as the first official on site, with his operational staff to be deployed for rescue missions in the disaster zone of the Eder reservoir.

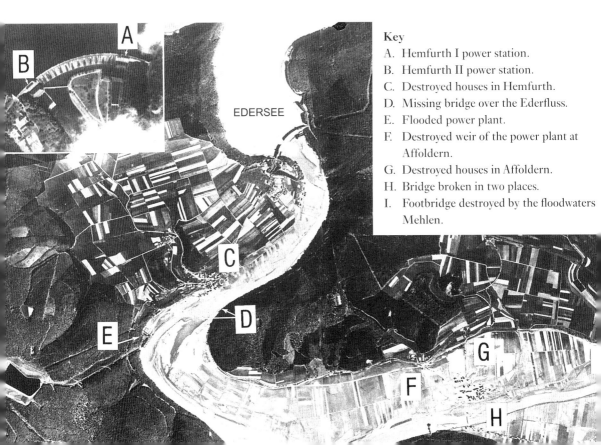

EDERSEE

Key
A. Hemfurth I power station.
B. Hemfurth II power station.
C. Destroyed houses in Hemfurth.
D. Missing bridge over the Ederfluss.
E. Flooded power plant.
F. Destroyed weir of the power plant at Affoldern.
G. Destroyed houses in Affoldern.
H. Bridge broken in two places.
I. Footbridge destroyed by the floodwaters Mehlen.

The village of Affoldern, the morning after the disaster, totally cut off from the outside world by the floods.

Above: Seemingly undamaged, in locked position, the closing units of the emergency releases at the waterside of the wall.

Above Right: The measuring unit, weighing several tons and constructed in order to keep tabs on the water level at the equalising pond at the Eder reservoir, is undermined and listing to one side. The water level was nine times higher than the highest known flood level of the Eder. Lower lying parts of Hemfurth, below the retaining wall, were turned into a stone desert by the raging sea. Sixty-eight people drowned in the area between the Eder Lake and the city of Kassel. The death toll was considerably lower here than in the Möhne and Ruhr valleys, as fewer people were living in the Eder valley, and as private telephone warnings had worked, in part.

The flooded Eder valley near Lieschenruh. In the background, the village of Affoldern.

A harrowing picture from Mehlen: drowned cattle are loaded onto trucks to be transported to the abattoirs. In Bergheim and Affoldern a shift of the real estate situations occurred through the flooding, and thus completely new interconnections between the various plots of land arose. In Affoldern more than 200 individual conveyances for the land registry were needed to legally convert the old status quo into new property relations.

Wilhelm Schätte, the director of the post office in Affoldern, was standing in front of the house with his wife and children, when the telephone rang inside. Due to the excitement and agitation in the village, Schätte's daughter and son had already fled towards the saving hills of Buhlen. Meanwhile the door to the hallway had slammed shut, and the key was inside. So Wilhelm Schätte climbed through an open window into the post office and seized the receiver. Mayor Ochse from Hemfurth announced: 'The water is coming, the Eder dam is broken, warn the village and relay the alarm!' which ensued.

In Bad Wildungen postmaster **Paul Danzglock** had seen the lightning bolts of the explosions near the Eder reservoir, shortly after the detonations trundled across. The civil servant hastened back to the post office. In the yard he heard the telephone ringing inside, unlocked the door, ran to the apparatus and heard a voice: 'Here is Schätte, Affoldern, the wall is hit, and the water is already coming.' Then, after an interlude of rumbling, the line went dead. Paul Danzglock immediately informed the police in Fritzlar and Bad Wildungen. They didn't want to believe him however, at first. Nevertheless they relayed the disaster warning. In the meantime a rifleman, who had stood guard at the power station of the equalising pond in Affoldern, had reached Schätte's post office and given the alarm. Together with Mr. and Mrs. Schätte, he escaped onto higher ground at the last moment. Two people following them drowned in the broiling sea.

Heinz Wiesemann during a taped interview:

"Here in Lieschensruh I could discern the pilots with their leather helmets inside the cockpits during the low-level flight. Tenants were living in a side room of our house. Suddenly there was a noise as if a chair had been moved. Nobody imagined that the Eder dam could possibly have been destroyed. When I looked out of the window, I saw in the distance a spray of water. I said to Mother: 'They are fogging up the valley.' There had been fogging installations before. My room was upstairs, looking towards Affoldern. Tired from the night shift, I was about to retire when I heard screams under the window. I said to my mother: 'There are drunks outside, come shouting from Buhlen Station.' Afterwards it turned out that they were people from Affoldern on the run.

Suddenly I heard my neighbour calling: 'Heinrich, out, I think the water is coming.' In the living room my father ripped a drawer with papers out of the cabinet, then we hastened through the garden, I dressed in gym clothes, through the water, up a nearby hill. Then a giant wave, around four metres tall, approached like a hay cart, mowing through the valley.

A horse manger with three horses tied to it drifted past. Now night settled in in earnest, my view was shrouded by mist. We could not see our hands in front of our faces. We walked along the railway embankment to Buhlen Station. In a room above the waiting lounge around thirty to forty refugees from Affoldern were sitting. Some were crying because they had lost relatives.

At 4.30 I returned. Our house was poking out of the water, but had withstood. The water was standing up to thirty centimetres below my bedroom window on the first floor. Two ducks swam through the branches of our tall chestnut tree. Behind the house, two mighty elms from the bridge at Affoldern were lying. They were so vast that their circumference couldn't have been embraced by two men. Rescue teams with storm boats searched for corpses.

I saw the corpse of an elderly man from Affoldern in a muddy rye field. His beard was still soaked in water, and worms were crawling through it. Men of the Organisation Todt then restored and plastered our house. As compensation, we received a kitchen cupboard and some chairs from the state."

Aerial Situation Protocol: Air Raid Warning Centre, Kassel

Information lifted from the official protocol reports, detailing the ongoing air situation on the night of the 16/17 May 1943, from the Air Raid Warning Centre in Kassel.

Time	Report
01.11	Möhne dam hit
01.12	Warning post Waldeck reports a low-flying enemy craft
01.14	Relayed to the police for orientation
01.15	Enemy aircraft above the Eder reservoir
01.17	Waldeck reports the dropping of red flares, probable attack on the Eder dam
01.25	Red flare bomb above the Eder reservoir
01.30	Four four-motor craft circling low above the Eder reservoir
01.32	Aircraft above the Eder reservoir
01.36	Waldeck, planes are circling over the reservoir
01.41	Aerial situation unchanged
01.43	Two four-motor craft above the dam
01.45	Smoke emission above the dam (Maudslay's failed drop?)
01.53	Two four-motor craft above the dam
02.04	Four-motor aircraft in the Waldeck area
02.05	Light above the dam
02.18	Enemy aircraft from the Eder lake area on return flight towards the north-west
02.35	One enemy craft is circling in the Marburg/Lahn area (Maudslay?)
02.36	Bad Wildungen from the warning post Mauser Works Waldeck: Affoldern is under water, houses are collapsing
02.12	Dam of the Eder reservoir hit
03.14	Aerial situation in the area settled down, west of Arnsberg-Münster, minor enemy activity

Anti-aircraft Batteries at British Dams

To come to the point: Winston Churchill's memoirs contain neither any information on the nature of the weapon used in "Operation Chastise" nor its assault tactics. At the time of the publication of these ten volumes in 1947-1953, the weapon used was still top secret. Only a brief

Christian Tilenius of the Reich Air Ministry photographed the flooded Eder valley near Bergheim from his plane. In the foreground the destroyed road bridge can be seen, behind it the torso of the railway bridge. Large patches of water are still standing in the fields.

Mehlen, Waldecker Street: in the early morning citizens of the place – women, old men, children and Hitler Youth members – follow the support measures at the destroyed houses in the background.

The railway bridge on the Bad Wildungen – Korbach/Brilon line between Giflitz and Bergheim has not withstood the water pressure. Elisabeth Schröder recalls: "A white wheel rolled against the edifice; suddenly the railway tracks flew into the air in a shower of sparks, and sections of the bridge collapsed."

The diaspora church of the 'Independent Evangelical Lutheran Church' in Bergheim defied the floods.

'Official Notice' at the railway station of Giflitz in May 1943: "Whosoever plunders will be punished by death!"

FLUGPLATZ FRITZLAR

On 18 May 1943 a British long-distance reconnaissance plane of the 592nd Squadron captured the Eder valley and the Fritzlar region section by section in a series of shots from a great height. The remaining bridge over the Eder in the town centre is clearly visible. The airfield of the German air force is completely flooded. Beyond the Eder raid the hangars are full of water, the barracks damaged, and the runway has become inoperative.

Rescue boats are in operation, the house walls mark the water level. At that time the airbase was not occupied by planes in operation.

Officers inspect the damage to the Fritzlar airfield.

Under the NSDAP emblem, the funeral for the flood victims took place on Friday, 21 May 1943, at 2pm at Fritzlar cemetery with intense involvement by the population. The memorial service was split into two denominations. Eight citizens of Fritzlar met with a watery death. After the district leader and the mayor, the Catholic parish priest and the Protestant dean Hans Scheffen spoke to their respective flocks. War had now most emphatically arrived in Fritzlar.

In Zennern near Fritzlar young men of the National Labour Service, working in aid of the disaster recovery effort, carry one of the flood victims to his grave. In the background, the Protestant church.

Wabern, on Wilhelm-Dilich Street: in front of the Reformed Evangelical parish church, two stunned citizens are standing in the floods. "From where is all this water coming? How could this happen?" Rescue teams with rubber crafts were deployed for rescue missions in Wabern as well.

Between Grifte and Wolfershausen, the railway bridge over the Eder was destroyed by the flood and thus the main line Kassel – Frankfurt/ Main (Main – Weser line) interrupted. The distance from the damage site to the Eder dam measures around forty-five kilometres, to Kassel twenty kilometres.

18 May 1943, Kassel as seen in an English aerial photograph, a sensational picture that was picked up by many British newspapers, gracing many front pages in the daily press. Clearly visible as the grey streak of water, the Fulda with the flooded areas in the low-lying districts of the city: 1. Karlsaue; 2. Karls' Meadow; 3. The Orangery and the Marble Bath; 4. Unterneustadt; 5. Flooded areas in Wolfsanger. On 17 May, at around 10am, the Eder flood wave reached Kassel. The flood rose until 3pm with devastating effects. From 7pm, the water level began to fall.

Enclosed by the brown floods of the Fulda, the Orangery and the Marble Bath in Kassel; as several hours passed between the report of the destruction at the Eder dam and the arrival of the flood wave, some preventive measures could be taken. During the night, flood warnings were relayed to those living in the endangered city districts; valuables could be retrieved from basements and lower floors and brought to higher ground. Many affected people put up resistance against the eviction orders. Besides the damage to military and industrial installations 1,130 residential buildings were slightly or moderately damaged.

Rescue operation with a pioneers' bateau on Flower Street in Hannoversch-Münden at the Werra.

Karlshagen is 139km away from the Eder reservoir. Citizens row in a boat to the milkman on Weser Street.

In Herstelle a flood billboard documents the highest levels of the Weser at 8.56cm on 18 May.

Curiously, the people merely look at the great flood in these images that belie the horrors of the catastrophe.

passage in the first volume can be found, in which Churchill relays instructions given to the authorities in charge, dated 17 May 1943, to inform him of the protection of British reservoirs undertaken against air strikes in the manner carried out by the RAF against the West German dams. This is the British Prime Minister's only clue to "Operation Chastise" in his memoirs. Immediately after the results of the attacks on the German reservoirs had been analysed, the Ministry of Defence investigated the vulnerability and importance of the reservoirs, dams and locks in their own country, in consultation with the special departments and experts. Hereby it was not forgotten that from now on the enemy would be fixated on water.

As in Germany, the focus now shifted to the air defence of reservoirs in Great Britain as well. Thirty-six 40mm guns and forty-eight spotlights were installed at the Sheffield reservoir, four guns and six spotlights at the King George Reservoir, twelve batteries with twelve spotlights at the Queen Mary Reservoir. Damage to these three reservoirs would not mean a significant loss to the industry, but it would have the gravest consequences for London's supply of drinking water. As in Germany, alternative measures of defence were thought of: balloon barrages, fogging installations with additional blinding effects at night, and mine fields in the lake which were supposed to throw up sixty-five metre tall columns of water with catastrophic effects on low-flying planes.

The aerial photographic reconnaissance for the collection of the necessary data was initiated at once to find the best positions for the anti-aircraft batteries and spotlights. The danger posed to the London Underground, used extensively as a network of air-raid shelters, from flooding as a result of bombing, had not changed. The risk remained high, throughout the remainder of the war. Investigations aimed to record the extent of resulting damage, in the event of a dam breach. They were carried out with an eye on the likelihood of population survival and the consequences of water shortage impeding industry and daily life. The question arose as to whether the great expenditure necessary in order to protect the reservoirs of Britain would be too high, in exchange for success against the German dams.

8 June, Churchill once again queried the protection of British reservoirs, stating his wish that a memorandum on the protection of the dams and reservoirs of the United Kingdom be printed as a note and distributed amongst the cabinet.

"Upkeeps" for Moscow? No Bouncing Bombs for Marshal Josef Stalin

On 1 June 1943 the Air Ministry in Whitehall, London, received an encrypted telegram from "Mission 30" Moscow. The Soviet general staff of navy and air force inquired after all the details of the successful RAF attacks on the Möhne and Eder dams. The Soviets showed great interest in this operation and potentially wanted to execute similar attacks. On the following points they wished to have all the information:

1. Complete description of the weapon used.
2. Number of bombs carried by the aircraft.
3. Number of planes needed for each reservoir.

4. Tactics of approach and method of deployment of mine or torpedo.
5. Structural details of the Möhne and Eder dams.
6. Evaluation of the damage to the individual dams including all available photographs.

The answers to these questions should be sent to the Soviet Union with the next courier plane. On 2 June 1943 the Chief of the General Staff of the RAF, Sir Charles Portal, reported the Soviets' desire to the committee and offered two alternatives: either we present the desired information and say that the Soviets shall not use it, or we say to them that we ourselves intend to further use the weapon and are not prepared to give information on this project, until the operation during which it shall be deployed has been carried out. Sir Dudley Pound pointed to the great potential dangers of the Soviet suggestion, concerning the secrecy and demanded time to consider. The committee agreed to postpone the decision on the telegram.

On 7 June 1943 the Soviets repeated their request and awaited delivery with the next air mail. After a short discussion, the committee decided to provide the requested information. All details and drawings might be delivered to "Mission 30" in Moscow via a secret and secure route. The Air Ministry should compile the necessary documents and make them ready for dispatch.

On 1 July 1943 Prime Minister Churchill agreed to proceed with project "Source". On the basis of this consideration, all negotiations with the Soviets regarding the "Upkeep" bouncing bombs should be postponed.

On 11 August the general staff of the RAF declared:

"Concerning your radio telegram 399 from 9 August: information will be sent as soon as possible, but we cannot say for the moment when the next air mail will depart. You should gain the greatest benefit possible from our knowledge of military technology and from this important and top secret information."

The information never reached Moscow, as it was supposed to be passed to the Soviet Union only after "Operation Highball" (mission against ships). But "Highball" wasn't utilised again for the remainder of the Second World War and nor was "Upkeep", the dam buster bomb.

In May 1991 Colonel Wjenkov, director of the historical department of the Soviet general staff in Moscow, answered the author's queries:

"Despite the best will to help you, no drawings or information on the 'bouncing bombs' can be found in the war archives of the USSR. Furthermore, no document of such an agreement can be found either. It is a certainty that deliveries of blueprints relating to the bouncing bomb were top secret. Therefore, no information relating to the talks was entered into our archive because it was subject to the highest levels of confidentiality. We regret that we are unable to give you a better answer. Nevertheless, we wish you good luck with your interesting research.
Colonel Wjenkov

In addition, US Air Force General Arnold required construction plans relating to "Upkeep" and "Highball". In principle, no objections could be made to the handover, as the Americans had already received the permission of Bomber Command to access technical drawings and related information.

Test installations should be mounted on US aircraft and filled model bombs should be sent to. Material Command Wright Field FAO Weapons Research Laboratory, namely in crates with specific markings in compliance with all manners of security measures. "Highball" had to be kept top secret so that the enemy would not use it against the ships of the allied forces. As "Highball" never achieved readiness for series production, however, no prototypes of the bouncing bombs were delivered to the Americans.

Speculations about the Restoration of the Dams at Möhne and Eder

After the successful attack on the reservoirs, the British military asked themselves how long it would take to rebuild the destroyed barrages and to fill the drained reservoirs with water.

The quickly initiated repair works did not remain hidden from aerial reconnaissance. The French resistance reported to London the withdrawal of thousands of men of the Organisation Todt from the Atlantic Wall for deployment in the German disaster zones and reservoirs, a sign of the importance of the reservoirs in Germany.

On 28 June 1943 a scientific advisor in the Air Ministry believed he had found a clue that could potentially explain the delays impacting upon the restoration of the Mohne dam: "I think it would be very useful, if detailed enlargements of the aerial photographs from before and after the attack on the Möhne dam could be made once more, especially if they were enlarged. There is the suspicion that the remainder of the foundations between the two Möhne dam towers may have shifted fifty-five centimetres down the valley.

Perhaps this shift is the result of distortion to the photographic paper, caused by gluing it onto a background. This possibility certainly exists. However, the movement of the foundation actually goes in the direction expected by us. To estimate the time for the restoration of the Möhne dam, more detailed examinations would be worthwhile. Would it also be possible to measure the gap in the Eder dam at the same time, by means of aerial photography, before and after the attack?

If the foundations had indeed been shifted, such a prompt restoration of the dam would not have been possible. The author writes about the rebuilding of the destroyed dams in his book "Als Deutschlands Dämme brachen" (Motorbuch Publishing Stuttgart).

An Open Balance: Statement on Losses and Damage

On 9 June 1943, the Higher SS and Police Leader of the government of Westphalia, Hanover, the governors of the Rhine provinces and the Reich governors in Lippe and Schaumburg-Lippe in the military district VI Munster, along with the Commander of the uniformed police, compiled the following overview of losses and damage during the Mohne disaster, according to the reports made so far:

Losses in life:

Identified German dead	403
Unidentified German dead	73
Missing German persons	60
Foreign dead	593
Missing foreign persons	156

Farms:

Totally damaged	6
Severely damaged	8
Moderately damaged	3
Slightly damaged	15

Losses in cattle:

Large cattle	571
Calves	7
Pigs	625
Small cattle	5113
Beehives	33

Crop damage:

Fields, meadows and pastures in total	4,073 hectare

Damage to property:

Residential houses completely damaged	95
Residential houses severely damaged	248
Residential houses moderately damaged	134
Residential houses slightly damaged	589

Factories:

Completely damaged	11
Severely damaged	41
Moderately damaged	40
Slightly damaged	33

Damages to bridges:

Railway bridges completely damaged	7
Railway bridges severely damaged	2
Road bridges completely damaged	18
Road bridges severely damaged	7
Road bridges slightly damaged	12

These preliminary statistics are largely incomplete. The damage to dams, power stations, water plants, sewage works, railway lines etc. is missing.

From the flooded areas of Eder, Fulda and Weser only a few imprecise damage reports exist. The Waterways and Shipping Office Hannoversch-Münden registers sixty-eight dead by the Eder flood.

A situation report from 19 May 1943 to the district president in Kassel lists the following damage in the Waldeck district: 103 buildings and fifteen farms destroyed, and damage to crops and roads not yet possible to survey. The village of Affoldern has been particularly badly affected. Here alone twelve drowned were recovered, seventy-five buildings destroyed, all food and fodder spoilt, 200 animals defined as 'large cattle' and 250 pigs have drowned, as well as forty horses. Thirty-one dead have been recovered (including the village of Affoldern).

District Fritzlar: 365 houses severely, 160 houses slightly damaged, three road and two railway bridges destroyed, very severe damage to crops. Losses in cattle, seventy large cattle animals and 500 sheep, so far four reported missing, water supply mostly impaired.

Town of Fritzlar: so far one drowned, eight missing (among them two Poles), another six persons missing from the Fritzlar airfield, water supply impaired, electrical light supply and telecommunication still disrupted.

District Melsungen: Many residential and farm buildings considerably damaged, 1,000 hectare of agricultural land flooded, three dead.

District Kassel: severe damage to crops, insignificant damage to property.

Town of Kassel: 17 May 1943, water level fell noticeably from 10pm onwards, municipal districts in the flooding area very silted up, water supply increasing during the course of 18 May 1943 from fifty per cent to eighty-three per cent. With the exception of shutting down the electricity for the tram and the Henschel company (only for a few hours), the supply of electricity is not disrupted, two alarm devices impaired, a number of half-timbered houses damaged in varying degrees. Considerable damage to crops, gardens and parks, especially severe devastation to roads (foremost Dam Street along the Fulda), one member of the fire police and one of the air raid precaution police drowned due to the capsizing of a bateau, around 1,900 persons homeless (among them also foreigners).

The vast material damage to buildings, fields, bridges, dams and railway installations by the Eder flood resulted in costs of millions of Reich mark. In fact, these sums were enough to surpass the damages caused by the Mohne flood.

Corresponding to the extent of the disasters, everywhere in the flooded areas support measures of all the rescue and clean-up services commenced. The district commissioner of Melsungen ordered the following immediate measures for the affected communities Niedermöllrich, Lohre, Altenburg, Harle, Rhünde, Felsberg, Gensungen, Böddinger, Neuenbrunslar, Altenbrunslar and Wolferhausen: "18 May 1943. All inhabitants aged between fourteen and sixty years of age, who are not directly affected by the Eder disaster in house or farm and who are not participating in external labour service, will be immediately assembled into gangs of ten to twenty men or women.

Reconstruction of the Möhne dam

As early as 18 May, the highest authorities decided to restore the Möhne reservoir as quickly as possible by all means available because of its decisive significance for the Ruhr area. The water masses had torn a gouge, eight metres deep, into the bedrock in front of the wall. The Ruhr Reservoir Society, owner of the barrage, was given the technical planning and the position of construction management with full responsibility. The Organisation Todt took on the execution of the construction tasks.

The construction site viewed from the water side.

The Organisation Todt, as representatives of the Third Reich, took on the task of bringing in building materials and developing construction companies with their machines, labourers and specialists.

At the Möhne dam, the companies Heinrich Butzler, Kehl & Co and others collaborated with labourers from France, Belgium, Holland and Germany. Many foreigners who had, in part, been redeployed from the Atlantic Wall with their firms, worked as volunteers, as they were often unemployed in their home countries or had joined the labour service in Germany.

View of the northern side of the breach in the 'Möhne dam quarry'

By 28 May, the clear-up had begun. The bottom of the breach had been washed away down to the hale core masonry and did not require further demolition. In contrast the two flanks of the breach, especially the northern side, showed that the masonry had been loosened and worn to a significant length and a considerable depth. Masonry still standing showed cracks and fissures.

On 9 July 6,950 cubic metres of unsound masonry had been removed. Only then could the rebuild begin in earnest. For safety reasons it was decided not to install a concrete seal inside the breach, as cracks in the joints or ones caused by shrinkage might have appeared. In order to prevent sabotage, only German masons were supposed to be employed at first. However, as only fifty construction craftsmen were currently available, further dry stone masons and miners were drafted in from Carinthia and Italy. They worked as freelance specialists with contracts.

The highest number of labourers employed on a single day amounted to 2,192 men, among them 748 French, 460 Germans, 441 Dutch, 340 Italians, 183 Belgians and twenty other foreigners. Thus the ratio between Germans and foreigners was 1:4. All had social security; their wages were paid by the local construction companies according to the tariff in force. The companies settled up with the headquarters of the Organisation Todt in Berlin. Later, deployed military internees (after the Badoglio putsch in Italy) were considered prisoners.

View of the southern side of the breach

The former chief of the OT headquarters in Berlin, construction engineer Xaver Dorsch, reported to the US Historical Division in March 1950: "The worst set-back was suffered by the building program of the OT Task Force West (Atlantic Wall, submarine bunkers), when the RAF succeeded in destroying the two great barrages of Möhne and Eder.

In summary it has to be noted here that the German military leadership would consider the war as lost if they did not succeed in rebuilding the dams as quickly as possible. The OT task force therefore received the order to transfer firms with their workers, tools and vehicles by the shortest route to the Reich, without regard to any possible losses to its own program, which consisted of the full extent of its new construction team (7,000 men). In terms of organisation, the rebuilding of the dams heralded a special era. The Organisation Todt is deployed on home territory, which was originally not intended." So far Xaver Dorsch.

As the utilisation of steel tube scaffolding was not possible due to cut-backs borne of the war economy, wooden transport scaffolding had to be used. As a precaution, a complete section of scaffolding was kept ready on the carpenters' square, to serve as a replacement after the event of a possible air raid. Revolving tower cranes and elevators delivered the building materials from the water side. On the 2 and 5 August, two fatal accidents occurred, killing French labourers Henry Hautefeuille and Rene Decaunes'.

Initially the German workers were lodged in the function room of the hotel Möhne Terraces, with foreigners lodged in the summer hall of hotel Seehof and in the shooting club Delecke, until residential and other barracks were erected. The provisions for the vast labour assignment were supplied by the OT stores and the army food offices Unna and Soest.

Despite the threat of air raids, work went on, even during the night under flood lights. The stone blocks came from a depot in the Bergisches Land and were actually intended for the construction of motorway bridges. Each stone had been cleaned using a high-pressure water device. The Ruhr-Lippe narrow-gauge railway performed brilliantly: one hundred freight cars with a capacity of 2,200 tons of building material arrived daily at 'Möhne Lake' station.

About one hundred Dutch carpenters built this giant wooden 'spider web', a masterpiece of carpentry. The transport scaffolding on the water side of the dam reached a height of 26.5 metres, as tall as an eight-storey house.

For security reasons, to prevent sabotage, spot checks on the material used were carried out repeatedly. Special attention was given to the mortar. Here a concrete sample is measured on a vibrating table. On the basis of existing experience and evaluations a so-called three-material binder of the TUBAG Company in Andernach was used as mortar.

The closing of the breach nears its completion with the finishing of the road surface.

"Quadruplets", an accurate defence weapon against low-flying planes

On 3 October 1943 the Möhne reservoir received distinguished guests. Armaments Minister Speer, also chief of Organisation Todt, gave a speech in front of the men of the OT including, amongst their number, 'construction soldiers', on the occasion of the renewed inauguration of the dam, the largest rebuilding operation during the Second World War in Germany. The closing of the breaches in the Möhne and Eder dams had been completed in record time (seventy-nine days at the Möhne dam).

After a tour by Speer, with task force leader Adam and the construction director of the Ruhr Reservoir Society Dr Prüss, he distributed praise and decorations among deserving men of the Organisation Todt.

OT chief Speer, senior site manager Quast and main site manager Voigt from the Eder dam listen to the leader of the task force 'Adam' reading a telegram by Hitler. On the left behind Voigt, we see Xaver Dorsch, director of the Operation Todt headquarters in Berlin.

In a photo album of the Organisation Todt, the speech of the Reich Minister is documented besides the construction phase. On 24 September 1943, six days before the set date, the gap in the wall was closed, and the refilling of the great 'water tower Möhne Lake' for the Ruhr area commenced. The rapid rebuilding of the dam, doubted by many, was a brilliant achievement on a logistic and technical level by all the engineers, construction companies and workforces involved, given the war situation.

On 29 September 1943 site manager W. Hennig made as a memento this etching of the valley side of the construction site with the scaffolding for the crane track, elevator tower and cranes. The mends in the dams of Möhne and Eder were still visible for decades.

Task force leader Adam later distributed some photocopies of the Hitler telegram of 2 October 1943 from the Leader's headquarters.

A triple chain of torpedo nets, attached to buoys of the navy, now protecting the dam.

Sea mines are waiting on the shore for their deployment.

From two one hundred metre tall steel posts, a curtain of steel rope is hung across the Möhne Lake. The 'plane catcher', 500m away from the dam, is furnished with 3.5kg contact mines.

Immediately after the end of the war, Barnes Wallis flew several times over the Möhne dam in low-level flight, to take film shots of his 'target'. He noted in his diary: "The Möhne dam is a great disappointment, a death valley lies before it". After his landing, he drove immediately to the Möhne wall and interviewed eye witnesses about the nocturnal air raid in the Seehof hotel.

On the valley side, bomb nets protected the dam against unwanted hits. An iron curtain of seventy steel mats is supposed to detonate bombs away from the masonry. A practical test never happened. On the waterside, bouncing bomb deflectors are installed underwater, attached to buoys. These were supposed to detonate the bouncing bombs away from the wall.

On the north tower of the Möhne dam the US soldiers find a wooden battery dummy directed towards the lakeside. It was installed by the air defence soldiers to deceive enemy aerial reconnaissance. At the approach of the western front, the air defence soldiers had retreated to the protection of the Arnsberg forest in the Ruhr basin.

7 April 1945: vanguards of the 8th US Tank Division reached the Möhne reservoir. From the north tower an American war correspondent photographed the Möhne dam, which had become famous in his homeland as well, due to the night raid. The roofs of the wall towers have been removed, so as not to serve again as a targeting aid during an air raid. Wooden railings replace the parapet.

Sorpe Lake

The Sorpe reservoir, with its rockfill dam, including a concrete core, withstood all the bombing raids of the Second World War. The 700m long and sixty-nine metre tall barrage stored seventy million cubic metres of water.

This aerial photograph shows damage to the dam crest for a length of 120 metres, including water tracks caused by the explosions on the valley side of the dam. The small white spots are barrage balloons, of which two cast shadows onto the slope of the dam. Twenty-four barrage balloons, anti-aircraft batteries and fogging devices are now forming the air defence. Also a torpedo net is now installed in the Sorpe Lake along the dam.

Basil Feneron described, in front of the author's camera, how he experienced the second night raid of 17 May 1943 on the Sorpe dam as flight engineer in his Lancaster AJ-F, with co-pilot Ken Brown.

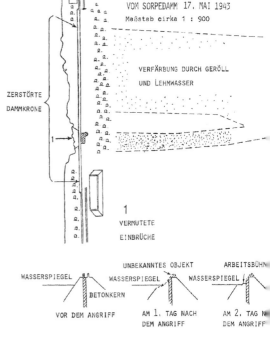

Left and Below Right: On 15 October the RAF had the Sorpe dam in their sight for the second time. Sixteen Lancasters of the 9th Squadron dropped a 5.2t "Tallboy" each from great altitude on the dam. The craters created were fifteen metres deep and thirty metres wide. The torpedo net chains are lying torn in the lake. Some bombs had time-delay fuses and detonated only sixty to ninety minutes after impact. A low water level prevented a draining of the lake.

Not all bombs exploded. In January 1959 this dud was found after the emptying of the lake and defused.

This is the only recorded German picture showing damage to the Sorpe dam from the night of 17 May 1943. Number 1 marks the impact of the bomb of the first attack. The crater is situated seven to eight metres below the roadway crown on the paved slope of the water side, around four to five metres below the water level and around forty metres away from the centre of the dam towards the southern slope of the mountain. Number 2 shows the impact of the second bomb; thirty metres away from the first bomb crater, five to six metres below the roadway crown, about two to three metres below water level. Both bombs were detonated after around ninety seconds by the self-destruction fuse, as the water at the crater sites was only a few metres deep, and as the hydrostatic fuses were set to 9.1m.

Nine barrage balloons are now protecting the dam directly. On German territory at that time there were around 220 reservoirs of which twenty-five to thirty were of the utmost importance. For these, immediate defensive measures such as anti-aircraft positions, fogging devices, balloon barrages, torpedo nets and camouflage had to be installed.

Diemel Lake

At the Diemel reservoir, sea mines of 1,000kg each are lying ready for the operation "Flowerpot". They were supposed to fling several giant water columns against low-flying bombers, when triggered by electric remote control, thus bringing them down. Many mines in the reservoirs exploded due to self-induction. In the Möhne Lake on 15 June and 29 July 1944 two explosive devices from the second defensive line detonated during a heavy thunderstorm in spite of grounding. Shortly after, two mines of the first row exploded under the same circumstances. The tremors were clearly felt on top of the dam. By this event the torpedo net chains 1 and 2 were torn apart. There were faulty explosions at the Eder Lake, too.

Trial run of an underwater detonation for the water curtain, hurled into the air by three exploding heavy sea mines, during the defensive operation "Flowerpot".

For every gang, an energetic man or woman (in a female gang) has to be assigned as leader. The mayor, as director of the local area, is responsible for the assembly and the deployment of the gangs. The gangs are considered as short-term conscripts for emergency services. Those who refuse this solidarity or defy the orders set, is immediately incorporated into a special forced gang whose supervision must be given to police officers or a reliable storm trooper, and be forced to work. All personal matters and work in one's own home has to be pushed to the background for now, until the economic life within the community takes on normal form again.

Male gangs have to be deployed in clean-up work outside the house, female gangs in cleaning the residential rooms, furniture, clothes, china and other household goods. In case of any form of failure, the mayors in charge will be held responsible and severely punished."

In Melsungen district alone the deployment of the following additional forces took place: army 851, police two, fire brigade 299, National Labour Service 1,050, political leaders eighteen, storm troopers twelve, Hitler Youth 105, League of German Girls ninety-five, National Socialist Women's League 230, National Socialist Public Welfare Organisation forty-eight, city watch twelve and country watch sixteen persons.

Legends: Treason, Sabotage, Espionage?

In Germany there were many speculations during and especially after the war about agent activity, espionage and even treason by the German military in connection with the attacks on the reservoirs. Even the Minister for Public Enlightenment and Propaganda, Dr Goebbels, expresses this suspicion in his diary. These successful night-time attacks by the British, the weak German air defence, as well as the missing protection against night fighters seemed unbelievable. During April and May of 1972, the author inquired about possible British agent activities carried out before the attacks on the reservoirs. He put his questions to Sir Barnes Wallis, who answered:

> "Concerning your query regarding agent activities before the attack, I say that we in England did not know such people. All our information was gleaned from German specialist journals such as "The Gas and Water Trade" and similar publications which are archived in the library of the 'Institution of Civil Engineers'. For our planning we assessed these publications, supported by aerial photographs from an altitude of around 9,500 metres which had been taken during the months, weeks and days before the attacks."

After the bombardment of the reservoirs there was "results espionage" from the Ruhr area, for during research in the "Public Record Office" the author found notes on the strike against the reservoirs in the diary of the RAF ("Operations Record Book"), jotted down a few days later, which could only have reached England via intelligence/radio communication. For during the war, there was no newspaper exchange with enemy and neutral states, much less with local newspapers.

In the diary of the Royal Air Force the following annotation is found on 27 May 1943 under no. 4130 in the balance sheet of the operations: the National Newspaper Essen published on 18 May 1943, a guideline that the water in Essen had to be boiled before usage. On 31 May 1943 under no. 4114 a similar sounding announcement of the Dortmund local press from 19 May is found, i.e. to boil the water due to the dangers to health from contaminated water.

One of the most inventive legends about the destruction of the Möhne dam, supported by Christian folkloric piety, was published by a Leipzig church newsletter in March 1967 under the heading "The crosses did return":

"During the Third Reich (1933-1945) the government in Germany waged war against Christianity, which so many Christians unfortunately did not recognise as a battle against Christ. In millions of humans the image of god was desecrated, in thousands of crosses, Christ himself. From the courts of law and schools, the crucifixes were removed, and in their stead the picture of the man Hitler was placed, worshipped like a god. Where to put all the crosses, however?

In the town halls or in the schools they were lying in heaps in attics and basements. So that they should no longer be accessible to anybody and would vanish forever, they were gathered onto trucks from many corners of Westphalia and slung into the hollow spaces in the immense dam of the Möhne reservoir. There, within the mighty stone wall, no man would be likely to free them. So those thought who had invented this wicked solution. And yet they have been freed. But in what terrible manner! English planes threw several torpedoes against the giant wall of the reservoir. The mighty bulwark shattered, and in the middle of the night the vast flood of one of the largest reservoirs rushed and roared with unimaginable force through villages and towns, flooded all the valleys bordering the river Rhine and swept houses and entire villages away; an horrific deluge claiming many, many people as victims. And on top of the floods, hundreds of crucifixes were floating. The bombs had liberated them from their prison, and now they swam upon the waves far into the land, floated towards the banks and shores. The crosses returned to the people."

The numerous publications, films and TV shows, even those which reported half-truth or errors, garnered a certain historical fame for the reservoirs far beyond Germany and provided unintended free advertising for tourism in these landscapes. Every year, many foreign tourists are among the visitors of the Möhne, Eder and Sorpe reservoirs.

The Hollywood Project "The Dam"

Shortly after the attacks a letter arrived at the British embassy in Washington from the "King Features Syndicate" in New York, one of the largest feature film syndicates in the USA, with the request to pass it on to the British Air Ministry in London. "No great deed in this war has elicited so much public enthusiasm as the bombardment of the Möhne and Eder dams.

There is an immense interest in the slightest information on the course of events and on Wing Commander Gibson and his men. We came up with the idea of collecting all data on the attack and its consequences. Perhaps you could send us further information in a kind of brochure. In addition we would also like to have photographs, sized at twenty by thirty centimeters, on the best quality high gloss paper, as the optimal master copy.

With regards the tremendous importance of a commercial utilisation it seems to me to be a very good thing to capture everything in documentation. The film department of the Ministry of Information may be inspired to produce a reproduction of this episode along the lines of the famous 'Zeebrügge' film made after World War I."

On 10 July 1943 a negative answer by the British Air Ministry was sent. Everything was subject to the greatest military secrecy, and except for the details already publicised, no further information was available. Military historians would gather the material and present it to the public at the appropriate time.

On 30 July 1943 another letter from the British aviation attaché in Washington arrived at the London Air Ministry: "As early as July 1943 information on the dam raids has reached Hollywood via the British embassy. The director Howard Hawks (later world-famous through several feature films, among them 'Gentlemen Prefer Blondes' with Marilyn Monroe) has a major film project in mind. He is planning to have a 100m-model of the Möhne dam built along with models of Lancaster bombers with a three metre wingspan. The costs for this alone are said to be 150,000 dollars. He needs detailed documents of anti-aircraft batteries, spotlights, balloon barrages and similar defence measures at the Möhne, the number of bombers deployed, the losses, the drops, the launch time, the number of damaged aircraft and injured. Is it possible to use the original names? Without particulars we would make a bad film. A representative of the British aviation attaché can read the script later.

The documents and photographs should be sent with the next sealed diplomatic bag to the USA. Howard Hawks wants to send his principal photographer immediately to England in order to film Lancaster bombers with their crews taking off. Please relay this telegram to the leadership of British Bomber Command."

On 9 August the encrypted answering telegram arrived with the British aviation attaché in Washington: "The British Air Ministry agrees to the Hawks project, but insists on various protocols for secrecy. It should rather be operated on a speculative basis. The Gibson report will not be made available and shall be carefully concealed." This is followed by detailed information on losses, training flights, briefing and maps with the targets as well as the names of thirty-four decorated aviators. Gibson met Hawks in Los Angeles. He wanted to assist in realising the film, when full collaboration with the British Air Ministry had been obtained. With a Lancaster from Canada, flight shots with actors in flight were supposed to be taken.

When the film script finally arrived at the London Air Ministry in November 1943, it was criticised by Squadron Leader Strachey: "I am sure that with the original documents you can make an interesting, exciting true story which the cinema goer wants to watch, and no-one in the 'Royal Air Force costume' will shudder or squirm in his seat whilst watching. I am therefore delighted that the author of the film script is coming to England to make contact with the squadron members and to take in some of the atmosphere. We can provide him with useful details from our own archives."

Barnes Wallis' judgement on the film script with the working title "The Dam":

"I was just shown the script for the film 'The destruction of the dams' which shall be made in the USA by Wing Commander Arnold from the Security Department. Apparently the permission for such a film has been given by the British aviation attaché in Washington. I have asked W.C. Arnold to show the script to Dr Pye, as I am so involved in the project and thus biased. I appear under a pseudonym in this film and am degraded to such a caricature, concerning which I am of the opinion, however, that no exceptions ought to be made for personal reasons. In my opinion the entire account is a mistreatment of the work of highly respected English scientists in general. The parading of a mad professor as the representative of the work of a large number of researchers has to be abhorrent to all of us and possibly damaging to the reputation of all scientists in England. For this reason, I wish for something to be done by the highest authorities in order to withdraw the permission previously given by the British aviation attache in Washington, or at least to insist that the scientific aspects of the film are set against an accurate background.

Barnes Wallis"

This American film project came to a standstill due to continual delays in receiving information on necessary details, but partly for reasons of secrecy, too. Not until the filming of a script based on elements of Paul Brickhill's famous book "The Dam Busters" did Barnes Wallis agree.

On the twelfth anniversary of the Dam's Raid, the 16/17 May 1955, the world premier of the English black-and-white feature film "The Dam Busters" took place in the Empire Theatre on Leicester Square in London. There were separate showings across two days, as very many prominent guests were invited. Two years of research and preparation had been invested into the project by the Associated British Productions Limited, before the film was finally filmed at Elstree Studios in Boreham Wood and at real locations in England. The film, a worldwide success, tells the destruction of the German dams from an English perspective and does not go into the devastation in the valleys and the effects on the armaments economy. In addition, at the time of shooting the film, details of the bouncing bombs were still subject to the greatest military secrecy.

The first extensive film documentary, which came about after many years of research and which could make use of eye witness statements in England and Germany and of the most recent military information no longer subject to secrecy, was presented by the author Helmuth Euler at the thirtieth anniversary of the reservoirs disasters on 17 May 1973 in the affected regions.

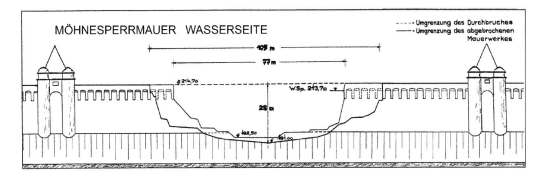

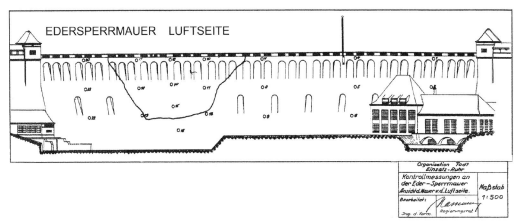

The breaches of the Möhne and Eder dams in comparison, regarding position and size

The drawings were made by the task force Ruhr of Organisation Todt. They show the Möhne dam from the waterside and the Eder dam from the valley side. In comparison, the difference in positions and sizes of the breaches in the walls is notable. The breach in the Möhne dam shows a length of seventy-seven metres, greatest height of twenty-two metres and an almost rectangular, sharp-edged contour. This confirms the statements of eye witnesses, according to which the break occurred suddenly, and at full volume, and not through enlargement of a smaller breach resulting from the water flow.

At the Eder dam the bomb that hit immediately tore an almost oval hole, like a gap in the mouth after a tooth extraction, into the wall south of its centre, seventy metres wide and twenty-two metres deep. The highest volumes of drained water deviated only slightly from each other. Through the hole in the Eder dam 8,500 cubic metres of water thundered per second, through the breach in the Möhne dam 8,800 cubic metres. However, there was a greater difference concerning the duration. The Möhne reservoir emptied within twelve hours, the drainage of the (1.4 times larger in volume capacity) Eder reservoir, took forty-eight hours due to the smaller gap.

On the insistence of the hydraulic engineering administration it was decided not to execute the repair on the Eder dam with a quick fix by a concrete seal, but also for reasons of propaganda. Commissioned by the Organisation Todt, the construction company Philipp Holzmann AG Frankfurt/ Main closed the breach by dry-stone masonry and thus securely linked new and old sections of the dam, a long-lasting, statically sound solution. Four of twelve emergency releases, around twenty metres below the mural crown on the valley side, which give the Eder dam its characteristic look, were not reinstalled during the repair measures. During the closing of the breach in the Möhne dam there was also no quick temporary solution with ferro-concrete, but a faithful rebuilding with granite and greywacke stone blocks.

As the measuring instruments for monitoring the stability of the Eder dam inside the wall were destroyed or damaged by the detonation to varying degrees, a new external measuring installation had to be created, with twenty-three control points at the valley side of the Eder dam.

Engineers of the Organisation Todt monitored its stability with a triangulation method from 26 March 1944 onwards. It was necessary to be able to monitor the movement of the wall, not only at the crown, but also in other sections, during the lowest and highest water levels in the lake.

Rebuilding the Eder dam

Of importance for the reconstruction of the dam, parallel to the aid and clearing works in the Eder valley by various organisations and the military, was the bridging of the Eder in Hemfurth. On 18 May 1943 the military district command IX ordered Company B of the Armoured Engineer Battalion 29 Hannoversch-Münden to establish a temporary bridge with a load-bearing capacity of twenty tons near Hemfurth. The company leader, First Lieutenant Dr Wilhelms, was the architect of the bridge construction.

After fifteen days of work, on 5 June 1943, the construction was handed over to the district commissioner

of Korbach, Fritz Marquart, and the population. In honour of General Otto Schellert of military district IX, the bridge was named after him. On the photo, it is situated next to the pillars of the destroyed road bridge of Hemfurth. In the foreground a light railway bridge led across the Eder to the dam construction site. In the centre stands a bridge for transporting the building material, both constructed by the Organisation Todt.

The armoured engineers perilously carry heavy iron beams to the construction site of the Schellert Bridge.

View of the construction site of the Organisation Todt in front of the dam. A light railway 'station' with turnout tracks has been installed for shuttle transport. Building supplies lie in readiness outside, while halls protect the sensitive materials. In the top left of the picture are the living barracks of the OT labourers, of whom around 1,500 were employed directly at the dam.

The OT personnel, predominantly labourers from France, Belgium, the Netherlands and Germany, were paid by the firm Philipp Holzmann AG Frankfurt according to tariff. The social insurances of these compulsory members were managed by the "German Health Insurance OT-West" within the former Health Insurance Fund of the district of Saarbrücken.

Above: Simultaneous to the repair of the Mohne dam, the restoration of the Eder barrage began. The firm Philipp Holzmann from Frankfurt, constructor of the dam thirty years ago, received the commission for rebuilding it from the Organisation Todt which was in charge. For the duration of the construction works, an "OT senior site management Eder" in Fritzlar was installed, just like there was an "OT senior site management Möhne" in Hagen for the Möhne reservoir and the Ruhr valley.

The repair works fell into the fourth and fifth year of the war, when almost all German men fit for military service had been sent to the front, and building materials and fuel were very scarce. Moreover the site lay in a sparsely settled mountainous forest region inconvenient for transport.

Right: View of the forty-eight metre tall (approx.) wooden scaffolding on the waterside of the dam.

From the 400m long retaining wall, 13,000 cubic metres of masonry had been broken off. At the base of the breach the wall measured eighteen metres. Ladders enabled the ascent and descent of the workers in the "Eder dam quarry". Two revolving tower cranes supplied the site with material, as well as two light railways. From the north tower of the wall, three tall wooden battery stands with quadruplet guns can be seen.

At the end of September 1943, after just under four months, the hole in the dam was closed. However, there were still difficulties with the cement slurry at the masonry during grouting. Vertical drillings for a drainage system from the mural crown to the tunnel in the dam's base could not be executed with the required level of accuracy. Only with the aid of a mini sender wrapped watertight and lowered into the drill holes, could the drill spot be located accurately with radio bearing, and thus the aim point of the drilling could be reached. A new drainage system could not be completed until the end of June 1944.

The closed breach from the valley side of the Eder dam.

Fifteen-year-old Air Force Auxiliary personnel, the first from the secondary school Bad Wildungen, are now defending the Eder dam in an exposed position with three quadruplet anti-aircraft batteries which were very dangerous for low-flying planes. Later, grammar school students from Kassel joined them. Their air defence stands were high up on the wall in front of the dam's north tower.

15 March 1945: British reconnaissance planes are still interested in the Eder reservoir. A triple chain of torpedo nets is now lying protectively in front of the wall. Fourteen days later, US soldiers stood at the "Waldeck reservoir" with their tank vanguards. The soldiers deployed for air defence of the dam, 1,300 to 1,500 men, had been dispatched to the approaching western front. The Americans had conquered and crossed the intact railway bridge across the Rhine at Remagen in a surprise move on 7 March 1945.

The air raid on 17 March 1943 and its consequences

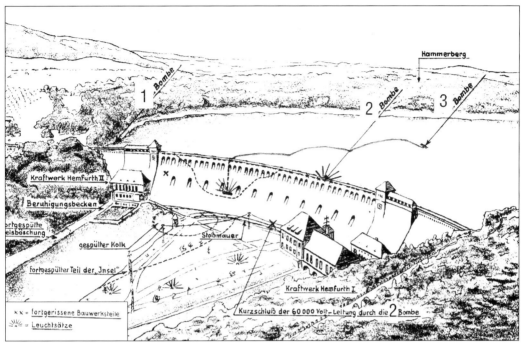

The attack on the Eder dam is illuminated by a sketch showing the sequence of bomb drops. Dave Shannon released the first bouncing bomb which exploded near the shore ahead of the retaining wall on the Hemfurth side of the lake. Bouncing bomb no. 2 deployed by Henry Maudslay exploded at the northern crest of the dam. Les Knight dropped the last available bomb. This was the only one that achieved three jumps across the dam, according to instructions, exploding at a depth of 9.1m, as predicted by Wallis, and tearing an enormous hole in the Eder barrage with a single strike.

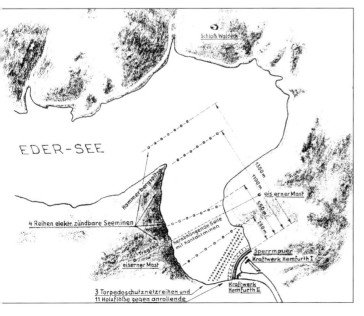

This sketch shows the passive air defence measures after the attack on the Eder dam. For this, twenty-four balloons of a low altitude battery (protection until 600m) were installed in a smaller circle, and twenty-four balloons of a high altitude battery (protection until 2,000m) in a wider circle, as well as a "fog company" with 500 smoke pots. Also in operation were one company of riflemen for the protection against landings by paratroopers, two anti-aircraft batteries with 12.5 centimetre guns, with quadruplet guns and four spotlights of sixty centimetres diameter. In addition, an anti-aircraft battery with four 3.7cm guns, two batteries with four 8.8cm guns each, a "shooting cart" battery with six "shooting carts", twenty-four guidance devices as well as three large-scale spotlights of 200cm diameter.

Altenburg in a British aerial photograph from 17 May 1943; settlement and valley are largely under water. Only the Altenburg with its tower on the higher ground of a steep basalt cliff, is protruding from the floods. In old times, the castle was a shield against attacks, a lookout across the land, and always a retreat in dire need. On this morning in May the old fortress became a refuge again. As in medieval times, the people escaped to this place from the deadly deluge; on top of the image the settlement of Rhünda.

The "Light Storm Boat Command 905" was called on during the night for a disaster mission in the Eder valley. Parts of the command were deployed as a pioneer construction company 'Rhünda' for the temporary restoration of two dam breaks on the railway line Frankfurt – Kassel at the outflow of the Schwalm into the Eder. With the castle ruin Altenburg as a backdrop, pioneers bridge the missing dam section with wooden bays. Heavy T-beams are set in place by hand; on the right the tower of the Altenburg mill.

Between Grifte and Wolfershausen the floods destroyed the railway bridge of the Frankfurt – Kassel line over the Eder. The damage to the construction is extensive; several pillars have vanished, burst or torn from their foundations.

Heinz Richter recalls: "Like a wall of fog, the 3.5m tall flood wave rolled towards Altenburg." Later, men of the Organisation Todt, Frenchmen and sixteen-year-olds from the National Labour Service came to clear up. In Altenburg they refilled the swept-away road with the aid of mine cars.

The mayor of the neighbouring places wrote letters of thanks to the district commissioner in Melsungen. The mayor of Niedermöllrich: "… The quick and decisive operation of the labour service was a true blessing for us. The National Labour Service has helped us not only with the removal of the damage caused by the disaster, but beyond this it has also seen us through the initial moral depression. When the company marched to their work in the early morning with their tools shouldered and a song on their lips, then the most pressing worries of the citizens were already banished."

Railway pioneers of the Reserve and Training Battalion 3 from Hanau/ Main have built a one-track temporary bridge from wooden posts parallel to the destroyed bridge, so as not to impede the later reconstruction of the latter. The technical senior site management was held by the president of the National Railway administration Kassel, Dr Ludwig Müller. With two heavy locomotives a load test is carried out. The coal cars of the locomotives bear slogans in white letters: "Wheels have to turn for victory; travels prolong the war!"

For the inauguration ceremony of the river bridge in June 1943 the deputy general of the 9th Army Corps and commander of the military district IX, Otto Schellert, arrived with a special train including a lounge car.

Below the hoisted Imperial War Flag the general made a speech, and even a marching band appeared. The pioneer Joseph Lejeune wrote this field postcard – "group photo at the railway embankment" – from Grifte to his family in St Vith. After completing the temporary railway bridge the pioneers departed. The population helps them to load the freight cars in Gudensberg station. Farmers have provided ox carts. Fathers among the soldiers carry their children and say goodbye.

German Model Rotational Water Bombs Tested in Berlin

Immediately after the attacks on the reservoirs in 1943, Dr Maecker – Ballistics Institute of the Technical Academy of the Air Force in Berlin-Gatow, Kladower Damm – received the commission to clarify the principle of operation of rotational bombs by model tests.

On the basis of the rotational bomb found intact near Haldern, models were manufactured at different scales: 1:12.7 – 1:20 – 1:50.

Every model was suspended from the bearings of a slide so that it could be put into forward and backward rotation with the means of a jet of water from a fire hose. The model trials at an ornamental pond between the buildings of the Technical Academy of the Air Force proceeded as follows:

> The slides were pushed back on an optical bench, and the retaining jig fastened. The rubber bands were stretched for release, the model bomb installed and put into rotation with a forceful jet of water. Its speed was indicated by a black-and-white disc. As soon as the desired speed was gained, the trigger of the retaining jig was pulled. Accelerated by the rubber bands, the model bomb sprang from the bearings and bounced across the ornamental pond, fifty centimetres deep. The trajectory was marked by metre signs. The assistant gathered the released models to be reused in further tests.
>
> A 16mm film camera followed the trajectories of the model bombs on the water surface in slow motion. In his report from 29 September 1943 with the title "Model tests with rotational water bombs" Dr Heinz Maecker could determine the operational principles of the bouncing bombs and develop defensive measures against a successful deployment at the dams. The jumping distances and speed observed by Dr Maecker correspond quite closely to the British trials. Three skips on the ornamental pond in Berlin-Gatow were the result of Maecker's tests. The following conclusions were drawn in a summary:

1. The bomb's direction of rotation must have been opposed to that of a wheel rolling on the surface of the water.
2. It has to be assumed that, after hitting the surface of the water, the bomb has made long jumps towards the retaining wall.
3. With increasing height of release, the bomb's ability to bounce decreases rapidly and probably disappears completely at a height of thirty-five metres, even with increased rotational speed.
4. Therefore the most effective protection against bombs of this kind has to be sought in a prevention of low-level attacks.
5. A covering of the water surface with wooden constructions, even if they are furnished with bumps, cannot stop the course of the bomb.
6. However, it seems sensible to create a sloping runway in front of the dam on its water side, on which the bomb can roll down after its impact on the retaining wall, supported by its rotation, and by this means it is kept at a distance sufficient for the dam's safety so that its detonation cannot cause devastating damage at any point.

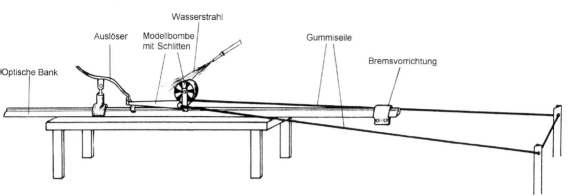

Launch device for the model bombs.

After the rebuilding of the Möhne and Eder barrages underwater, deflectors made from tree trunks were installed, equally at other objects to be protected. In July 1997, in a film interview at the Möhne reservoir, Prof. Dr. Dr. E.H. Heinz Maecker explained his bouncing bomb research in Berlin-Gatow to the author.

Forty-five Years On: Memories of the Dam Busters

Len Sumpter, born in 1911, bombardier in D.J. Shannon's Lancaster AJ-L: "In April 1941 I joined the RAF. At that time, England was heavily bombarded by the German Air Force. City districts were reduced to rubble, many people died. So I thought to myself: you have to join the RAF to do something against this, furthermore since the Germans had attacked Poland and other European nations. For his new squadron, Gibson only chose experienced pilots personally known to him. In most cases they brought their own crews along. Some crews were still in the process of being assembled, as there was a lack of men here and there, e.g. our radio operator only joined us at the end of April. It was important that the people got along and like each other. The assembly of the crews was not undertaken on the basis of interviews, only confirmed achievements mattered. I only talked with Gibson himself two days before the attack, when we dropped a 'concrete bouncing bomb' at the beach of Reculver near the Reculver Towers (church ruin). Two posts with white sheets tied to them simulated the dam towers, through these the trial bombs were supposed to bounce.

The original aiming device was developed by a technician from Farnborough, Wing Commander C.L. Dann. A plywood triangle with an eye cup for sighting across two pins worked on the principle of triangulation. If the eye saw the two pins in alignment with the dam towers during the approach, the critical point to release the bomb was reached. During training, however, we found that this device could not be held steady during the approach, moreover as we had one hand on the bomb release and could not support ourselves. I and another bombardier named E.C. Johnson from Les Knight's crew thought the matter over and found the solution.

Dr Maecker with his assistant during test no. 128; the pond had not been dug just for ornamental purposes, but as a cooling water reservoir for a test installation for aircraft engines. Today the communal hospital "Havelhöhe am Kladower Damm" is standing in its place.

The launch device with a model bomb at the scale of 1:12.7 ready for test no. 124.

Right: After the raids on the reservoirs, Dr Heinz Maecker received the order to uncover the mechanism of the dams' destruction by the bouncing bombs through model tests within the Technical Academy of the German Air Force in Berlin-Gatow. In addition to his report, he shot a 16mm reversal film from which these images were taken.

Göttingen protocol   Institute for Geophysics

1) 00:27:29.8 Uhr DSZ

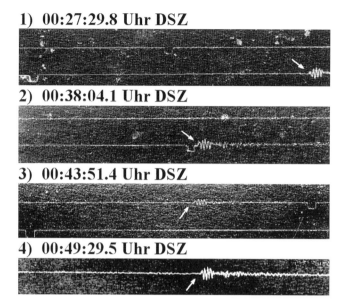

2) 00:38:04.1 Uhr DSZ

3) 00:43:51.4 Uhr DSZ

4) 00:49:29.5 Uhr DSZ

Explosions on 17 May 1943 at the Möhne dam
Figure is enlarged five times.
The arrow marks the initial onset of the registration. Recorded is the electro wave component with the seismograph by Wiechert which plays back the ground movement in 2000-fold enhancement. From this results a movement of the ground in Göttingen of around one to three micro metres. At a distance of 130km and a wave travel time of c.6.5km/s, this translates into the following explosion times at the Möhne dam:

1) 00:27:29.8 GST   2) 00:38:04.1 GST
3) 00:43:51.4 GST   4) 00:49:29.5 GST

1) 01:37:28.1 Uhr DSZ

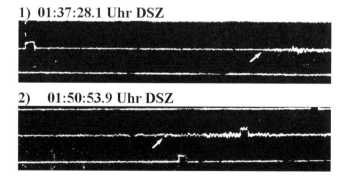

2)   01:50:53.9 Uhr DSZ

Explosions of 17 May 1943 at the Eder dam.
Figure is enlarged five times.
The arrow marks the initial onset of the registration. Recorded is the electro wave component with the seismograph by Wiechert which plays back the ground movement in 2000-fold enhancement. From this results a movement of the ground in Göttingen of around one to three micro metres. At a distance of seventy-five kilometres and a wave travel time of c.6.5km/s, this translates into the following explosion times at the Eder dam:

1) 01:37:28.1 GST   2) 01:50:53.9 GST

If you fix two cords to the screws holding the windscreen and attach them to one eye, a triangle is formed, similar to the operating principle of the wooden device. You calculate the length of the cords from the screen to the eye in relation to the distance between the dam towers, which were indicated by two marks on the screen. So both arms could be placed on a support and the aim was steadier. One hand held the bomb release, the other the ends of the cords. With the wooden sight, aiming was an imprecise and shaky matter. Many bombardiers used the 'string method' (chinagraph). The distance between the two target marks on the windscreen measured twenty-two centimetres. If you now held the strings to the nose and sighted across them (angle, marking and distance to the dam towers were very precisely matched with each other) until the towers drawing near came into alignment with the markings, the exact point of release was reached. The exact distance between the dam towers was known through specialist journals and aerial reconnaissance. These chinagraph aiming devices have worked better then the wooden models. Each bombardier could choose between wooden or string model and decide on the method which suited him best.

Approximate times are given for Hopgood and Maudslay
The "soft" explosions not registered in Göttingen are detonations which did not take place underwater at the retaining wall or which deflagrated at the slope of the Sorpe dam. Due to this, little pressure was exerted on the rock formations which transported the shock waves as with an earthquake. The destructions of the Möhne and Eder dams followed at an interval of one hour.

Institute for Geophysics Göttingen

The symbolic inscription of the
measuring station by Emil Wiechert:
"Far away tidings are brought to you
by the swaying rock – read the signs!"

Shockwaves of Rotation Bombs

Time	Pilot	Duration	Length of Deflection
		MÖHNE RESERVOIR	
00:27:29.8	Gibson	40.8sec	0.6mm
00:38:04.1	Martin	14.0sec	0.8mm
00:43:51.4	Young	2.6sec	0.2mm
00:49:29.5	Maltby	40.5sec	0.8mm
Destruction			
		EDER RESERVOIR	
01:37:28.1	Shannon	34.0sec	0.4mm
01:50:53.9	Knight	57.0sec	0.2mm
Destruction			
		ENNEPE RESERVOIR	
03:38:00.0	Townsend Misfire		

Of eleven rotational bombs dropped, four were registered as "soft" explosions in the Gottingen records.

1) 00:33	Hopgood	"Soft" explosion at the Möhne reservoir.	
2) 00.45	McCarthy	"Soft" explosion at the Sorpe reservoir.	
3) 01:43	Maudslay	"Soft" explosion at the Eder reservoir.	
4) 03:14	Brown	"Soft" explosion at the Sorpe reservoir.	

During the training period, I really only knew my own little crew of seven. With the other crews I had very little contact. We were in competition with each other for the best drop results and the most turning marks hit correctly. Usually a bombardier does not have much work at an altitude of 8,000 metres. He waits for the target and assists the navigator a little. For example, Hamm comes into view. We are six kilometres off-course, so the order is 'Correct that!' During the extremely low-level flight against the dams we could not relax for a moment, we had to concentrate completely and think of nothing else.

Then there was this joke about a hotel in Lincoln called the 'Saracen's Head'. It was a great joke, but it came true once or twice. It was said: 'If you go for a drink at the 'Saracen's Head' at lunchtime, the bartender tells you which target you have to attack in the evening'. Apparently, this was true. However, I personally do not believe it, even though she was right with her tips a few times. The standard joke was: 'Ask the girl behind the bar, she will tell you where the journey is going tonight'.

The morning of the attack, I helped to mount a bouncing bomb to Gibson's aircraft, the first original bomb I had seen. We called the Lancaster the 'pregnant one', because in profile the aircraft with the protruding bomb was as large as a pregnant woman. The launch took place in formation. Before Soest we disbanded and flew towards the Möhne dam individually. Passing over one of the dam towers, we were showered with tracer projectiles which I do not like very much. I asked the pilot why he was approaching so closely, for the aircraft had received two or three hits, which did not cause us any difficulties, though.

We then flew a holding pattern with the other aircraft in left turn, ten kilometres south of Völlinghausen, in an orbit of 200m altitude and waited for Gibson's call. The board communication remained switched on, so all crew members could listen to what was happening. I heard Gibson saying: 'I will attack now'. I saw him diving towards the lake and approaching the Möhne dam, saw the air defence aiming for him, saw the tall column of water, but nothing happened. Gibson returned and ordered Hopgood to attack as number two. Hopgood was hit. His bomb exploded inside the power station, his aircraft caught fire and crashed five kilometres to the north-west.

Then Mickey Martin attacked. Gibson accompanied him to draw the anti-aircraft fire to himself. At this point the battery on the south tower was no longer firing. That made attacking slightly easier. Martin's bomb was not positioned horizontally, swung off and exploded near the shore. During Dinghy Young's attack, Gibson and Martin were flying as well. Young's bomb did not hit the surface accurately either. It bounced more to the left of the dam's centre, and exploded before the torpedo nets.

Then it was number five's turn, Maltby, with company. We were supposed to be next. The immense mushroom of explosion loomed over the Möhne dam. Shortly afterwards Gibson made contact: 'The dam is bust, abort the approach'. After some circles around the Möhne Lake we saw the unique spectacle. Gibson ordered Les Knight, Dave Shannon and Henry Maudslay who still carried their bombs and Squadron Leader Les Young as his deputy (without bomb) to fly as quickly as possible to the Eder dam. Nobody from our aircraft did know the situation at the Eder Lake in detail. We had seen no model of the Eder dam before the attack. It was quite hellish to descend there at night. Past the Waldeck castle, through a ravine, we dived towards the lake.

It was very difficult to gain the required height of 18.3 metres on the last 1,000 metres above the water behind the summit of the Hammerberg, for then the aircraft is already passing the retaining wall. Then the pilot had great difficulty pulling it over the next mountain to regain a left course past the Waldeck castle. During our first approaches the height was only right when the Lancaster was already passing the towers. The navigator said: 'The height is right' and I: 'It is too late'. At that moment the towers had long since passed out of sight. Finally we made a correct approach and I released the bomb, it bounced more towards the Hemfurth side and exploded near the shore. Our tail gunner saw a column of water, 300 metres tall, but the dam was holding. Maudsley, who attacked after us, released his bomb too late. At that time we thought that he had blown himself up. Les Knight managed the deed with the last available bomb, and the dam broke, his bouncing bomb hit the right side of the barrage.

At the Eder dam we needed three bombs, at the Möhne five. We saw the water rushing through the breach in the Eder dam and tumbling towards Kassel, like the Niagara Falls. The crews were overjoyed; we circled a few times and watched the 'show', until Gibson urged us to fly back. All exertions and hardships during training had led to success after all. Only years later I have learned that we flew the raid against the dams on a Sunday. It was a 'Sunday Raid'. Inside the aircraft we were cheering, in the lovely light of the moon the small village of Hemfurth was clearly visible.

Actually there was no difference in the 'Dams Raid' to the training flights, only that we could be shot down and that we transported a live bomb. The most thrilling and exciting moment for me was the instant when I was circling in the holding pattern over the Arnsberg forest and had to attack the Möhne dam as number six. Then you think: 'Now it begins', descend to the one-minute approach, release the bomb, during which you receive thirty seconds of anti-aircraft fire, and then you are beyond it.

Fortunately there was no air defence at the Eder. Despite the mountainous surroundings, an attack there is actually easier than over a large city, where you are fired at for more than half an hour, and searched for and blinded by spotlights. After the successful attacks I did not understand why the RAF did not disrupt the rebuilding works by intense high altitude bombardment. An air raid with one hundred aircraft could easily have destroyed the installations on the construction sites and by this postponed the recommissioning of the reservoirs for a year. So the dams were standing again after four months.

After the return to Scampton we were very tired due to the long flight duration and the constant concentration on ground observation. We disembarked, congratulated each other and went to the debriefing room. Here we drank coffee which was offered to us by a girl after every sortie. I believe this night there was whiskey or brandy if desired. That was unusual as far as I can remember. We sat there and talked about those who had not returned, among them many friends. Somebody said that he saw Burpee crash, another Astell or Hopgood. So we waited in the debriefing room, until we knew that nobody could return any longer and went to bed.

Two hours later we rose again, met in the sergeants' casino and spoke with the other crews who had also survived. Here the mood was not quite so great, for it was an expected fact in the RAF that you might never again see the comrade beside you after the next raid. Yet everybody hoped to return from the sortie. According to my memory, by contrast, there was a great party in the officers' mess. All were tipsy, and later the mood improved in the sergeants' casino, too. After all, you climb into a plane, take off, and in the end it is fate if you return. My crew always called me Satan, for I had said to them that I was too evil to die, so they could never crash with me on the plane. Then everybody laughed about it and said: 'We have Len Sumpter with us, don't we'. The next day the newspapers printed sensational articles on the 'Dams Raid'. The locals now knew that the raid had been flown from Scampton. All who had participated in the attack received their honours immediately, just as you present a soldier in the field with his decoration. 'Bomber Harris' sent a telegram. Everyone found it in his mail box. For me with the annotation: 'You will receive the Distinguished Flying Medal'. Then you went to a shop, bought a strap and put it on your uniform jacket.

We saw the photographs of the damage in the river valleys. For a long period water and electricity were off, but it was nowhere near the great damage foreseen by our superiors."

John Fraser, bombardier in Hopgood's Lancaster AJ-M, Pilot Officer of the Canadian air force: "When my aircraft was shot down over the Möhne reservoir, I released the bouncing bomb too late. A direct hit destroyed the power station. With luck, I myself could leave the aircraft by parachute shortly before the crash in Ostgönnen. After I had been taken prisoner,

I gave detailed information on the function of the bouncing bombs to the military authorities. In Stalag Luft III, I witnessed the end of the war.

I clearly recall the launch of the raid. We were still standing about for a little and we talked. Our navigator was Kenneth Earnshaw from Alberta, Canada. With him I flew my first mission with the 50th squadron. He had the gift of seemingly being able to predict future events. He said: 'This or that crew will soon not return from a sortie, perhaps they still have one or two trips.' And as we were standing there, I asked him: 'What do you think about the flight tonight?' He answered: 'I believe we will lose eight aircraft tonight, perhaps we are among them.' He was exactly right with his opinion.

During the mounting of the bouncing bombs to the Lancasters, there occurred an incident which might have endangered the whole operation. An attractive blonde girl from the WAAF had cast an eye at the men of the 617th squadron, especially Mickey Martin. She climbed into the cockpit of the Lancaster AJ-P and waited for him there. Out of boredom or curiosity she played with various switches and unwittingly pulled the handle for immediate emergency release. The heavy 'devil's egg' fell onto the concrete floor. Almost 200 men who made their aircraft ready for launch ran for their lives. Fortunately the bomb did not explode, as the self-destructing trigger had not been primed yet. The bouncing bomb was mounted once more to Mickey Martin's Lancaster.

(Later commentators on this incident were keen to see it counted amongst the created myths and legends of 617 squadron, and to see it portrayed as a mere technical error, moving forwards.)"

Dave Shannon, Flight Lieutenant, born in 1922 in Australia. In November 1942 he came with a troop carrier from the USA to Liverpool in England, but remained a member of the Australian Air Force. He piloted the Lancaster AJ-L against the Eder dam.

"It was 'great sport' to fly approaches towards the Lincolnshire canals and to frighten the people on the ships and on the shores during training. Everybody in the squadron was a volunteer. Gibson asked them all to say yes or no, nobody backed out. Most of them had the feeling that a great strike against the enemy was supposed to be made, but nobody knew where. The battle of the Möhne reservoir was supposed to start at midnight. Fourteen aircraft took off first, five were held back in reserve, until the first radio reports were made available, detailing which dams had been destroyed. After the destruction of the three main targets, the other dams should be attacked, of which we did not see any models during the briefing, only photographs. I took off at half past nine, flew without incident to the Dutch coast where light air defence opened fire on us. The flight led past Terschelling over the Zuiderzee. On the marked routes, the flak-free zones were not always correct. So there were a few surprises, or we flew over a German airfield which was heavily defended. The spotlights mostly pointed straight into the sky and could not capture us with their beams. They roamed about like the light air defence with its tracer ammunition. Enemy night fighters could not have operated against us at our altitude.

The Möhne Lake with its dam was lying beautifully in the light of the moon. Just as I wanted to launch the attack as the sixth aircraft, there were loud yells in the headphones: 'The wall is broken, the dam is bust.' Gibson said to me: 'Abort the attack and remain in holding position.' I can hardly describe the mood inside the plane, the shouts and the wild excitement: 'It is broken, it is broken'. We then continued our flight to the Eder reservoir in the Waldecker Land.

Mist rose from the valleys and clung to the mountains. In some places, the water in the lake was hardly distinguishable from the mist. The dam itself was very difficult to discern in the landscape, as there were several large branches of water in the vicinity. Above the Eder Lake, Gibson called his aircraft together. I was not quite sure if it actually was the Eder dam. So I made a 'dummy run' at something which showed some similarity with a dam, but it was another branch of the Eder in the moonlight. Gibson marked the Eder dam with a flare, and all flew towards that light. It was quite a hairy matter to descend towards the Eder Lake, past the tall castle of Waldeck, like an eagle's nest on a forested spot. The scenery surrounding the Eder dam revealed itself to be extremely beautiful, but the landscape wasn't particularly well-suited to ascending and descending with a heavy four-motor Lancaster at almost 400kmh. All reservoirs in Germany are located in enchanting landscapes. I believe we were positioned correctly with the Lancaster, when our bouncing bomb ran against the Eder dam and exploded at the southern side of the lake. At first it seemed as if a small breach was showing, but the wall was holding. We were very happy, when finally Les Knight's bouncing bomb – the last available one – led to success. Without doubt the destruction of the dams was a heavy blow against Nazi Germany's armaments industry. Yet almost fifty per cent of losses to aircraft with their crews gave some food for thought. The Germans managed to rebuild the dams more quickly than we had considered possible."

Edward Johnson, born 1912, Flying Officer, from Lincoln, bombardier in Les Knight's Lancaster AJ-N. At the beginning of the war he volunteered for the RAF:

"I went to the new squadron with my comrades and was glad to be able to continue flying with them. During training we speculated mostly about the target. Many were concerned about what it might be in the end. Most favoured submarine bunkers as targets, where we would drop the bombs into the entrances to blow them up. The submarine bunkers were located in harbours along the French Channel coast. We did not think of the reservoirs in Germany. Scampton was a typical pre-war airfield with good accommodation, hangars and beautiful casinos. By contrast it was unfortunate that there were no concrete airstrips, only a runway on grass.

Our crew was a mixture of different nationalities, Australians, Canadians, and I was British. The navigator and I were much older than the others in the crew, but we got along well. The pilot did not touch alcohol, was religious due to his upbringing, and all were non-smokers. As aiming device I used the chinagraph method which I had helped to develop, two marks with chinagraph pencil on the windscreen and two cords.

With this I achieved success at the Eder dam. During simulated night flight training, the flight engineer did not wear special glasses and thus followed the low-level flight without sight impairment, in order to be able to warn the pilot if an obstacle appeared. The Air Ministry had approved several regions for low-level flight, but the squadron was showered with complaints about the noise.

When I saw the bomb for the first time, I was very surprised. I said to myself: 'This is impossible. That thing, a large heavy cylinder, is supposed to be rotated as well.' The many trial bombs we had dropped had been much smaller with less weight. We never actually trained with a live bomb, of course. In fact, we only saw the 'Upkeep' weapon on the day of the operation itself. During the briefing in the afternoon before the launch, I learned of the targets. For one and a half hours we listened to the speeches of Barnes Wallis, of AOC Cochrane and of the 'weatherman'. There was much display material, models of the targets, maps and boards with section drawings of the dam constructions. In addition, the 'radio' men explained frequencies and codes again.

The air defence situation on route was discussed. We belonged to the main group flying to the Möhne. I personally was slightly tenser during this raid than usual, because we went against a specific target in low-level flight. The flight to the target area passed by without any problems arising with regards map reading or navigation.

At the Möhne dam the last aircraft of the first wave had just arrived. On the spot Gibson determined the order of attack. In the clear moonlit night, with extremely good visibility up to ten kilometres, the event could be very clearly observed; a truly indescribable picture of how the explosions drove the water upwards and flooded the wall. Due to the fantastic range of vision we could see the bouncing bombs jump across the Möhne Lake. Soon we asked ourselves whether the 'things' would actually work.

So in the end there was great excitement when the Möhne dam finally broke, with a single bomb as predicted by Wallis. So his calculations were correct, after all. The approach to the Möhne dam was straighter and much easier than the approach to the Eder. At the Möhne there was air defence, yet in exchange we had to descend onto a 'trickier' terrain at the Eder reservoir. With the rotating bomb this was a difficult manoeuvre to fly. The wall itself was not easy to locate, being situated in a vexing corner. I still clearly recall the attacks on the Eder dam. At first Dave Shannon made four or five attempts to get into the right position for bomb release. Then Gibson stopped his 'trial series' and ordered him to wait. Now Henry Maudslay started two failed attempts. After him, Dave Shannon attacked once more and, after two failed approaches, released the first bouncing bomb which exploded near the right-hand shore before the dam. Gibson gave Maudslay the order to attack. Twice he tried. During the third run-up he approached the wall too high to release the bomb. Yet the bombardier triggered the weapon, it bounced too violently, catapulted onto the crest of the dam instead of sinking into the water, and exploded with a terrible flash of lightning. We saw Maudslay's Lancaster as a silhouette against the light. It must have been shortly behind the explosion's mushroom, for during this stage of the flight the bomb was still almost as fast as the Lancaster.

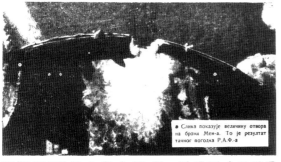

УНИШТАВАЊЕ НЕМАЧКЕ
РАТНЕ ИНДУСТРИЈЕ НЕ ПРЕСТАЈЕ

Ова слика показује боље него речи силину и прецизност бомбардована Р.А.Ф.-а. У својим непрекидним уништавајућим нападима на велике индустријске центре Немачке Р.А.Ф је нанео један тежак удар Руру.

Тешки бомбардери надлетели су као олуја бране Мен и Едер. Бране су провљене и најважнија индустријска област Немачке поплављена. Железнице, мостови, електричне централе и фабрике услед ове поплаве постале су неупотребљиве. Велики део ста-

новништва остао је без крова над главом. Број жртава је веома велики.

Немачка штампа, заборављајући своје одушевљење приликом бомбардовања Београда, Ротердама, Варшаве и Лондона, жестоко протестује против „варварства" ових напада, којима је циљ уништавање немачке ратне машине и ослобођење земаља које су под немачким јармом—Ово је најбољи доказ колико је бомбардовање Р.А.Ф.-а успешно.

● Рурска индустрија је парализована.
● 4.000 људи удавило се приликом поплаве,
● 120.000 Немаца без крова над главом.
● Потпуно уништење електричних централа.
● Велики простори су опустошени поплавом.
● Канали покварени и неупотребљиви.
● Опсадно стање је проглашено.

Тако Немачка почиње да плаћа цену својих злочина. т. 10

A leaflet in Cyrillic letters dropped over Yugoslavia.

The French "Courriere de l'Air" informed the citizens in France and Belgium about the successful raids on the German reservoirs and their consequences. In the Netherlands similar "aerial news" in Dutch fell from the sky, too. Even the intact Sorpe dam was reported as destroyed. Reading and passing on leaflets as well as listening to enemy broadcasts were forbidden in Germany under maximum punishment.

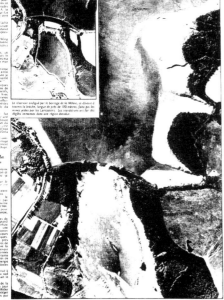

Ови јадници који избегавају дејство британског бомбардовања, уништени су поплавом.

Besides the radio, British propaganda employed leaflets for allied and enemy territories as well as caricatures in English newspapers.

Flight Lieutenant K.G. Hesketh, officer in the Royal Australian Air Force, was an enthusiastic collector of souvenirs relating to the missions of the Australian Air Force in Europe. So he dismantled the bronze inauguration plaque from the north tower of the Möhne dam. Hesketh's collection was presented to the War Museum in Canberra by the Royal Australian Air Force in 1948. There this "booty" points to the Australian participation in the raid and touts the Möhne dam as a significant monument of military history.

Auch dieser Viermotorige sah England nicht wieder

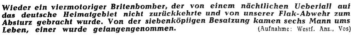

Wieder ein viermotoriger Britenbomber, der von einem nächtlichen Ueberfall auf das deutsche Heimatgebiet nicht zurückkehrte und von unserer Flak-Abwehr zum Absturz gebracht wurde. Von der siebenköpfigen Besatzung kamen sechs Mann ums Leben, einer wurde gefangengenommen. (Aufnahme: Westf. Anz., Vos)

The debris of Ottley's Lancaster AJ-C lay in Ostbusch near Heessen. The "Westfälische Anzeiger" in Hamm published this photograph without mentioning the context. Fred Tees became a prisoner of war, as he survived the downing by chance.

Malte Schrader, battery commander of a Hamm anti-aircraft unit at that time, found this singed, blood-smeared flight map with the approach routes via the Möhne to the Eder reservoir and back to the Sorpe dam.

Fred Tees then and in 1981 during a visit on the occasion of the inauguration of a memorial at the crash site. As the front board gunner he had switched his place with the tail gunner Sergeant H. Strange before launch. At the impact of the aircraft the rear gunner station broke off and was hurled away from the centre of the explosion. Only slightly injured, Tees was taken prisoner.

The aircraft must have been damaged by the explosion. Gibson saw that immediately. He asked over the radio: 'Are you okay, Henry?' Everyone in the three remaining aircraft – Dinghy Young, Gibson's deputy, without bomb, was already on the return flight – thought that Henry Maudslay had crashed. We heard nothing of him at first, until he reported with a very weak and sad voice which did not sound like him at all that he believed he was okay.

Then it was our turn. Three trial runs we flew before our last attack. My pilot got us down quickly with a correct approach. I saw the towers very clearly, was happy with my aiming device, the position and everything else. I released the bomb and for a moment forgot everything about it, because we were flying directly towards a mountain beyond the retaining wall. That is perhaps the most terrible instant, if you see the mountain hurtling towards you at maximum speed. I was afraid that we could not pass over the obstacle in time, but the Lancaster just managed to lift over the mountain top with maximum force.

The entire success of the attack depended on the fact that the pilot brought the Lancaster into an absolutely horizontal position during the release of the bomb. For this a synchronisation of the navigator for the altitude, of the radio operator for the exact rotation of the bomb, of the flight engineer for the speed and of the bombardier for the precise aiming was necessary.

I myself could not see the Eder dam collapsing, as it had run out of my sight. Yet by the shouting of the tail gunner Harry O'Brien over the board communication it was clear to me that a section of the dam must have fallen.

For a moment we forgot all about our safety and followed the immense flood wave shooting down the valley. I saw a car chasing along the road in front of the water, its headlights like fearful eyes in the dark. Closer and closer the flood came. It caught up with the car. In the spray, these eyes suddenly shimmered greenish, became darker and finally vanished altogether. Gibson said: 'Boys, you have done well. It is high time for the return flight.' Ten minutes we circled above the destroyed Eder dam. For many years I could not believe that Maudslay was shot down only on the return journey over West Germany. I assumed that he had crashed in the Eder region.

Our return route led past the Möhne reservoir. Here the water was still running in a great torrent through the breach. In a short while the river banks appeared, the power station in front of the dam had vanished completely. Large pieces of debris were lying along the Möhne valley as far as we could see. The flight engineer reported sufficient fuel to be flying home at full throttle. The return flight passed without firing and other incidents. We were very glad to see the Dutch coast again. Later the tail gunner said that we had nearly rammed a large concrete construction during the flyover which the pilot had not seen.

We were surprised and astonished not to be received by German night fighters, for the Germans must have known that we were on our way home. Yet with the radar of those years we could not be located during low-level flight. At the Möhne reservoir no night fighters were looking for us, either, although we were circling for almost three quarters of an hour. We must have been seen by many people. Fortunately the Germans had no communication links for such an attack. In my opinion it would have been good if we had had our own long distance night fighters as an escort.

After the return we were shocked by our losses which we had not expected to be so high. The sensitive Wallis, a gentleman, left the celebration very early. He was deeply affected and simply could not grasp the fact of having lost so many men. Wallis was a father figure with determination and looked like the typical scientist. Later in life I was reprimanded again and again to have killed so many people with the draining water. That is an impossible accusation, because you are in a battle situation and do not think about it. You received an order and you had to carry it out.

Certainly, that was my greatest special operation, a much publicised raid, but not my most dangerous one. I flew a low-flying operation in September 1943 with the same tactics against the Dortmund-Ems canal with special bombs and bombers to blow up the canal dykes, which ended in a disaster for most of us. Only three aircraft returned. During the return flight, I was the first to jump out of our burning plane at 300m. The Dutch resistance smuggled me to England via Belgium, France, Spain and Gibraltar."

Harold Hobday, Flying Officer, navigator in Les Knight's Lancaster AJ-N:

"I came to Squadron X with my crew. We wanted to stay together, our performance was good, and thus we were selected. Gibson was the heart and soul of the mess parties. He switched bomber jackets with his comrades. Yet if somebody drank before the training flights, he came down on them like a ton of bricks. We believed that we were training for an attack on the Tirpitz, the great German battleship which was bristling with guns. Later we were very glad not to have had to face the ship.

The selection of the first nine crews for the main targets was decided by the best trial drops of a bouncing bomb filled with concrete at the beach of Reculver in Kent. The crews hitting most closely to the target were chosen. So we got into the main group with a very good drop. An ambitious pilot who did not count among the 'chosen' begged Gibson to let him fly in the main group instead of us. Although this pilot was a friend of Gibson, the latter did not grant his request. The idea with the headlights was first class. During the descent in the course of the attack I looked onto the water through my Plexiglas bubble in the cockpit until the recumbent eight was forming. The moonlight was no disruption. Some of us had concerns about the illumination, as the German gunners had a better aim at us. Yet these were seeing us in the moonlight anyway. The 'Gee' radar device on board the Lancaster guaranteed a good navigation. Mostly it only worked until the Dutch coast, since from here on it was disrupted by the Germans. I personally still had 'Gee' directional contacts far into Germany and lost these only shortly before the Möhne Lake. At a specific frequency the device delivered visible markers to a small screen, which were transmitted onto a special map.

So we always knew precisely where the aircraft was. On the night of the attack I had to take along a parachute. In the bag there were also a large sextant, maps, navigational aids, dividers, ruler and an oxygen mask. Personal items were not allowed to be taken along on a sortie. At the Möhne Lake we saw the exciting spectacle. Then during the third attack on the Eder dam we managed a repetition. During this I was sitting on a swivel chair in order to talk the aircraft down with the headlights. First class visibility prevailed starboard. Usually I am sitting in front of a blank wall with instruments and other things. On the return flight, the Möhne reservoir offered a fantastic view. It showed itself to be half empty. The water was still racing down the valley. Yet suddenly the air defence fired on us from behind. Tracer ammunition passed closely, but fortunately did not hit us. We veered off quickly. We did not deploy our own night fighters. It would have been wrong to send them to the dams. They would have revealed the target and alerted German night fighters. A synchronised approach did not lend itself, either, for then too many aircraft would have impeded each other during the circling above the target. Above the barrages the Germans could have listened to our perfect frequency-modulation communication. A pilot whose bomb had not hit the Eder dam tried to give us tips via radio on how to go in during our approach. That was disruptive and we turned him off. Back in the mess, I fell asleep in an armchair and woke only in the morning.

Splendid times followed. During leave we were passed around everywhere. If we had also managed to bust the third target, the Sorpe dam, even greater damage would have been inflicted upon Germany's armaments industry. I also believe that the attack had its value. An enormous sum was invested by us, too. Barnes Wallis with his experiments, the modification of the Lancaster bombers, the mechanism for the bomb's propulsion, the weeks in training and the time which we were not in action because of it.

The 'Dams Raid', the strike against the reservoirs, was a vital means to maintain the population's morale in wartime England."

Flight Sergeant **Robert Kellow** operated the radios in Les Knight's Lancaster AJ-N. "In Scampton only five people were aware of the targets of the attack until the very morning of the raid. During training I had a forty-eight-hour leave in London where my relatives and acquaintances asked me again and again what I had been doing the last few weeks. I said to them that I had been over Berlin. They answered: 'But you have already been there before.' Then I said: 'We were flying around England all the time.' They simply could not understand why I was being so secretive. Even the 57th Squadron 'next door' did not know what was going on. They believed that we were only sitting around, did nothing and did not contribute to the war effort. Many were jealous of us, because Squadron X made more of an impression on the girls in the vicinity as we were better looking.

At the Eder dam we flew the last available bouncing bomb against the wall. All responsibility was now resting on us. After several failed approaches with the wrong altitude or speed the crew was actually quite frustrated. Gibson became worried, as dawn was near. I still recall how the navigator said: 'Lower, lower, stop, the height is absolutely right, the spots are standing correctly.' The aircraft was now flying at a speed of 385kmh. Everything worked perfectly, and the bombardier pushed the trigger. In vertical flight we passed over the mountain beyond the retaining wall and, looking back, we saw the bouncing bomb explode. The impression was created of a giant fist punching a hole in the Eder dam.

Our tail gunner O'Brien recounted later: 'At my station, a splendid front row seat, I had a fantastic view which probably nobody else will ever have again. There is no comparison to this bird's eye perspective.' The water column rose almost as high as the mountains behind the Eder dam, around 300 metres. I had not expected that the explosion mushroom would shoot up so quickly behind me, almost reaching the Lancaster's tail in which I ascended almost vertically as if inside an elevator."

William Townsend, born 1921, flew his twenty-seventh mission as pilot against the Ennepe dam. From the 49th Bomber Squadron he was transferred to Special Squadron X, with all of his crew but one: "We were also training low level flight in a 'link trainer'. This flight simulation installation is a static plane with many cockpit instruments which is controlled externally by an instructor. You learn how to fly a course in bad weather and various kinds of winds. No crash follows a mistake. There was also 'Dinghy Drill' in case of an emergency water landing. The survival aid 'dinghy', a static tank with a rubber craft, was stored inside the wings of the Lancaster. During an emergency water landing, it was triggered automatically, was tied to the aircraft and thus could not drift away. The crew had to climb over the wing into the rubber boat. From Manston I flew towards the coast, at which two dummy towers were erected, and dropped a concrete bouncing bomb, my only actual trial with a model bomb.

Pilot Munro of our squadron had an uncomfortable experience. He seemed to have released his trial bomb slightly below the prescribed altitude, as the height of release could only be estimated during daylight. The bomb dropped onto the water and bounced against the tail of the Lancaster. The lower section of the gun turret near the fuselage side was damaged, evidently not too badly. Yet I made the very unpleasant realisation that the Lancaster would vibrate violently due to the rotation of the bouncing bomb, something that I had not expected in practice. During the attack on the Ennepe dam, this rattling effect occurred again. It might also have been the cause for Maudslay's failed drop at the Eder dam. The vibration did not occur immediately after the bomb had started turning. It took almost fifteen minutes until the heavy weight took its effect. On the day of the attack there were two briefings.

The pilots and navigators were let into the mission's secret in the morning, the rest of the crews in the afternoon. Nobody was allowed to leave at that point. I believe that this was actually a blessing, for if one word had slipped under these circumstances, the entire operation could have ended a fiasco. Too many factors stood in opposition to survival on the trip. I believe it was no easy task to approach at night, at twenty metres altitude, above enemy territory, with a heavy aircraft of more than thirty metres wing span and a very heavy bomb load. The losses speak for themselves. It was a hazardous game to carry the bombs to the other side of the heavily defended Ruhr area. We belonged to the 'flying reserve' which was supposed to fill the gaps in the other waves having launched earlier, wherever others had dropped out on route to their targets.

One and a half hours after Gibson's take-off we followed him on his route under direct radio control by the centre of the 5th British Bomber Fleet. In my aircraft, O for orange,

On the initiative of Bernard Droste, a memorial was erected at the crash site in September 1981 by the "Don Bosco" scouts of St Mary's parish in Heessen. Fred Tees was invited to the inauguration ceremony.

Above: On 18 May 1943, after the debriefings, 617 Squadron went on leave, and Wing Commander Guy Gibson wrote fifty-six letters to the relatives of those aviators who had not returned from the sortie.

Below: Small crucifixes with red poppies are placed before the rock with its hortative inscription.

Above: Almost fifty years after the crash, with the aid of a metal detector, Werner Ruffing found a movable disc from the aircraft's navigation section and a whistle to be used during an emergency landing on water.

Former enemies, friends today: a British tourist is throwing a wreath into the Möhne Lake dedicated to the dead of both sides.

On 19 September 1976 there was a meeting of veterans of the former Dam Buster Squadron. From left to right: Pilot Officer G. Rice who had to abort his run-up prematurely, Sergeant H. E. O'Brian – tail gunner in Les Knight's Lancaster which destroyed the Eder dam – Sergeant F. Tees who survived the crash in Heessen near Hamm, Sergeant J.H. Clay – bombardier in Munro's Lancaster whose mission had to be aborted – author Helmuth Euler, Flying Officer E.C. Johnson who busted the Eder dam as bombardier, and Sergeant H.B. Feneron – flight engineer in K.W. Brown's Lancaster during the attack on the Sorpe dam.

Air defence corporal Karl Schütte, who downed the second attacking Lancaster, described the nocturnal raid from his viewpoint to Len Sumpter on a day in May 1990.

In August 1990, Karl Schütte and Len Sumpter, bombardier in Dave Shannon's Lancaster who released the first bomb against the Eder dam, exchanged tokens of friendship. Karl Schutte is holding up a drawing that was given to him, showing the memorial at Woodhall Spa that was constructed in memory of the aviators of 617 Squadron who fell during the war.

The sixtieth anniversary of the Dams Raid, 2003 in England: thousands of spectators have travelled to the coast at Reculver to experience the flyby of Europe's last airworthy Lancaster at the Reculver Towers; a memorial day for the legendary Dam Busters. The photo was taken by the English photographer Ben May who had seen the secret trials of the RAF at the beach of Reculver as a seventeen-year-old boy. In 1943 he did not know anything about the purpose of the trials, but some weeks later news came thick and fast in the British press about the spectacular destructions of the Möhne and Eder dams. Now the secret of the bouncing bomb was revealed.

The sixtieth anniversary of the Möhne disaster in Wickede/ Ruhr: with the rolling of drums, the flags are dipped to honour the dead of 17 May 1943. As usual for these anniversaries, flag delegations of clubs and societies accompany the citizens to the memorial for the community's flood victims on the banks of the Ruhr. In the presence of representatives from the political community, the parishes and societies, wreaths are laid down. Orators condemn the never-ceasing madness of war. The 118 civilian victims of the Möhne flood from this Ruhr community will never be forgotten.

In Affoldern, below the Eder dam, this sculpture recalls the night of horror. A mother holds her child high above the deadly flood.

An imploring appeal to finally turn towards peace and remember the brevity of human existence.

In Neheim a 5.5m tall lantern of the dead in front of the Sauerländer cathedral, the parish church St John the Baptist, commemorates the terror of the disaster night. From the representation of the broken Möhne dam and a harrowing scene of drowning people, the gaze travels upwards over the inscription to the top where a light is burning inside the lantern.

I received no radio instructions guiding us to a specific reservoir. We were already beyond the Ruhr area behind the mountains in low-level flight and perhaps that was why we weren't receiving any group radio reports. As every aircraft had an alternative target, I attacked the Ennepe dam. Above Holland there was only one hairy situation, when we had to fly around a defensive chain of light flak and spotlights to return to course again.

The Ennepe dam was very difficult to identify. There were pockets of mist resembling several small lakes. In addition, an island was marked in front of the dam on our map which in reality did not exist, only a headland, causing confusion at first. The surrounding mountains were not so high here, and so we could descend reasonably well onto the reservoir, even with the vibrating bomb. It was very easy to approach the dam head-on, as there was no air defence. During the third attempt we were positioned absolutely accurately. Altitude per spotlight and speed were correct. The bomb dropped into the water at a specific distance from the dam, bounced along with the Lancaster for a while and exploded, which I could not see at the front of the aircraft. The image presented itself only to the navigator and the tail gunner.

The return flight led us past the Möhne dam, only ten minutes away by plane, across which we had also approached. In the meantime the flood was already foaming for miles through the Ruhr and Möhne valleys. Church towers and roofs protruded from the water, villages seemed to drown.

When we were back in Scampton, nobody wanted to believe this report, until the images of the long distance reconnaissance confirmed it. The crew showed themselves to be distressed by the broken Möhne dam and regretted that they had not succeeded at the Ennepe reservoir. We were filled only with the desire to get away from here as soon as possible.

Between Terschelling and Texel we had to circumvent a German fighter airfield in order to find the 'hole' on the continent between the two islands. Light projectiles reached for us, dropped onto the water and jumped up again higher than our Lancaster. Fortunately we were not hit. At that time we were flying with only three motors, a rather bad thing. Usually you can fly pretty well with three motors, but four motors are better. I had to stop one motor losing much oil and smearing the windscreen. When I wanted to turn off the motor, the pressure had dropped, and even more oil splashed onto the screen. I suspected a defect in the oil line. I was already counting on a landing in Scampton with two motors, which I wanted to avoid at any cost. Yet in reality only an instrument on the dashboard was malfunctioning. So the erroneous information was given that another motor had failed. After six and a half hours of flight I then made a very bad landing with an oil-smeared windscreen and in strong winds, against the sun from an altitude of thirty metres. After some great leaps across the runway, the Lancaster at last came to a standstill. Everywhere people were waving and running out of buildings onto the runway. We were almost forty-five minutes overdue. It had been thought that we were missing. When we appeared thereafter, they were very pleased. A part of the 'welcoming committee' was waiting in the parking areas, another came to the aircraft from which we lowered the ladder.

An officer with very much fruit salad on his cap wanted to be informed before the debriefing. I said to him that he had to wait until the debriefing. The curious gentleman was none other than the Commander-in-Chief himself, 'Bomber' Harris. He took it calmly and did not grouse. Before the raid I was very sceptical about the success and our chances of survival. The losses made that clear. Again and again I heard: 'When you do this and that tonight, you will shorten the war.' If you hear this a dozen times, you become sceptical. If seven men are sitting in an aircraft, but only one is able to fly it, then this is not good on a 'special trip'. So I found it advisable that another could take my place as pilot in an emergency. The other positions should be exchangeable, too. For example, I could take over the operator's position and he could fly the Lancaster. My men were not forced to learn additional skills. They did it voluntarily, and that has turned out well during other raids."

George Chalmers, born 1921, joined the RAF straight from school. The Flight Sergeant operated the radio in Townsend's Lancaster AJ-O. "In Scampton I had one and a half hours to study the security instructions and then had to present myself to the Commander of the airfield. The web of secrecy was very dense. In the pubs and bars, agents were placed who listened to our conversations, eavesdropped on telephone calls made from the airfield and recorded them. We were told, too, that there was security personnel on the airbase, perhaps from London, whom we did not know. Our post was censored. On board we initially used the standard radio equipment, a radio receiver type 1154/1155 which had an enormous reach during summer time in great altitudes at a high frequency. The apparatus (twenty to thirty centimetres) was mounted onto a small table in the fuselage opposite the motors. Later we received the improved radio device type T.T.1143.

Inside the aircraft above my station was a Plexiglas dome (astrodome) for astronomical navigation. During the flight I frequently looked through this to observe the stars and at the same time operated the radio. The reports from the aircraft to the base were encrypted with code words, a list of which we had to hand. I can no longer recall in detail the call signs and frequencies today. Only during the briefing did I learn of the target, the dams. I have only trained in radio operations and communications. The bouncing bomb itself I only saw half an hour before the take-off. I enjoyed the low-level flight training at this speed, when the landscape, houses and trees were rushing past me so quickly. To me, slightly further back in the Lancaster, it did not look that dangerous, but for the comrades at the front it must have been thrilling to see obstacles like high-voltage lines, poles and chimneys racing towards them and then to pull over them. With our growling motors we frightened the people. Once I saw horses escape from a farm and gallop across the fields. I saw Wallis during the briefing. For me he was just a civilian. Only later did I learn that he had conducted research and developed the weapon.

We took off as the last chain of the first wave at dusk. It got darker and darker, and in contrast the moon grew brighter and brighter, like a russet weather balloon. The Germans were awake. At the Dutch coast their tracers awaited us. Each aircraft of our wave had to answer a group radio report on short wave which was sent every half hour, simply by sending the plane identification letter, O for Orange in our case. When we flew across enemy territory in Holland, I saw an aircraft crashing, it must have been Burpee.

We reached the draining Möhne reservoir: the flood was spectacular, houses, treetops in the water, swimming rooftops in the Ruhr valley. By radio we learned that the Eder dam had been destroyed, too, and veered off towards the Ennepe dam. Here it was very difficult to find the right reservoir, for there were several in the area. We found our dam and attacked it. It was situated in a forested, hilly landscape without air defence. The bombardier looked through his sight, the ends of the wall merged with the nails, and he released the bomb. I did not see the bouncing of the bomb, only the water column rising, when I looked back through the astrodome. During the approach I sat on the floor and had to monitor the number of revolutions of the bomb.

After the war it was speculated that we might have attacked the wrong reservoir. However, we most certainly attacked the one that we were charged with. The navigator was responsible for the fact that it was the right dam. I still take him by his word today. Radio communication with the base was without incident; perhaps I missed a series of reports during the outbound flight. This I was told later, after our return, by the Chief of the Radio Division. There was no contact with other aircraft. At that time we did not have the sense, either, that people might drown in the valleys. We fulfilled our task and did our job. We sat in the last plane to return. Bomber Harris, Cochrane, the Airfield Commander and Wallis were already waiting. After landing, you are always relieved to set your feet on firm ground.

The attack caused great difficulties for the Germans. That was our intent. Perhaps it has shortened the war a little, for thousands of labourers were withdrawn from the Atlantic Wall for the clean-up and rebuilding of the dams."

Joseph McCarthy, Flight Lieutenant, born in the USA. He came to England via the Canadian Air Force. During the attack on the Sorpe dam he flew the Lancaster AJ-T. McCarthy counted among the aviators who were Gibson's 'right hands'.

"Gibson had a very friendly relationship with all crew members. He indulged in two hobbies, shooting in the local surroundings and visiting all the pubs in this corner of England.

The situation with the female personnel at Squadron X brought about an interesting event. Six ladies were required on site. The first three had to be dismissed, due to their circumstances. At this point, the other three had no interest in the new squadron and asked for transfer. All pilots went to the flight school of jumping hedges à la Lancaster during training.

The day of the attack, during take-off, my right outboard engine did not start, so we had to change to a reserve plane. To save time we threw some pieces of equipment through the aircraft's window. When the flight engineer threw out a parachute, the rescue parachute got stuck on a hook, opened like a balloon and covered me completely. In great haste we piled our equipment on a trolley and drove to the reserve craft AJ-T. Upon arrival, the compass deviation maps of the Lancaster were missing, and these were absolutely necessary to determine the exact course of the plane. Panic stirred up, the maps had to be fetched. From the authorities in charge we received a correctional map for the outbound flight with the bouncing bomb on board. That naturally posed problems for the return flight.

Our Lancaster had nearly made up the twenty-one-minute delay at the Sorpe dam. I approached the dam itself parallel to the crest several times, and descended via Langscheid as ordered.

During the tenth attempt I released the bouncing bomb without rotation, in a conventional drop, onto the centre of the dam at the water side. We could not use spotlights as an altimeter,

In Wickede, not far from the Ruhr, a memorial in the form of a bronze plaque commemorates the victims of the community. The artist Josef Baron gives an impressive account of the night of terror in stylised form – in reality bouncing bombs were deployed at the reservoirs.

because the reserve craft did not have them. A heavy detonation shook the dam, but it withstood. Back we flew along the route whence we had come and traversed the meanwhile 'wandering' Möhne Lake.

Without the heavy bomb on board, naturally the magnetic field of the plane changed. So the needle of the compass had turned twenty-five degrees to the west. I only noticed this, when a town appeared in front of me. I ordered my navigator to check this and he answered: 'We are on course.' Suddenly flak opened fire on us, spotlights flared. Now we knew we had veered off-course and were flying over the heavily defended town of Hamm. Sometimes the spotlights could not be circumvented, so we simply shot them out. Above Holland we occasionally saw German night fighters high above us. Yet they could not find us and probably had not expected us so low, either."

Basil Feneron, flight engineer in the Lancaster AJ-F with the pilot Flight Sergeant Kenneth Brown, flew against the Sorpe dam as part of the reserve. "From afar, the dam looked white in the moonlight. Banks of mist were lingering in the farther surroundings. At the centre of the dam, damage could be discerned, large chunks of rubble were strewn about. We circled for a few minutes and then approached the dam from the lake side, with the spotlight altimeter turned on, which the navigator could control through the domed cockpit screen during the descent. The moon was shining onto the water surface almost at a right angle. At 3.14 my bombardier delivered his load very precisely on target. When the bouncing bomb broke away from the Lancaster, the aircraft made a slide jump. At full speed we zoomed across the dam and the valley beyond. Suddenly the water seemed to lift, muddy, up to one-hundred-metres high, and then fell back, like in slow motion. We had a clear view of the explosion site. A shock wave and a ring of smoke circled around the base of this column of water. The shock wave of the explosion could be felt inside the Lancaster. To the letter, without rotation, the bouncing bomb was released at the Sorpe dam. Otherwise it would have leapt over the target. Near dawn we were still above Reich territory, but had little enemy contact. During the flight we witnessed two crashes of our own aircraft."

List of Sources

The author wishes to express his thanks to the many people who have provided information, photographs and, over the course of many years, their valuable time. Without their assistance, this book could not have been completed.

Detlef R. Albrecht, Manfred Bäcker, Evelyn Bäppler, Gerard Bellebaum, Karl Bergmann, Helmut Bladt, Udo Bleidick, Grete Blumenroth, Ignatz Böckenhoff, Karl Böhmer, Dr. Volker Brendow, Lotte Buerstätte, Heinz Büttner, Gertrud Caspari, Paul Claudius, Dr. A.R. Collins, Günter Danzglock, Werner Dettmar, Jan van den Driesschen, Bernard Droste, René Elshout, Karl Ludwig Ensuleit, Henriette Euler, Walter Fischer, Eckhard Fisseler, Foto-Dülberg/ H. Windgassen – Soest, Heinz Gerlach, Dipl.-Ing. Gluch, Jürgen Grewe, Otto Grünwald, André Guillon, Albert Günther, Michael Gosmann, Ulrike Hake, Wilhelm Hellwig, Didier

Hindrycks, Rudolf Hirschfeld, Major Tonie Holt, Ludger Horenkamp, Friedel Junker, Hermann Kaiser, Dr. Jörg Kaltwasser, Paul Keiser, Agnes and Uwe Kerinnes, Dr. Gerhard Köhn, Hartmut Kraatz, Heinz-Wilhelm Kramer, Günter Krause, Friedrich-Wilhelm Kretzer, Norbert Krüger, Randolf Kugler, Hans Lauer, Anne Marie Laurenz, Heinz Leiwig, Leon Lejeune-Steils, Heinrich Lehn, Dr. Richard Litterscheid, Luise Lorenz, Prof. Dr. Dr.-Ing. E. H. Heinz Maecker, Otto Mantel, Rolf Matzen, Ben May, Jan-Olov Molin, Alfred Müller, Wilhelm Neuhaus, Wilm Nöke, Franz-Josef Obermeier, Harry O'Brien, Hans A. Peters, Joachim Prölss, Friedhelm Quast, Hermann Quast, Winston G. Ramsey, Roswitha reining, Anton Riediger, Walter Rocholl, Theo Röttlingsberger, Wilfried von Rüden, Manfred Schaake, Kurt Schiefelbein, Hermann Schmidt, Heinz Schnelle, Pastor Franz Schnütgen, Herbert Scholl, Dr. Johann-Henrich Schotten, Harry Schürmann, Karl Schütte, Engelbert Schwingenheuer, Jim Shortland, Karl Heinz Stammschulte, Wilfried Steinhoff, Albert Stieglitz, Bernd Stobrawa, Hubert Stolle, Len Sumpter, Christoph Tauchert, Gerhard Teriet, Christian Tilenius, Bill Townsend, Alan Thompson, Sir Barnes Wallis, Fred Wauters, Siegfried Welt, Dr. H. Wilhelms, Les Wilson, Klaus Winter, Dr. Ursula Wolkers, Andreas Wörmann, Paul Wunderlich.

Thank you for the kindness and support provided by the following institutions:

Municipal archives
Affoldern, Arnsberg, Baunatal, Bergisch-Gladbach, Berlin, Düsseldorf, Edertal, Ennepetal, Essen, Felsberg, Fritzlar, Fröndenberg, Hagen, Hamm, Herdecke, Kassel, Korbach, Marburg, Melsungen, Münster, Solingen, Witten.

Companies, institutions, newspapers and archives
Associated Press Pathe Limited, Australian War Memorial/ Camberra, British Aerospace, British Aircraft Corporation Limited/ Weybridge, British Museum/ London, Federal Archive Aachen, Federal Archive Berlin, Federal Archive Coblenz, Federal Archive Freiburg in Breisgau, Federal Film Archive Berlin, Canadian National Archives, Commonwealth War Graves Commission, Elstree Studios/ Boreham Wood, Ennepe Wasserverband Gevelsberg, Cemeteries Department Soest, Hessian State Archive Marburg, Hessische/ Niedersächsische Allgemeine (HNA), Institute of Hygiene of the Ruhr Area Gelsenkirchen, Imperial War Museum/ London, Institute for Geophysics of Göttingen University, Institute for World Economics Kiel University, Institute for Contemporary History Munich, International Tracing Service Arolsen, Museum Bad Wildungen, National Archive Berlin, Air Force Museum Berlin-Gatow, Ministry of Defence/ London, Research Office for Military History Freiburg in Breisgau, National Archives/ Washington, Parsonage Archive St. John the Baptist Neheim, Public Record Office/ London and kew, Radio Canadian Army Europe, Regional Museum Fritzlar, Royal Air Force Museum/ Hendon, Ruhr Valley Museum Schwerte, Ruhrverband Essen, Municipal Works Remscheid Limited, Science Museum/ London, Astronomical Observatory Bochum, Traffic Museum Nuremberg, Geramn war Graves Commission Kassel, Waldeckische Allgemeine, Waldeckische Landeszeitung, Waterways and Shipping Office Hannoversch-Münden, Westfälischer Anzeiger und Kurier, Westfälische Landeszeitung Rote Erde, Meteorological Office Essen, Wupperverband Wuppertal.

Before and after the war Wilhelm Strotkamp was captain of a pleasure boat on the Möhne Lake. In 1942 he was assigned as auxiliary policeman to guard the Möhne dam and experienced the effect of the explosive physics of the dam buster bomb during the attack on the dam. In May 1968 he gave Helmuth Euler a film interview. Strotkamp had watched as the retaining wall moved back and forth between the towers, before the centre piece broke off suddenly, in one enormous block of masonry. Shock waves had initiated the collapse of the wall, as it had been predicted by the bomb's constructor Dr Barnes Wallis.

On 12 August 1990 the bombardier Len Sumpter described his memories of the raid on the Eder dam to the author Helmuth Euler in front of a camera. "Our pilot Dave Shannon flew the Lancaster AJ-L in low-level flight at eighteen metres altitude past the Waldeck castle across the tip of the Hammerberg against the Eder dam." Len Sumpter released the first bomb against the Eder dam, and it exploded at some distance near the southern shore on the Hemfurth side of the lake. Wing Commander Guy Gibson had observed the earthquake at the Eder retaining wall, too, and how the tremors had forced the centre piece of the wall to suddenly break off completely.

Inside flap at the back: The most dangerous British bomber of the Second World War, the Lancaster, became the carrier of the bouncing bomb. Put into service in 1943, twenty-three aircraft of this type were modified for the operation against the German dams. Rolls Royce provided the 'Merlin 28' engines which generated 1,460hp at an altitude of 3,500 metres. Aircraft data: crew seven men; maximum speed 435kmh; reach 2,600km, weaponry six board guns.

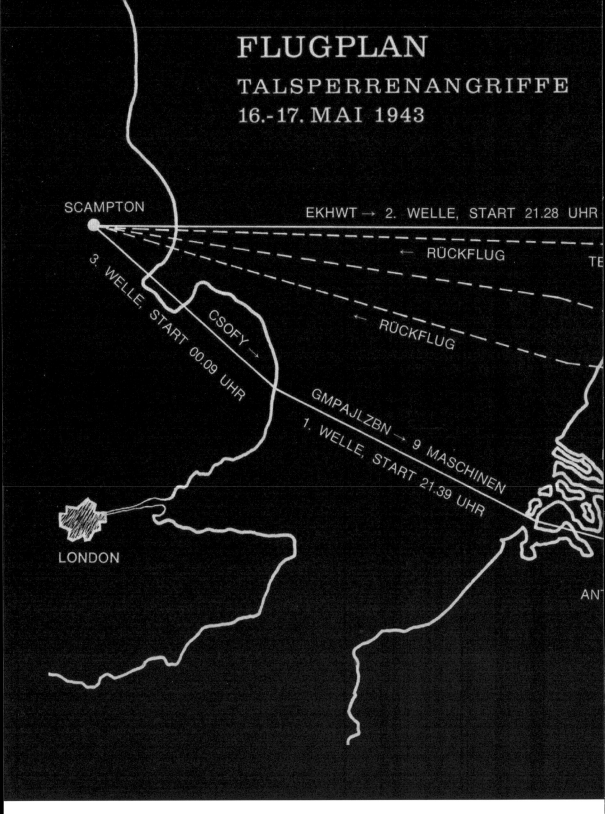

FLUGPLAN
TALSPERRENANGRIFFE
16.-17. MAI 1943

SCAMPTON

EKHWT → 2. WELLE, START 21.28 UHR

← RÜCKFLUG

TE

3. WELLE, START 00.09 UHR

CSOFY →

← RÜCKFLUG

GMPAJLZBN → 9 MASCHINEN

1. WELLE, START 21.39 UHR

LONDON

ANT

Inside Front Cover.

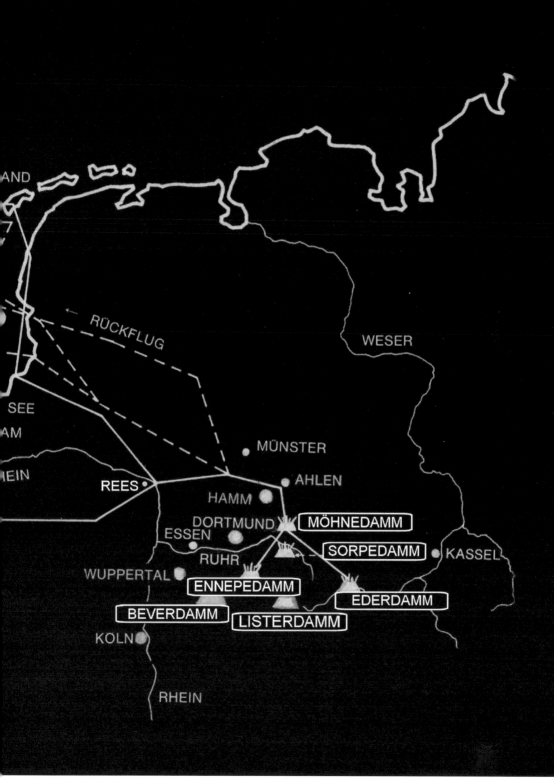